EVERY DAY W MARY

Reflections by the Affiliates of Mayslake Ministries

Edited by Dr. Mary Amore

Our Sunday Visitor

www.osv.com
Our Sunday Visitor Publishing Division
Our Sunday Visitor, Inc.
Huntington, Indiana 46750

Our Sunday Visitor Publishing Division
Our Sunday Visitor, Inc.
200 Noll Plaza
Huntington, IN 46750
1-800-348-2440

ISBN: 978-1-68192-145-7 (Inventory No. T1867)
eISBN: 978-1-68192-147-1
LCCN: 2017943412

Cover design: Lindsey Riesen
Cover art: Shutterstock
Interior design: Dianne Nelson

PRINTED IN THE UNITED STATES OF AMERICA

Dedication

To Lauren Nelson, thank you for your inspiring idea to write this book. You were the seed of hope and vision for this project, and I am forever grateful. May our Blessed Mother continue to lead and guide you in life as you serve the Lord in your vocation as a daughter, sister, wife, mother, and disciple.

To the gifted affiliates at Mayslake Ministries, thank you for your gracious acceptance of my invitation to share your bountiful wisdom and spiritual gifts through the pages of this book so that people may come to know and love our Blessed Mother.

To my family: my husband, Joe; my son, Joey; and my daughter, Lauren. Thank you for your willingness to help me see this project to completion. Your love and support will be forever appreciated. May this book be a reminder of our commitment to always be there for one another!

Lastly, to our Mother Mary, thank you for your fiat, for your incredible gift of courage and faith that brought Jesus into our world and into our lives. We are forever grateful.

Contents

Introduction

Mary's life as a young Jewish girl, wife, mother, and disciple has much to teach us about living in today's fast-paced world as a follower of Christ. From the cradle to the cross, Mary never lost faith in the Lord; her entire life bore witness to her unfailing love of God. We are called, and empowered, to do the same.

Every Day with Mary is a daily devotional written to help you begin — or deepen — your relationship with our Blessed Mother, Mary. These short reflections are intended to enable you to connect Mary's life experiences with those of your own life. Each of the twelve months of the year carries the theme of a particular fruit of the Spirit. By encountering the fruits of the Holy Spirit in Mary's life, we can begin to see how that same Holy Spirit can bear the fruit of faithful Christian discipleship in us.

No one voice or perspective can speak to all people, but we are all enriched by experiences and perspectives that are not our own. That is why this book draws from the spiritual wisdom and insight shared by a diverse group of thirty Catholic men and women. These authors, who comprise the affiliate staff of Mayslake Ministries, include lay and clergy, single and married; their ages range from twenty-seven to seventy-six. Each person, in his or her own way, has sought to make the presence of Mary in our lives of faith accessible, understandable, and inspirational.

Day by day, I pray that the pages of this book will draw you into the heart of Mary and inspire you to follow her example of living the fruits of the Spirit. Whether you are a business professional running to catch a flight, a stay-at-home mom or dad struggling to raise your family, a college student studying for a test, or a person enjoying retirement, these timely and relevant reflections will inspire you on your spiritual journey and invite you to live *Every Day with Mary.*

— Dr. Mary Amore, executive director, Mayslake Ministries

~ PEACE ~

January 1
Solemnity of Mary, Mother of God

"Mary kept all these things, pondering them in her heart." — Luke 2:19

The events surrounding the birth of Jesus were extraordinary and Scripture tells us that "Mary kept all these things, pondering them in her heart." Is it any wonder? After all, who can understand the mind of God? As the mother of Jesus, Mary chose to prayerfully reflect rather than react. This brought her great peace even in the midst of difficulties.

Our world is in turmoil often because so many people act without thinking. Sometimes we openly disagree with others because they are different from us or try to persuade people to think the way we do. Both of these impulses can disturb our peaceful relationships. Mary's life invites us to prayerfully bring our conflicts and misunderstandings first to the Lord, trusting that God will give us his wisdom and courage to know when and how to act.

— Dr. Mary Amore

HOW DO YOU RESPOND to people and events that you don't understand? Is your first inclination to disagree? To win people over to your side? Reflect on why you behave in this manner. Seek the wisdom of the Spirit to reflect before you speak and act.

Prayer: Mary, help me to place my difficulties and conflicts into the hands of your Son, Jesus, that he may lead and guide me to live in his peace.

January 2

"Seek peace, and pursue it." — *Psalms 34:14*

When asked what they would like for Christmas, many harried mothers and fathers immediately respond, "Peace!" When beauty-pageant contestants are asked what they would work for if they won are similarly quick to answer, "World peace." Peace is a gift of the Spirit that the hearts of humans seek at all levels.

In modern times, Mary is associated with a message of peace and tranquility in our broken world. Her message, especially as she gave it to the three children at Fátima, is one of peace for all humankind.

The peace that Mary speaks of is the peace that Jesus brings. Peace should be the goal in our dealings at work, in our encounters with family members, as well as in the world arena. Our role as Christians is to bring the peace of Christ to all people and situations.

— Lauren Nelson

WHAT SORT OF PEACE do you think Mary sought in her life? What moments of peace can you pursue today? How can you give others the gift of peace?

Prayer: Mary, be with us as we pursue peace in our lives. Help us to give peace to others through our words and actions.

January 3

"Glory to God in the highest / and on earth peace among men
with whom he is pleased!" — Luke 2:14

Mary gave birth to a baby boy, born on a peaceful winter's night in a cave, in an unfamiliar city. Mary wrapped him in swaddling clothes and laid him in a manger.

My wife gave birth to a baby girl, born on an autumn afternoon, in a neighborhood hospital. After she was born, I wrapped her in a soft swaddling blanket. Back in those days I didn't think much about Mary; in fact, I had abandoned my faith and was busy pursuing worldly dreams. Two months after my daughter was born, however, she needed life-threatening surgery. Fearful, I turned to Mary and to God. I surrendered my life and promised that if my baby pulled through, I would return to church. The surgery was successful and for the first time in years I felt at peace.

As a result of surrendering her life to God, Mary gave birth to the Prince of Peace. When I surrendered myself to God, the gift of peace was reborn in my soul.

— Bob Frazee

CALL TO MIND A SITUATION you can give over to the Lord in the hope of finding peace.

Prayer: Mary, pray that I may have the grace to be open to God's plan for me. Help me to live in this world as a person of peace.

January 4

"For I am sure that neither death, nor life, nor angels, nor principalities, nor things present, nor things to come, nor powers, nor height, nor depth, nor anything else in all creation, will be able to separate us from the love of God in Christ Jesus our Lord." — Romans 8:38-39

These powerful words bring us a sense of peace. They reassure us that no matter what happens in this life, God will never leave us. We may forget about him, but he never leaves us to face our trials alone. Nothing can separate us from the love of Christ Jesus.

Mary had peace in her heart because she knew firsthand that the Lord would never leave her. Throughout her life, Mary experienced unfathomable difficulties, even the death of her Son. And yet, Mary stayed strong in her faith. She never lost her way; peace reigned for Mary.

When we are experiencing painful situations that test our resolve, we can reach out to Mary and seek her help in restoring our peace and increasing our faith in Jesus.

— Sheila Cusack

HOW WILL YOU TALK to Mary today and ask her to bring God's peace to your heart? Ask Mary to be a model of peaceful living for you, knowing you are so loved by God.

Prayer: Mary, help me to know I am never separated from God, even when I walk on rocky roads.

January 5

"Be still, and know that I am God." — Psalms 46:10

I recently attended a winter wedding in a Wisconsin bayside resort town. As we traveled the country roads, I was moved by the serenity of the winter landscape. It was stark, snowy, and peaceful. As far as the eye could see Midwestern farm country was hunkered down, quietly awaiting the return of spring. Across the fields were leafless trees, dark against a gray sky, often with a bird of prey perched on high branches. The landscape invited me to quiet solitude.

Mary's life echoes the peaceful serenity that I experience in winter. In the Gospels, Mary is the woman of grace who willingly surrenders to God's action in her life. She serves, prays, and suffers, yet she is at peace because God is with her.

Like Mary, I've learned through the years to embrace the contemplative dimension of our Christian faith that invites us to be silent and reflective. Deep interior prayer opens us to seeing God's presence in everything. It brings us inner peace.

— Bob Frazee

CONSIDER THE WAYS that you are being called to a deeper prayer life. Set aside ten minutes today to sit in prayerful silence. Listen for the voice of God.

Prayer: Mary, help me to turn away from the busyness of life so as to enter into deep contemplative prayer with the Lord.

January 6

*"And going into the house they saw the child with Mary his mother,
and they fell down and worshiped him." — Matthew 2:11*

Ask any mother and she will tell you that birthing a child is no easy task. Like all pregnant women, Mary had to give herself to this new physical and emotional experience as it unfolded in her life. In Mary's case, the setting for the birth of Jesus was less than ideal, for it took place in a stable surrounded by barnyard animals. But I suspect that Mary's experience of birthing faded away to utter peace and tranquility as she gently held and caressed Jesus in her arms for the first time.

As people of faith, Mary's life inspires us to seek God's peace in the midst of the ordinary and hectic moments of our everyday lives. She shows us that when we give ourselves fully to God's will, the result is peace.

— Sharon A. Abel, PhD

CONSIDER THE MANY WAYS that you might honor God each time you meet his divine presence on your spiritual journey.

Prayer: Mary, I thank God for your example of how to live in this world with a peaceful heart. Help me to look at the world today through new eyes, that I may seek and find the peaceful presence of the Christ Child.

January 7

"Great peace have those who love your law; / nothing can make them stumble." — Psalms 119:165

When I was a parish music director, I was blessed to have my grandma's dear friend Mabel in my choir. Mabel always did her best to honor God and always came with a cheerful disposition and a sense of peace about her. She loved the Lord! In time, Mabel lost her eyesight and dropped out of choir. Years later, I was blessed to join Mabel and her husband's sixtieth anniversary celebration. Mabel beamed with joy. When I asked her how she was, she replied, "I'm wonderful!" That encounter made me wonder how anyone could be at peace with less than ideal circumstances.

The answer is visible in the life of Mary. Raised as a faithful Jew loving God's law, Mary had the gift of peace. She knew the Lord's heart, and it was a joy for Mary to make his law the hallmark of her life. No matter what hardships or stumbling blocks our Blessed Mother experienced, she remained at peace.

— Christine Grano

Do we love the law of the Lord? What might be our stumbling blocks to peace? Turn to Mary for inspiration and strength.

Prayer: Mary, intercede for us as we aspire to be like you, loving the law of the Lord that brings peace.

January 8

"Finally, brethren, rejoice. Mend your ways, heed my appeal, agree with one another, live in peace, and the God of love and peace will be with you." — *2 Corinthians 13:11*

In this reading, St. Paul encourages us to extend the peace of Christ to one another as brothers and sisters. In this broken world of ours, peace is not readily attainable; nor is it easily sustainable. What does peace look like for you? For our world?

While we may all have different ideas of what peace is and how it can be achieved, Mary invites us to look beyond our earthly realities. As our spiritual mother, Mary shows us how to put on the gift of the everlasting peace of Christ, obeying the commandment to love God and our neighbor.

— Lauren Nelson

THE NEXT TIME you are at Mass, focus on the kiss of peace. Truly pass on Christ's peace by looking others in the eye and saying a prayer for them.

Prayer: Mary, help me to work for peace. Give me the strength to continue what you began.

January 9

"Do whatever he tells you." — John 2:5

The Wedding at Cana is one of only a few Gospel stories in which we see Jesus and Mary interacting.

First-century Jewish culture placed a high value on family honor. The wedding celebration was the final step of the ritual marriage process. Running out of wine would have been more than an embarrassment; it would have been a loss of honor for both families.

Mary's words to Jesus — "they have no wine" — display a compassionate concern for the host. Jesus' reply, though, seems to lack any concern. Mary responds with peaceful confidence that Jesus will grant her unspoken request. She tells the servers to do whatever he tells you. In the end, they have an abundance of wine, and the host is honored for saving the best until last. Without saying much, a composed Mary quietly directs the action to its amiable resolution.

Mary's example invites us to be at peace in our personal surrender to God's will. It also implies that at times it may be uncomfortable to do so.
— Bob Frazee

IF YOU'RE AVOIDING something difficult in your life, pray to Mary for both courage and composure.

Prayer: Hail, Holy Queen, I pray to you for the courage to bring my needs and the needs of others to God and to peacefully accept what God has planned for me.

January 10

"You keep him in perfect peace, / whose mind is stayed on you, / because he trusts in you." — Isaiah 26:3

Jen is a bubbly, outgoing, loving individual. I met her at the parish where her husband served as a deacon. Together, they have three beautiful children and a close extended family.

Jen's life changed forever when her fifty-one-year-old husband died of cancer just days before their oldest daughter's wedding. The following year, her mom died. And just about six months later, Jen's forty-seven-year-old sister died of a heart attack, suddenly and without warning. In just two short years, Jen's life was turned upside down. Yet, when we would talk, there was an incredible sense of peace she carried because of her deep faith in God.

Gabriel's announcement to Mary disrupted her whole world. As a betrothed woman planning a life with Joseph, this was not what Mary thought her life would be. Yet, because of her deep faith in God, Mary was able to remain in peace as she walked a new and unfamiliar road. Mary is our inspiration to stay the course when life is not what we expect.

— Christine Grano

TAKE A MOMENT to recall a time when your life was significantly disrupted.

Prayer: Mary, you can understand fully when life does not go as planned. Pray for us that, in those times, we may receive peace by fixing our eyes on your Son and learn to trust his plan for us.

January 11

"Peace I leave with you; my peace I give to you; not as the world gives do I give it to you. Let not your hearts be troubled, neither let them be afraid."
— *John 14:27*

Jesus warns us not to be fooled by the feelings of contentment that can accompany money, power, fame, or success. These do not bring us lasting peace. True peace comes from being in relationship with Our Lord. Jesus can give us peace and restore peace when our souls are troubled. His presence can calm our fears and help us when we meet obstacles in life.

In spite of many hardships, our Blessed Mother lived each day with a peaceful heart, because she and Jesus were united in mind and spirit. As the mother of Our Lord, Mary seeks to walk with us on our spiritual journey. She longs to lead us to her Son so we may experience the profound peace that only Jesus can bring.

— Gina Sannasardo

WHERE IS THE SOURCE of peace in your life? This day, invite Mary to help you to deepen your relationship with Jesus.

Prayer: Blessed Mother, please come close to me. Guide me in my life today so that I might receive the peaceful presence of your Son.

January 12

"And the peace of God, which passes all understanding, will keep your hearts and your minds in Christ Jesus." — Philippians 4:7

While traveling to Ephesus (in Turkey), I had the opportunity to visit what is believed to have been Mary's last home. Walking the grounds, I was struck with such a sense of peace. Mary's life had so many different dimensions, and peace was among them. Luke's Gospel tells us that Mary listened to the shepherds who came to honor the baby Jesus and reflected on what they said in her heart.

Do we keep the messages that God sends to us in our hearts? When troubles or challenges arise, that is the time for us to be still and listen to what God is saying to us. He may be asking us to change something. Or he may be asking us to just sit peacefully, trusting that he has everything under control.

Mary's life is a testament to following God's guidance. And because of that, her life reflected peace. The same is true for us.

— Suzette Horyza

PRAYERFULLY CONSIDER the ways that you can invite the peace of the Lord to fill your heart this day.

Prayer: Mary, help me to be still when difficulties arise, that I may be open to receiving the peace that only Jesus can bring.

January 13

"Her ways are ways of pleasantness, / and all her paths are peace. / She is a tree of life to those who lay hold of her; / those who hold her fast are called happy." — Proverbs 3:17-18

This beautiful Scripture speaks eloquently about the peace that comes when one finds wisdom. But we can easily substitute "Mary" as the subject of this prose. In Scripture, few adjectives are attached to Mary. Regardless of what is happening, her demeanor is at peace because she walks with Christ. Mary is also a tree of life, inviting us to cling to her in times of unrest or struggle, to take refuge by her during the great storms of our lives, and to seek shelter and peace in her motherly embrace.

When we cling to Mary, the road to Jesus becomes clear. Her paths are peaceful ones for they lead us to her Son, Jesus, the Prince of Peace.

— Lauren Nelson

HAVE YOU EVER FOUND PEACE with Mary's help? Spend a few moments asking for her to bring you peace today.

Prayer: Mary, I seek the peace that only you can help me find. Lead me to your beloved Son and keep me safe within your love.

January 14

"Mary kept all these things, pondering them in her heart." — Luke 2:19

As God's plan of salvation unfolds, there are three key moments when Mary deeply reflects on her experiences in her heart: the Annunciation, the Christmas visit of the shepherds, and finding the lost child Jesus in the Temple.

Interior silence and peace are integral to reflective prayer. St. Mother Teresa of Calcutta provided some insight into the connection. She wrote:

> The fruit of Silence is Prayer
> The fruit of Prayer is Faith
> The fruit of Faith is Love
> The fruit of Love is Service
> The fruit of Service is Peace

Mary's life offers us an example of how silent reflection will deepen our prayer, enrich our faith, increase our capacity to love, draw us to serve others, and fill our heart with peace.

Mary models and invites us to silent reflection, and Mother Teresa models and invites us to serve. When we do so we receive the interior peace that Jesus promised to us. This is how and where world peace begins, in our hearts.

— Bob Frazee

How CAN YOU embrace quiet, reflective prayer today?

Prayer: Blessed Mother, help me to discover the peace that comes from a life of prayer and service to your Son, Jesus Christ.

January 15

"Strive for peace with all men, and for the holiness without which no one will see the Lord." — Hebrews 12:14

If we seek to live in holiness and peace, then others will come to Jesus through our words and actions. Being the presence of Christ is not an easy task, because we live in a world filled with sin, criticism, judgment, and condemnation. How can we strive to be holy? Who can help us to live in this world as people of peace?

Mary's life offers us a pathway to holiness and a way to a peaceful heart. Mary did not wish harm to those who turned her away from the inn when Jesus was to be born; nor did she attack those who rejected her Son — even those who crucified him. Throughout her life Mary remained a woman of peace. Our mother Mary invites us to follow her example of holiness when dealing with difficult people and negative situations.

— Gina Sannasardo

HOW CAN YOU EXHIBIT holiness today? Invite Mary's peaceful spirit to help you, especially when dealing with difficult people.

Prayer: Blessed Mother, we look to you with eager hearts. Help us be righteous in your Son's eyes so that one day we may enter into his glorious kingdom.

January 16

"And his name will be called … Prince of Peace." — Isaiah 9:6

As a devout Jew, Mary was among those who were still living with hope for the Messiah. She would have been very familiar with the wonderful prophecies of Isaiah. Yet little did Mary know that she was the one that God had chosen to bring his Son, the Prince of Peace, into the world.

Our world, though, is so very far from peaceful. There are divisions between nations and within them. Friends have falling-outs, and family members are not talking to one another. We might well ask, where is this Prince of Peace?

Mary birthed peace into our world. Like Mary, we are charged to bring the Prince of Peace into our world. But that peace begins in our own hearts. With Mary's help we can find Jesus alive in us and bring the presence of the Prince of Peace into our troubled and broken world.

— Christine Grano

WHAT IS THE STATE of my heart? Filled with peace? Or am I full of anxiety, anger, or fear? How can I carry peace inside me like Mary did, and birth peace into my circle of influence?

Prayer: Mary, pray for me that I allow the Lord to change my heart and infuse me with peace to birth into my world.

January 17

"And he said to the woman, 'Your faith has saved you; go in peace.'"
— *Luke 7:50*

Almost everyone is moved by the powerful image of Michelangelo's *Pietà*, in which Mary cradles the lifeless body of Jesus after the Crucifixion.

But recently, I came upon another Pietà statue in which Mary's posture was uniquely different. Instead of wrapping her arms around Jesus, Mary's arms are extended outward. The palms of her hands are facing upward in a posture that expresses her complete openness to the will of God.

Grief is a fact of life. Loss can come when we least expect it. Like Mary, we can cradle the memories of more peaceful times. But Mary's life can also inspire us to extend our arms and hearts to accept God's will and allow his grace to bring us to a new place of peace.

— Chris Hannigan-Wiehn

IS THERE A LOSS in your life that causes you to long for peaceful times gone by? Can you cradle those memories in your heart and open yourself to God's gift of peace?

Prayer: Mary, Queen of Peace, sit with me today as I extend my arms and open my hands to God asking for the healing peace of his divine love.

January 18

"For everything there is a season; and a time for every matter under the heavens: / A time to love, and a time to hate; / a time for war, and a time for peace." — *Ecclesiastes 3:1,8*

As the mother of Jesus, Mary experienced the full range of human life. She felt love in her family; she witnessed acts of hatred, too, some directed toward her Son. Similarly, we witness acts of rejection and self-ishness even among families and friends. We see violence in neighbor-hoods, sports arenas, workplaces, all around the world.

Through it all, Mary was able to keep peace in her heart, and we can, too. Mary's life invites us to seek the Lord's abiding peace, especially in times of trouble. Praying the Rosary is a favorite spiritual practice for many. The Rosary can be a powerful weapon of prayer, one that enables us to meditate with Mary and Jesus on the mysteries they shared in life.

— Mary Beth Desmond

THINK OF A TIME when you truly felt loved and at peace. Recall an ex-perience of feeling rejection or opposition in your personal or profes-sional life. Pray a Rosary, or part of the Rosary, and bring those times to God.

Prayer: Mary, pray that the Rosary may become a weapon of choice for me, to find peace and bring peace to the world.

January 19

"Let him turn away from evil and do right; / let him seek peace
and pursue it." — 1 Peter 3:11

It is easy to give into what looks glamorous and popular, but these passing elements will not bring us everlasting peace. The apostle Peter warns us about giving into evil ways and tells us that peace is something we must seek and pursue. We must actively look for where God plants seeds of peace and then be on watch for where it grows and spreads.

Our Blessed Mother is here to help us to do just that. We are given daily opportunities to turn away from evil and to do good, but we sometimes fail in that task. The next time you have a choice to make, turn to Mary for the inspiration and guidance to lead you away from evil and seek peace.

— Gina Sannasardo

WHAT PREVENTS YOU from being a peacemaker in this world? Invite Mary to help you to notice where peace can grow today.

Prayer: Mary, as the mother of Jesus and our spiritual mother, be with us as we wrestle to do what is right, and help us to seek and pursue peace in our lives.

January 20

"Deceit is in the heart of those who devise evil, / but those who plan good have joy." — Proverbs 12:20

God's word teaches us that deceitful hearts seek revenge and harbor maliciousness. In contrast, the Scriptures also assure us that those who spread peace will have joy, both now and for eternity.

As the mother of Jesus, Mary knew how deceitful the human heart could be. But through her own commitment to God's peace, Mary found deep joy, an attractive and genuine joy that radiated warmth for all. Our Blessed Mother waits for us to seek the peace that only her Son can bring. When we do, we, too, will find unexpected joy.

— Gina Sannasardo

CONSIDER THE OPPORTUNITIES in your life in which you can promote peace in the face of dissension or bitterness. Invite Mary to walk with you today, and to help you discover joy.

Prayer: Blessed Mother, come to our aide and be present with us as we stand against the deceit that tries to enter our hearts. Help us to live as sons and daughter of the Lord, that we may choose peace and find joy every day of our lives.

January 21

"For you shall go out in joy, / and be led forth in peace; / the mountains and the hills before you / shall break forth into singing / and all the trees of the field shall clap their hands." — Isaiah 55:12

After my husband and I became empty nesters, we were able to travel to Israel. There, the imagery that Isaiah used in his writings became fully alive to us. The beautiful landscape brought us to tears. Our hearts overflowed with peace as we realized that these were the very places the Holy Family walked.

Jesus frequently invited his disciples to come away with him to a place for rest, to receive the peace that they needed to continue in their work. When we look to Mary as Jesus' mother, we often forget that she was also his devoted disciple. Mary raised Jesus, but she also listened attentively to him. Surely Mary found peace in those same beautiful places in the countryside so she could return to the demands of her life as wife, mother, and disciple.

— Christine Grano

WHERE ARE THOSE PLACES in nature that fill you with God's peace? Take some time to intentionally place yourself in the peace of God's creation as Mary did.

Prayer: Dear Mary, you found refreshment and peace in God and in creation. Pray that we take time to follow your lead, and that we find for ourselves places of rest and peace.

January 22

"The fruit of the Spirit is love, joy, peace, patience, kindness, goodness, faithfulness, gentleness, self-control." — *Galatians 5:22-23*

Jesus gifts us with the fruits of the Spirit to help us in our times of need and weakness. They serve as a guide and reminder that we are not alone, nor separated from the One who sent the Spirit. Jesus is always with us, providing, nurturing, and peacefully empowering us.

As the mother of Jesus, Mary's entire life reflects the full complement of the Holy Spirit's gifts. Mary knew what it meant to have peace, love, kindness, and joy in her daily life, for she walked each day with Jesus. As the mother of our Savior, Mary's life is a living model for us to follow on how to act, serve, and walk in the footsteps of her Son. Mary offers us a road map of where to go and to whom we should turn to in times of need.

— Gina Sannasardo

Turn to Mary today and invite her to show you the pathway to peace. Seek Mary's assistance in deepening your relationship with the Lord, for then peace will reign in your heart.

Prayer: Blessed Mother, we joyfully look to you as our mother, help us as we seek to cultivate peace, kindness, and joy in our daily living.

January 23

"And let the peace of Christ rule in your hearts, to which indeed you were called in the one body. And be thankful. And whatever you do, in word or deed, do everything in the name of the Lord Jesus, giving thanks to God the Father through him." — Colossians 3:15,17

When we allow Christ to control our hearts, Scripture assures us that we will be at peace. Then we can do everything in the name of Jesus and give thanks to God through Jesus.

As the mother of Jesus, Mary is here to help us draw closer to her Son, Jesus. As our prayer advocate, Mary gently shares our burdens so that we can have peace again in our hearts. Mary will walk with us when we are afraid. She will take us by the hand and lead us in the direction of her Son. Let us seek Mary's motherly help in restoring peace to our weary souls.

— Lauren Nelson

IN WHAT WAYS does your life reflect the peace of Christ? Ask Mary to show you how to welcome peace in your life. In all of your actions, ask her to guide your every step and the choices you make.

Prayer: Mary, help me to go about my day with the peace of Christ in my heart directing my steps.

January 24

"Be still before the Lord, and wait patiently for him." — Psalms 37:7

A number of years ago, a small art gallery announced a contest to create a painting that captured the theme "Peace." Submissions poured in from all over. Finally, the day arrived to publicly announce the winner.

When the winning painting was unveiled, the crowd was stunned. A massive waterfall was depicted with water cascading down the rocky precipice. The gray sky was filling with ominous dark clouds. A spindly tree clung to the rocky cliff with its small branches reaching toward the waterfall. On one branch, a bird was nesting. Her wings spread serenely over three small eggs.

Mary lived in a tumultuous world. Her homeland was occupied by a foreign army and those in power were often brutal. Beatings, scourging, forced military service, slavery, confiscation and destruction of property were common. In the midst of this was God's picture of peace: Mary.

Mary's peace flowed from her closeness to God. She never lost sight of God and never forgot God was there. Mary knew that even if chaos surrounded her, she could lean on God. Mary "nested" in the Lord.

— Joseph Abel, PhD

MAKE TIME THIS DAY to sit in quiet solitude with God. Know that God is present. Invite him to fill you with his peace.

Prayer: O Mary, may we learn to trust God as deeply and completely as you did.

January 25

"Finally, brethren, whatever is true, whatever is honorable, whatever is just, whatever is pure, whatever is lovely, whatever is gracious, if there is any excellence, if there is anything worthy of praise, think about these things. What you have learned and received and heard and seen in me, do; and the God of peace will be with you." — Philippians 4:8-9

St. Paul teaches on what enables us to discover the peace of God. The qualities that Paul speak of are those that Mary models for us. Mary is genuine and has integrity; she is chaste, caring, kind, and welcoming. Mary lived all that is needed to have a peace-filled and loving relationship with God and others. It is no wonder, then, that one of Mary's honorary titles is Queen of Peace.

These same qualities can also serve as a guide for us. When we make them part of our lives and choices, we will find peace.

— Mary Beth Desmond

CONSIDER YOUR OWN LIFE. In what ways can you integrate the qualities mentioned above into your life so that you may experience the peace of Christ?

Prayer: Mary, may your loving qualities serve as a model and guide for all I think, say, and do.

January 26

"Let the peace of Christ rule in your hearts, to which indeed you were called in the one body. And be thankful." — Colossians 3:15

Peace can dwell in our hearts if our focus is upon Jesus. Since we are all one in Christ, we are brothers and sisters called both to receive and to give peace.

Mary allowed peace to rule in her, and the peace that lived in her heart touched others in a most profound way. Despite the difficulties and challenges that Mary faced as the mother of Jesus, her life radiated peace and thanksgiving because she was at peace in her relationship with the Lord. Our Blessed Mother models for us a life of faithful discipleship, a life of the trust that brings peace.

— Gina Sannasardo

HOW CAN YOU LET PEACE reign in your heart? In what ways can you allow peace to become your gift to those around you? Today, ask Mary to place the peace of her Son in your heart.

Prayer: Blessed Mother, we pray that we, too, would learn to let your Son's peace rule in our hearts so that we might serve one another with love and peace.

January 27

"She was greatly troubled at the saying." — Luke 1:29

The Annunciation must have been quite an emotional experience for Mary. The Scriptures tell us she was initially troubled and afraid, then confused, because she didn't understand. By the time the angel left her, Mary was at peace.

Mary's interior peace was revealed in the most ordinary way: she went to help her cousin Elizabeth. Helping meant doing the laundry, cooking, and cleaning. It meant making preparations for a new baby's arrival.

There's a wonderful lesson for us in these ordinary gestures. We don't need to do great heroic deeds, just loving ones. Loving others starts with a desire to respond to God's grace. That desire grows into an intention, then a free choice to act. As Mary shows us, it can be as simple as offering help to a relative or friend.

When we answer the call of God in our lives, we may start out troubled, fearful, or confused, as Mary did. But we can also experience the interior peace that comes from surrendering to God's will.

— Bob Frazee

HOW CAN WE CHANGE one ordinary deed today into an act of love?

Prayer: Mary, help me follow your example. Show me how to surrender, intend, and then act.

January 28

"The LORD lift up his countenance upon you, and give you peace."
— *Numbers 6:26*

I was raised by my mother after my parents divorced. She was plagued with alcohol addiction and mental illness. Sometimes my mother became suddenly agitated and made me the target of her unhappiness and despair. Everything about my life growing up was unstable and unpredictable.

Desperate for peace, I developed a close relationship with Jesus and a love for his mother. I often shared my burdens with Mary and asked her to help me find peace. She became a mother to me.

Mary is here to help us on life's journey. She leads us to our gracious Lord, who longs to give us the gift of his peace.

— Michael Grano

RECALL A TIME when you sought and received peace in a difficult situation, perhaps one that was out of your control. Be grateful for that moment, and ask God to "look upon you kindly" with peace again today.

Prayer: Mary, please ask Jesus to send agents of peace to my life through friends and family, and help me to bring his peace to others.

January 29

"Jesus came and stood among them and said to them, 'Peace be with you. If you forgive the sins of any, they are forgiven; if you retain the sins any, they are retained.'" — *John 20:19,23*

Witnessing her Son's execution at the foot of the cross, Mary was challenged. At the time, she may not have fully understood why Jesus had to die as he did. But Mary knew that to be at peace and live in peace she had to accept God's will and live a heart-centered life trusting in God's mercy and love. Despite injustice, violence, abandonment, and betrayal, she forgave.

Mary's life challenges us to focus on peace and forgiveness, rather than injury and pain. When we are wronged, it is easy to hold on to negative thoughts and feelings. We can choose to turn the offense over and over in our minds and hold on to the injury as if that will somehow punish the perpetrator or justify our bitterness. That choice will never bring us peace.

— Jane Zimmerman

SEEK MARY'S HELP this day in letting go of any anger and hurt that is in your heart. Choose peace for your heart.

Prayer: Dear Mary, help me to forgive and to focus on the blessings all around me, so that my heart may be filled with the peace of Christ, your Son.

January 30

"If I then, your Lord and Teacher, have washed your feet, you also ought to wash one another's feet." — John 13:14

I wonder if Jesus remembered his own experiences as a child with his mother when he washed the feet of the disciples. Certainly, this ritual highlights the importance of humility and the peace and comfort it brings. No one modeled that better than Mary.

Mary must have washed the feet of her Son many times. Some of my fondest memories of fatherhood are of bathing our children when they were newborns. Warm water, cooing, stretching of arms and legs, and that prolonged baby gaze often gave way to their first smiles. Those were peaceful moments. I'm sure Mary treasured many such moments.

I recently had the honor of assisting at a sponge bath for a hospice patient I was visiting. The aide's gentle respect for the patient's dignity was humbling. This bath was peaceful, too. It was one of the final preparations for this man's journey into eternal life.

— Bob Frazee

How can you respond to Jesus' invitation to wash one another's feet?

Prayer: Mother Mary, teach me to seek peace in humble acts of service to others.

January 31

"Peace I leave with you; my peace I give to you; not as the world gives do I give to you. Let not your hearts be troubled, neither let them be afraid."
— John 14:27

Apart from Jesus we can find no peace. Thankfully, he is always with us; he will never abandon us. When our lives are difficult and filled with troubles, we may feel that the Lord has forgotten about us or that he is angry with us. We may be tempted to distance ourselves from God. But when we walk away from God, we also walk away from peace.

Mary shows us how to find peace in the midst of uncertainty. Her entire life was woven with the steel threads of a faith strong enough to keep it all together in good times and in bad. Peace lived in the depths of Mary's soul, not because her life was easy, but because she understood that God was always with her. Left to fend for herself, Mary would have been in trouble. But the knowledge that she walked with God gave Mary great peace and strength.

— Dr. Mary Amore

HOW CAN YOU COME to a deeper realization that you are not alone, that Jesus is present in your life today and will be there for you tomorrow?

Prayer: Mary, life without Jesus is unbearable. Help me to walk with Christ, that I may have peace in my heart each day.

February 1

"For God so loved the world that he gave his only-begotten Son, that whoever believes in him should not perish but have eternal life. For God sent the Son into the world, not to condemn the world, but that the world might be saved through him." — John 3:16-17

Are you in a loving relationship with the Lord? How would you describe this divine relationship with God to another person?

Mary experienced the fullness of God's love as the mother of our Savior. In the face of uncertainty, Mary gave her life over to God because she loved him. In the face of hatred, Mary witnessed Jesus offer mercy and compassion. At the hands of those who betrayed him, Mary saw Jesus offer pardon and forgiveness to his persecutors. Mary tasted the promise of God's unending love through the birth, death, and resurrection of Jesus.

As our spiritual mother, Mary invites us to enter into a loving relationship with Jesus so that we might experience the fullness of God's love and bring it to others.

— Dr. Mary Amore

JESUS CALLS US to love one another, not to condemn or judge. Seek Mary's help in bringing God's love to all people.

Prayer: Mary, help me to offer the fullness of God's love to everyone I meet today.

February 2
The Presentation of the Lord

"Behold, this child is set for the fall and rising of many in Israel / and for a sign that is spoken against / (and a sword will pierce through your own soul also), / that thoughts out of many hearts may be revealed." — Luke 2:34-35

Mary's heart was pierced, not only as she endured the suffering of her Son, but also as she has witnessed our own natural tendencies toward sin.

Five years ago, I finished reading a popular romance novel and was looking for a new book to read. The Holy Spirit led me to a Catholic radio program at a time when Catholic radio was never on in my car. Tuning in, I was intrigued by a conversation about a book about Marian consecration. I decided to read it. Mary's love came through the Scripture passages and Rosaries that lead to my own consecration. Her love led me back to her Son in the Sacrament of Reconciliation (after a long absence), which freed me from the sin that had trapped me.

If we open our hearts, Mary's love will lead us right to her Son.

— Katie Choudhary

HAVE I ACCEPTED Mary's love? Have I allowed her to lead me to Christ Jesus?

Prayer: Mary, Queen Mother, help me to open my heart to your love, so that I may know the love and mercy of Jesus.

February 3

"I love you, O LORD, my strength. / The LORD is my rock, and my fortress, and my deliverer, / my God, my rock, in whom I take refuge, / my shield, and the horn of my salvation, my stronghold." — Psalms 18:1-2

The beautiful words in Psalms 18 could have been penned by the hand of our Blessed Mother herself, for they are reflective of Mary's relationship with God. For Mary, the Lord was a rock, the foundation on which she built her life. God was Mary's strength, every day and especially in times of adversity. He was also her refuge. Mary trusted that the Lord was her shield and would keep her safe from all harm.

Because Mary knew God's love for her, she returned God's love completely. As our spiritual mother, Mary invites us to love the Lord God with our entire being as she did. She is here to help us build our lives on the love of her Son, Jesus. When we do so, we, too, will experience the unconditional love of God that Mary knew every day of her life. Let us turn to Mary seeking a deeper, loving relationship with God.

— Lauren Nelson

WHAT PRAISES OF LOVE can you give to God today? How has the Lord been your foundation or your refuge?

Prayer: Mary, teach me to praise God in all I do and to love God with all that I am.

February 4

"You shall love your neighbor as yourself." — Matthew 22:39

When our friends suffered a house fire a few days before Christmas, their newly married daughter and son-in-law took them in. Across the street from the house that had the fire was a vacant house for sale. When they heard about what had happened, the owners of the vacant house took down the "For Sale" sign and told our friends, "It's yours, live here." What a beautiful example of the way we are all called to love our neighbors as ourselves.

I imagine that Mary was the perfect neighbor. Her heart brimming with love, Mary surely baked bread and shared it, or took an extra jar to the well to draw water for a neighbor. Mary understood that it was impossible to love God without loving the people God created. Let us seek our Blessed Mother's help to see and respond to the presence of God in all people.

— Mary Beth Desmond

How do you show love to your neighbors? Have you received love and kindness from others who have seen you as their neighbor?

Prayer: Mary, your love for others inspires me to take care of my friends and family. Help me to see God's presence in all people and to count them as my neighbors.

February 5

"Blessed are the meek, for they shall inherit the earth." — *Matthew 5:5*

Mary was "blessed." The angel Gabriel was the first to announce this gift of God's grace in the young Mary's life. Elizabeth, too, recognized that Mary was blessed. Mary was the Mother of God, but she did not consider anything beneath her. Love, and a willingness to serve, inspired Mary to go and visit her cousin Elizabeth. And this act of love opened Mary to a new world, one with the wisdom and insight an older family member like Elizabeth could give her.

— Larry Dreffein

HOW CAN THE LOVE that Mary demonstrated for Elizabeth manifest itself in your life? Is there someone you love who could use a helping hand? Sometimes just growing old creates new needs and dependence on others' loving kindness.

Prayer: Mary, your loving ways prepared you to be the mother of our Savior. Your love lived out each day with your Son gives us insight into his life as well as our own. May I embrace lowliness in the love I show others. May the loving example you gave inspire me to be a willing servant in my world.

February 6

"As the Father has loved me, so have I loved you; abide in my love."
— John 15:9

Have you ever wondered how glue works? Have you ever noticed that if you pull a peanut-butter sandwich apart that the peanut butter is stuck on both pieces of the sandwich bread? Scientists still don't fully understand all the details of how gluey substances make one thing stick to another. If you want a short answer, the word is "forces."

Stickiness is a wonderful metaphor to use in the spiritual life when thinking of Mary and Jesus and our relationship with them. In a way, Mary can be the binding agent who brings us to Jesus. Her love for humanity draws us into a loving union with Jesus, one in which we learn to rely on — and "stick" to — him. Mary is like glue in our spiritual lives. Without Mary, we would not have the gift of Jesus. As the mother of our Savior, Mary's role in salvation history is to lead us all to her Son, that we may remain in his love all the days of our lives.

— Joseph Abel, PhD

I INVITE YOU to sit in prayerful silence and reflect on the ways that Mary's life can lead you to Jesus.

Prayer: Mary, draw us closer to your Son, Jesus, that we may live and move and have our being in his love.

February 7

"A woman in the crowd raised her voice and said to him, 'Blessed is the womb that bore you, and the breasts that you sucked!' But he said, 'Blessed rather are those who hear the word of God and keep it!'" — Luke 11:27-28

Many people think of being "blessed" as a divine favor that is merited or earned. Jesus, however, proclaimed that blessedness belongs to all who hear the word of God and act upon it. That is because they encounter God's word as an invitation to love. Mary is the example par excellence of one who was blessed in this way.

Luke presents Mary as one who pondered the wonder and joy of being loved by God and allowed that love to take root within her and bear fruit in the manner in which she lived her life. Her pondering was an encounter with love.

Mary's pondering is an invitation for us to move beyond simply hearing God's word to an encounter with love that takes root in our lives.

— Father Tom Borkowski

Do I PONDER God's word? Do I see obedience to his word as a response to his love? Do I consider myself blessed?

Prayer: Mary, woman of joy, be my guide to ponder God's word so that it becomes an encounter with love that bears joyful and abundant fruit.

February 8

"Love one another; even as I have loved you." — John 13:34

When I picture Mary, I see the eyes of motherly love, a beautiful gaze. I imagine Mary's look of love when she saw her newborn Son for the first time. I imagine, too, the many times Mary looked through the eyes of love to Joseph, Jesus, and her cousin Elizabeth. I can also see her eyes pouring out tears of love for her Son as he hung on the cross.

My eyes always fill with tears whenever I see someone serving in the military return home from deployment and reconnect with their families. Can you think of a time when you saw someone's eyes light up or sparkle when they spoke about someone they love? I believe that expression of love is God's divine light shining through. But loving one another as Christ has loved us also means loving oneself. That is not being selfish but rather learning to fully appreciate the divine presence within.

— Mary Beth Desmond

RECALL A TIME when you truly felt loved through the eyes of another person. Look in the mirror and tell yourself you are a beloved son or daughter of God. Imagine the eyes of Jesus looking at you with love.

Prayer: Mary, help us to love one another as God has loved us. Help us to see one another through the eyes of love.

February 9

*"As he landed he saw a great throng, and he had compassion on them,
because they were like sheep without a shepherd; and he began
to teach them many things." — Mark 6:34*

Mary was the first disciple of Jesus. Can you imagine all that she must have learned from him as she spent day after day teaching and caring for him in their home in Nazareth? Even more so, on the cross Jesus entrusted Mary with the great duty to be a mother for each one of us.

A few weeks ago, I was overwhelmed with the responsibilities of adulthood. My calendar was filled to the brim with tasks, meetings, and activities. I called a friend for help, and she listened and offered practical and loving advice that gently led me back to the living waters of Jesus. She was Mary for me.

— Katie Choudhary

How can Mary help you bring the loving heart of Jesus into your world?

Prayer: Blessed Mother, Our Lady of Perpetual Help, thank you for having pity on me. Bring me to the feet of Jesus so I may experience his divine love.

February 10

"That Christ may dwell in your hearts through faith; that you, being rooted and grounded in love, may have power to comprehend."
— *Ephesians 3:17-18*

Our Blessed Mother is the vessel of pure love by which God came to us in the person of Jesus Christ. Through her selfless act of love and her willingness to do the will of God, we are graced to have Christ dwell among us. Mary was an utterly selfless human being and her love for the Lord had no conditions.

All too often we put conditions on our love for God. In our prayers we might say, "Lord, if you do this for me, I will go to church." Or, "God, if you heal me, I will read the Bible more." The list of our conditions for God is endless. It is because we are not rooted or grounded in love.

Mary's life shows us a better way, a more perfect pathway to holiness — namely, unconditional love for God.

— Lauren Nelson

WHAT CONDITIONS do you put on your love for God? How can you work on making your love for him unconditional?

Prayer: Mary, your love for God knows no bounds. Teach me to give God all my love without boundaries or conditions.

February 11
Our Lady of Lourdes

"O daughter, you are blessed by the Most High God above all women on earth; and blessed be the Lord God, who created the heavens and the earth."
— Judith 13:18

On February 11, 1858, Mary appeared to Bernadette Soubirous, a young peasant girl in southern France. For six months, Mary came to Bernadette with one special message: "God is love. He loves us just as we are." The message that the Blessed Mother delivered at Lourdes is one of hope for all who seek a loving relationship with God.

In the time leading up to the Annunciation, young Mary of Nazareth prayed daily to the God of Israel. She loved God with her whole heart and soul. When the time of fulfillment came, God bestowed upon Mary the highest honor of our human race: he made her the mother of God.

Mary is here to help us come into a loving relationship with God. Her mission, like that at Lourdes, is to let her children know that God loves us in spite of our imperfections.

— Dr. Mary Amore

WHAT IS KEEPING you from cultivating a loving relationship with the Lord?

Prayer: Mary, in giving Bernadette a message of love, you gave the human race the gift of hope. Help me to spend my life loving God above all else.

February 12

"Who can find a good wife? / She is far more precious than jewels. / The heart of her husband trusts in her, / and he will have no lack of gain. / She does him good, and not harm / all the days of her life." — *Proverbs 31:10-12*

Mary was a worthy wife to Joseph, a treasured pearl beyond compare, and Joseph entrusted his heart to her. Mary's life of grace brought him only goodness, and the love between Mary, Joseph, and Jesus remains a role model of family life for us today.

When I was young, my mom dreamed of buying a strand of pearls, so she put one on layaway and paid for it little by little over time. When the purchase was complete, my mom treasured her pearls and wore them only on special occasions. After she died, the pearls came to me. Now, when I wear them on special occasions, I always think of her. The pearls remind me of her love. Their value lies in the strands of unfailing love and goodness my mom provided me. Someday I hope to give the pearls to my only daughter.

— Mary Beth Desmond

Do you have a gift that you treasure? Reflect on the loving relationship that accompanies that treasured item.

Prayer: Mary, pray for families, that together we may learn to value one another as a priceless pearl, and to entrust our hearts to one another.

February 13

"O give thanks to the LORD, for he is good, / for his mercy endures for ever."
— *Psalms 136:1*

A favorite painting of mine depicts our Blessed Mother sitting cross-legged in the foreground while removing freshly baked bread from bowls. Behind her are two women. One is forming the dough into loaves. The other is placing the bread into a stone oven.

A Jewish friend had gazed at the painting in a store, then bought it. I tried to explain the scene, but she stopped me. "I know who this is," she exclaimed. "It's Mary. She's one of us. She's doing what we do, celebrating the story with bread. I'm hanging this in my kitchen. Now let's eat!" The painting is now proudly displayed in a kosher kitchen in Brooklyn, New York.

It's amazing that two thousand years later Mary is recognized in her tradition as well as ours. The grace and love that Mary received from God as the handmaid of the Lord is still in our world. Mary remains the one hailed, "full of grace." She is God's declaration that grace never leaves us and that God's love endures forever.

— Joseph Abel, PhD

HOW CAN YOU HONOR the ever-present love of God given to us through Mary?

Prayer: Hail Mary, help us see that we, like you, are filled with grace. God's love for us endures forever. In fact, the whole world is full of grace.

February 14

"With all lowliness and meekness, with patience, forbearing one another in love, eager to maintain the unity of the Spirit in the bond of peace."
— *Ephesians 4:2-3*

When we reflect on the life of Mary and Joseph, we often think of them as the earthly parents of Jesus, but forget that they were also a loving married couple. Joseph loved Mary. Scripture tells us that when he found out Mary was expecting a child, Joseph planned to divorce her quietly. Joseph wanted to spare Mary both embarrassment and the full force of Jewish law.

The bond of love that Mary and Joseph shared helped them get through difficulties they faced. Shortly after Jesus was born, they had to flee to a foreign land in fear for their baby boy's life; and years later they suffered great anxiety when they lost Jesus for three days only to find him in the Temple. Mary loved Joseph, and she made a loving home for him and Jesus.

Through it all, the Holy Family exemplified the virtues of humility, gentleness, and patience.

— Lauren Nelson

PRAYERFULLY CONSIDER the ways that Mary and Joseph's love for God and one another can inspire you to live in love.

Prayer: Mary, help me to live my life with others in the perfect love that you and Joseph shared.

February 15

"If you really fulfil the royal law, according to the Scripture, 'You shall love your neighbor as yourself,' you do well." — *James 2:8*

When I think of a perfect neighbor, Mary comes to mind. In the village of Nazareth, surely Mary was one who reached out to friends and neighbors before they even asked for help. I am sure Mary performed many acts of kindness for her neighbors: making a meal for someone in need, watching a neighbor's child, or praying with a sick friend. Mary ministered lovingly to all those in her life. She loved her neighbors as herself.

I have a friend who is a nurse practitioner, and I see so much of Mary in her. My friend lovingly cares for her patients at work, but also cares for two elderly parents and provides medical advice for her friends and family via text messages and phone calls. She is our first point of contact when we need help figuring out our next course of action. Mary and my friend each offer a beautiful example of love of God and love of neighbor.

— Katie Choudhary

Do I LOVE my neighbor as myself? Think of one act of love you can do today for your neighbor.

Prayer: Immaculate Heart of Mary, help me to love like you do, so that my actions may demonstrate my love of God and neighbor.

February 16

"And over all these put on love, which binds everything together in perfect harmony." — Colossians 3:14

Our society obsesses about clothes. Every year new styles come out and we are encouraged to go out and buy them. Whether we are stepping out on the red carpet, attending a friend's wedding, or simply going to work, wearing the right outfit is a priority for many people. Some have lost sight of the fact that clothes do not make the person.

Mary's clothes, as depicted in works of art, were simple and plain. Mary's life was not about her "look," but rather about who she was. As a beloved daughter of God and the mother of Jesus, Mary was clothed in love, which binds everything together. Mary was dressed in love when she visited her cousin Elizabeth, journeyed to Bethlehem for the birth of her child, and stood at the foot of the cross.

Our Blessed Mother invites us to wrap ourselves in love, the true garment for those who follow Jesus. Love never goes out of style.

— Mary Beth Desmond

WHAT ARE WAYS you can clothe yourself in love? Consider giving away items of clothing you no longer wear to those in need.

Prayer: Mary, help us accessorize ourselves with grace, purity, and love, that we may build a more loving, kind, and harmonious world.

February 17

"Hatred stirs up strife, / but love covers all offenses." — *Proverbs 10:12*

Love conquers all. We have heard these three little words since we were young. Even in the fairy tales we read to our children this line is used to assure us that in the end all will be well, because love will win out.

As a child, Jesus heard this same message in the stories that Mary told him about his ancestors: Noah, Abraham and Isaac, Moses, and David. Throughout all of their struggles, love conquered.

Today, much of our world is embroiled in disputes. Children are bullied in school, threats of terrorism loom over us, and political battles are a daily occurrence. Our gentle mother Mary, who gave birth to the Son of God, is here to remind us that love still conquers all. God is love, and there is nothing in this world that love cannot, or will not, overcome.

— Lauren Nelson

HOW CAN YOU SHOW the love of God today to your friends, family, and those that God sends your way?

Prayer: Mary, show us how love can cover all of our offenses. Teach us how to turn away from conflict and to focus on the love that Jesus brings to us.

February 18

"If anyone would be first, he must be last of all and servant of all."
— *Mark 9:35*

As the mother of the house, I imagine Mary served wonderful meals to Joseph and Jesus. Mary loved her family, and cooking for them was certainly an expression of that love.

I have great memories of my mom making perfect pancakes on Sunday mornings. Mom would serve up three nice stacks of hot, buttered, silver-dollar-sized pancakes at the table so we could enjoy them right away. My dad, brother, and I would gobble them up, and she would then take the plate back to the stove to refill it, repeating this ritual until we were all full. One by one we would leave the breakfast table.

One day, as I was rinsing my plate in the sink, I heard my mom say, "Now that everyone is full, I am left alone with the leftovers." I sat back down and talked with her while she enjoyed her lukewarm pancakes. Mom was always serving us and was the last to eat. Lasting love is sacrificial love.

— Katie Choudhary

WHAT IS THE NAME of someone in your life who has put himself or herself last so you could benefit?

Prayer: Mary, please lift up (insert name) to your Son's care today. I am thankful for the example of love you and this person have given me.

February 19

"There is no fear in love, but perfect love casts out fear." — *1 John 4:18*

When the angel Gabriel first spoke to Mary, she was deeply disturbed. She questioned his words, yet complied with the angel's request out of her love for the Lord. We are often deeply disturbed or have serious questions when we face something overwhelming or incomprehensible. Underneath those feelings and thoughts lies fear: fear that evil may befall us or a loved one, or fear we that won't be able to handle the suffering, or that we can't possibly do what's required.

If we proceed with love, however, we gain the strength we need. We can say, with Mary, "My soul proclaims the greatness of the Lord and my spirit rejoices in God my Savior." We are able to model our lives after Mary who was able to meet her questions and her challenges with trust in God's love for her. The perfect love of God drives out all fear.

— Jane Zimmerman

IT TAKES COMMITMENT to learn to know oneself, to be mindful of one's thoughts, feelings, and impulses. How can the love of God help you overcome fear today?

Prayer: Dear Mary, help me to know when I am anxious and fearful, to be aware of my thoughts and urges, and to turn to God's love with hope.

February 20

"We know that in everything God works for good with those who love him, who are called according to his purpose." — *Romans 8:28*

Mary was called — personally handpicked by God — to fulfill his purpose for her. Mary said yes to an unknown future, a life that was filled with trials and difficulties. Mary's yes to God came from her deep love for him. She partnered with the Lord in helping all things work.

Our calls from God are also very personal. We have all been created for a purpose. Our lives are spent making choices, decisions that ultimately affect relationship with God. Whether we are making a decision on where to live or where to work, our loving relationship with the Lord invites us to take into consideration God's will for us. Mary's life invites us to partner with God as we make decisions. God loves us and desires only our good.

When we choose God's purpose for us, just as Mary did, we can know that things will work for our benefit.

— Mary Beth Desmond

HAVE YOU EVER MADE a decision you were uncertain about? How could God's purpose for you become part of how you consider the choices you make?

Prayer: Mary, help us to hear and answer the Lord's personal call to us to fulfill his purpose.

February 21

"I am the mother of beautiful love." — Sirach 24:18*

Mary is our mother, not according to the flesh, but through love.

It is absolutely impossible to analyze the love Mary has for us or to know the true depth of it. Because Jesus gave his mother to us from the cross, all of Mary's love is for us. We are her adopted children, and Mary, the mother of God, is a refuge and an advocate we can turn to in our daily lives. We know that because Jesus loved her completely our love for Mary can never be too much.

Mary has set a high standard for how we, as her children, should live our lives and love one another. Mary asks us to live each day in love for Jesus. She offers to form and mother that love in our hearts.

— Deborah O'Donnell

TAKE TIME TO THINK today about how you can put others first and show love to everyone around you. Ask Mary to be "the mother of beautiful love" in your life.

Prayer: Mary, guide me on this journey to love and help me to be a humble servant of the Lord in all that I do.

* Some ancient texts omit this verse.

February 22

"Judge not, and you will not be judged; condemn not, and you will not be condemned; forgive, and you will be forgiven.... For the measure you give will be the measure you get back." — Luke 6:37-38

When Mary found Jesus in the Temple after he had been lost for three days, she did not yell at him, tell him how bad his behavior was, or lecture her twelve-year-old Son for disobeying his parents. Instead, Mary treated Jesus with love and respect.

As our heavenly mother, Mary invites us to take the same approach. If we want family members who have walked away from the Faith, given up on God, or chosen lifestyles that are in conflict with the values of our faith to come back to the Lord, then we must offer them love and mercy, not judgment or condemnation. Mary is our advocate, and she can help us bring our family members back to the Lord with love, kindness, and compassion. Then these are the measures which will in return be measured out to us.

— Dr. Mary Amore

CALL TO MIND one family member in need of God's mercy and forgiveness. How will you reach out to that person today without judgment?

Prayer: Mary, help me to live in this world with the compassionate and loving heart of Jesus.

February 23

"His mother said to the servants, 'Do whatever he tells you.'" — *John 2:5*

You can picture the scene, can't you? The son says, "It's not time yet." The mother knows otherwise, ignores the protests, and starts everything rolling. Did you ever stop to think of the great love and courage it took for Mary to nudge Jesus into his public ministry? All the things she carried in her heart included the knowledge that difficulties lay ahead for her Son. But she also knew that this was what must be done.

As our spiritual mother, Mary is here to nudge us along the way, too. Sometimes we avoid things that are presented to us; we may be fearful, indecisive, or unprepared. In those moments, we can turn to Mary for guidance and inspiration. She seeks only for us to do the will of the Father.

The next time you say to yourself "I don't want to" or "it's not time yet," think about Mary's great love. Feel the nudge offered to take that next step and know that our Blessed Mother will be there to support you.

— Suzette Horyza

RECALL A TIME when you felt the nudge of God's love.

Prayer: Mary, help me to be in tune with my heart, that I may listen to God's voice speaking to me.

February 24

"Love bears all things, believes all things, hopes all things, endures all things."
— 1 Corinthians 13:7

As a nurse, I have been blessed to see love come to life. When patients are surprised by a sudden illness or an unexpected admission to the hospital, they often feel disconnected from what is meaningful in their life. They long for the simple pleasures they love, whether the presence of family, prayer time, a pet, music, a morning walk, Mass, a cup of coffee, or just being able to go to work. They long for love in their lives.

I am inspired by Mary and her life experiences. As the mother of Jesus, Mary endured many moments of disconnection from things that were meaningful to her life. She was a refugee in a foreign land, the mother of a lost child, and a witness to the crucifixion of her beloved Son. Yet Mary's love for God never wavered. Loving God can help us reconnect to all that is meaningful for us, for love bears all things, believes all things, hopes all things, endures all things.

— Mary Beth Desmond

CONSIDER THE WAYS that you can offer love and support to someone who is struggling.

Prayer: Mary, help me to bring the love of Jesus to my family, friends, and those that Jesus sends my way.

February 25

"Above all hold unfailing your love for one another." — *1 Peter 4:8*

The writer of this epistle is telling Christians to have deep, earnest love for one another so that they can remain strong in their faith in spite of persecution. It is also important for us to foster a loving faith and family unity despite our differences and diversities.

When we look at Mary, sometimes it's difficult to imagine her as a housewife, mother, and active disciple who had many of the same difficulties we have with our families and friends: irritations of marriage, frustrations of motherhood, disagreements with others.

Mary was devout and faithful in her relationship with God. His intense love was a soothing balm for all the human difficulties Mary may have encountered. Instead of family challenges causing division, Mary's intense love for God brought a cohesive bonding to her family, and ultimately enabled Mary to hold the disciples together after Jesus' death and resurrection.

Mary invites us to draw close to God so we can allow the love of Christ to flow through us.

— Christine Grano

TODAY, SPEND SOME QUALITY TIME in prayer so that you may grow in intimacy with God.

Prayer: Mary, pray for us to stay close to the Lord and let his divine presence flow through us so we may be agents of love in the world.

February 26

"For this is the message you have heard from the beginning, that we should love one another." — 1 John 3:11

Love is important because it is eternal. God, who is love, will always be with us. The love we show toward God and our fellow brothers and sisters in Christ will remain with us forever. The way in which we love one another at this moment will continue to manifest in heaven.

The best and most devout example of love is Mary, second only to God's love for us. Mary is an advocate helping us to love God. As our spiritual mother, Mary shows us how to give ourselves to her Son.

Our personal shortcomings erode the union of the body of Christ in our own personal relationship with God and with others. Mary challenges us to accept and give love as the highest and greatest of all God's gifts, and to allow this gift to inspire our thoughts, words, and actions. If we do everything in "love," we are in union with the body of Christ.

— Nanci Lukasik-Smith

WHAT ACTIONS CAN YOU DO today with love and charity for all?

Prayer: Holy Mother, encourage me to show love and respect to my dear ones. Gently redirect me when needed and soften my heart when others are acting unloving toward me. Hold me closely as I work through the day, and let others see love in all of my actions.

February 27

"Well did Isaiah prophesy of you hypocrites, as it is written, / 'This people honors me with their lips, / but their heart is far from me." — Mark 7:6

Jesus called out the Pharisees and scribes for not practicing what they preached. Unlike these hypocrites, Mary remained true to the words she proclaimed to the angel Gabriel: "Behold, I am the handmaid of the Lord; let it be to me according to your word." Mary freely consecrated her life to the will of the Lord. She honored God by giving her heart to him, and she lived this reality every day by lovingly caring for Jesus and following him.

Mary's life inspires us to be better Christians. We've learned the great commandment to love God and our neighbor. But are we kind to other people, or quick to criticize those whose opinions differ from ours? Do we honor the Lord with our hearts, or do we just give him lip service?

Let us seek Mary's help in living out our faith so that our actions will align with what we say we believe.

— Katie Choudhary

PRAYERFULLY CONSIDER the ways you can cultivate authentic love of God and love of neighbor into your daily living.

Prayer: Mother most pure, help me to act with purpose for Jesus. May my acts lead me closer to him.

February 28

"So faith, hope, love abide, these three; but the greatest of these is love."
— *1 Corinthians 13:13*

My uncle was part of the Greatest Generation, those who lived through the Great Depression and World War II. No matter how difficult his life was, he and his family always demonstrated a strong faith, hope in the future, and unconditional love. When my uncle's health declined, I witnessed his children care for him on a daily basis with the same faith, hope, and love they had experienced.

My extended family's legacy of faith, hope, and love was rooted in strong devotion to the Blessed Mother. Mary was their role model, and her life of faith in God gave my family hope that anything was possible, as long as the love of Christ was at the heart of their actions. Mary's love — pure, radiating beauty, grace, gentleness, and kindness — is always present and available to us. I hope that Mary's love will help me to pass on my family's legacy to my children.

— Mary Beth Desmond

WHO HAS MODELED faith, hope, and love to you? What spiritual practices help you grow in the three things that last?

Prayer: Hail Mary, full of grace, please fill the hearts of the faithful with the desire to share Christ's message of faith, hope, and love.

~ SURRENDER ~

March 1

"Be still, and know that I am God." — Psalms 46:10

My husband and I often spend time at a lake in northern Wisconsin. At dusk, once the fishermen retire, the lake becomes quiet and still. We like to drift with the tide on a pontoon boat and watch magnificent sunsets. This is followed by a clear view of a breathtaking night sky which features billions of stars. There the breadth and depth of God's creation is set before us. With minds free from distractions, we are ready to embrace the silence and totally surrender to God's loving presence.

Total surrender to God means that we, like Mary, accept that we are not in control of what God may call us to do. Mary's life invites us to trust in God's providence, to let go and allow our creator God to work within us. We are his, and God has a plan for us. Stillness and silence invite God to lead. When we finally surrender our lives to God, we will come fully alive.

— Sharon A. Abel, PhD

TAKE TIME TODAY to be still. Surrender to the presence of the Lord. Listen for what God is speaking to you. May your response be, "Lead me, Lord."

Prayer: Mary, you have taught me how to be still before the Lord. You listened, God spoke, and his plan for our salvation fell into place. May I listen, and surrender, to God's plan for me.

March 2

"At the end of eight days, when he was circumcised, he was called Jesus, the name given by the angel before he was conceived in the womb." — Luke 2:21

When the time came, Mary and Joseph chose to name their Son, Jesus. This was not a family name, but rather the one that had been given to the child by the angel Gabriel. Mary surrendered her preferences and was obedient to the angel's instruction.

Obedience is not a popular concept in our culture. But many misunderstand what true obedience is. Obedience to the will of God is not something imposed upon us; it is something we must freely choose to do. Obedience doesn't mean that we don't think for ourselves or that we have lost all sense of our identity. On the contrary, obedience to God means that we have found our true identity as beloved sons and daughters of the Lord. Then it is a joy for us to follow the ways of the Lord, as it was for Mary.

— Dr. Mary Amore

CONSIDER HOW YOU MIGHT DEEPEN your obedience to God and renew your spiritual journey.

Prayer: Blessed Mother, help me to be obedient to the will of God, that I may freely surrender my life into his loving care.

March 3

"And Jesus said to her, 'O woman, what have you to do with me? My hour has not yet come.' His mother said to the servants, 'Do whatever he tells you.'"
— *John 2:4*

At the wedding feast in Cana, Jesus listened to the prompting of his mother and changed water into wine. When Mary says, "Do whatever he tells you," she is also speaking to all of us. If we follow Mary's directive and adhere to the will of the Lord, then the watery events of our lives have the opportunity to be changed into choice wine as well.

Jesus' words are clear and straightforward; yet how often do we fail to do what the Lord asks of us? At times, it seems that our broken world takes great delight in meeting conflict and diversity with hatred and condemnation. Spiritual transformation is possible, but only if we are willing to surrender our own willfulness over to the Lord so that we may follow Mary's example and do whatever Jesus tells us.

— Lauren Nelson

IF YOU WERE STANDING in the presence of our Blessed Mother and she told you to do whatever he tells you, what would your response be?

Prayer: Mary, help us to listen to the words of your Son, Jesus, that we may do whatever he asks of us.

March 4

*"Greater love has no man than this, that a man lay down his life
for his friends." — John 15:13*

At the age of thirty-two, I was diagnosed with breast cancer. Alone and frightened, I opened up to my friends and church community about my diagnosis not long after surgery. I was overwhelmed by the great outpouring of support through meals, visits, prayers, child care, and acts of love. My friends and family laid down their lives for me by surrendering their fears to visit me and entering into my pain to comfort me with their love.

During this dark time, I prayed to Mary daily and begged her to ask Jesus to heal me. Blessed Mary was my strength; she was there to help me when I was alone and afraid.

Mary held me when I cried, soothed my fears and sorrows, and invited me to surrender my cross moments to her. She will do the same for you.

— Dr. Barb Jarvis Pauls

HOW CAN I SURRENDER my fears of reaching out to others today and be present like Mother Mary? Is there someone I know who needs a friend to inspire faith and give reassurance of God's abiding love?

Prayer: Holy Mary, Mother of God, thank you for all the ways you have been my friend and confidante. Help me to open up and surrender to the faith and love that you share in Jesus, your Son.

March 5

"Yet with a contrite heart and a humble spirit may we be accepted /... / for there will be no shame for those who trust in you." — Daniel 3:39-40*

In our business-as-usual reactive mode, it is often difficult for us to be contrite and humble, much less forgiving. Mary's life inspires us to prayerfully reflect upon things before we act or react. In times of difficulties and great challenges, Mary prayerfully surrendered the events in her life over to the Lord. In this responsive mode, she was able to fulfill God's plan for her.

Surrender is a choice we make of our own free will and with God's grace. With Mary's help, we can prayerfully surrender our anger, our desire for control, and our need for security over to the Lord. When we do, we grow in our spiritual life.

— John Holmes

CHOOSE A TIME TODAY, even if only for five minutes, to sit quietly with God. Prayerfully ponder the following: What are the one or two major blocks to God's grace in your life? Pray to let go of those obstacles so that you can become more receptive to God's grace.

Prayer: Dearest Mother Mary, continue to lead me to your Son and help me to be in a better position to do what God calls me to do.

* *Some texts identify this passage as part of "The Prayer of Azariah in the Furnace" (vv. 16-17) within Daniel 3.*

March 6

"Yet, O LORD, you are our Father; / we are the clay, and you are our potter; / we are all the work of your hand." — Isaiah 64:8

It is startling to learn how deeply we have been living in delusion, or to come face to face with the realization of how we have not been relying on God, really.

My twenty-year-old son had never had any health issues more serious than a pitching injury during high school baseball. On a recent study-abroad program, he had trouble breathing and Italian doctors found a large tumor in his sinus and cranial cavity. The life that we knew, his and mine, immediately came to a screeching halt. There had been absolutely no warning signs of a detour ahead. After a twelve-hour operation, six weeks of recovery, and daily radiation for six-plus weeks, they found more cancer. Now more radiation is scheduled. Daily, I ask God, "Where are you?"

— Betty Crane

IN MOMENTS OF DESPAIR, I think of Mary at the foot of Jesus' cross, looking up at his brutalized, crucified body. What were her thoughts? How was she able to surrender to the Crucifixion? In the darkness, let us cling to Mary for help in surrendering to our heavenly Father.

Prayer: Mary, help me learn to surrender to God's plan for me and for those I love just as you surrendered your life to your heavenly Father. Help me to accept how God shapes my life and my heart.

March 7

"But as for me and my house, we will serve the LORD." — Joshua 24:15

Mary's decision to serve God came in the form of her unconditional yes, her willingness not only to bear Jesus, the Son of God, but to raise him and accompany him through life. As his mother, Mary freely and completely devoted herself to this divine calling. When Jesus grew up and took on public ministry, Mary continued to offer her life in supporting Jesus as he healed the sick, gave sight to the blind, and offered mercy to those in need.

Today's families come in all shapes and sizes, and not everyone's household is in perfect order; yet Mary's life gives us hope. Mary invites us to follow in her steps as we place God at the center of our family life. Then we and our house will be able to serve the Lord.

— Lauren Nelson

CONSIDER YOUR OWN FAMILY. What could you surrender so that you and your household could better serve God? What does serving the Lord look like in your particular family?

Prayer: Mary, help me to surrender my heart and the lives of all those that I love over to the Lord, so that our house may love and serve God all the days of our lives.

March 8

*"This is eternal life, that they know you the only true God,
and Jesus Christ whom you have sent." — John 17:3*

There is a Navajo tale that tells of a warrior who searched for God. Seeing God on a mountaintop, the scout rode up and dismounted. He took three arrows and held them high above his head, then placed the arrows at God's feet. God waved the scout away.

The scout returned to his horse, took the woven blanket, held it high above his head, and laid it at God's feet. God waved the scout away. Then the scout took his most prized possession; he led his horse to God, and placed the reins in God's hands. God waived the scout away. The scout extended his arms toward God and dropped to his knees. God looked at the scout and smiled. The warrior realized he could not negotiate a relationship with God on his terms. He must surrender all.

Mary made a total surrender to God. She held nothing back. She did not negotiate. All she was and had she handed over to God to do as he pleased. Surrender brought her freedom, and surrender can bring freedom to us as well.

— Joseph Abel, PhD

WHAT DO YOU CLING TO? How can you surrender it to God today?

Prayer: Mary, your life shows us the way of surrender. May we follow that path and come to true freedom.

March 9

*"And he called to him the multitude with his disciples, and said to them,
'If any man would come after me, let him deny himself and take up
his cross and follow me. For whoever would save his life will lose it;
and whoever loses his life for my sake and the gospel's will save it.'"*
— *Mark 8:34-35*

To those of us who want to follow Christ, the challenge is clear. Denying ourselves and taking up our crosses is an act of surrender. We surrender our desire for security, affection, and, most of all, control. We surrender those ego drivers we think are so important. Mary did this from the outset. She surrendered in perfect trust to God's will for her.

When our crosses seem more than we can bear, we can turn to Mother Mary, who can help us find the courage to surrender our lives to God. When we surrender our crosses, we gain the strength to carry them, and a better perspective on bearing the trials in our lives.

— John Holmes

WHAT CROSS ARE YOU CARRYING at the moment? Ask Mary's help in placing this matter into the hands of our loving Lord.

Prayer: Holy Mother, thank you for your example of trusting in the Lord. Help me to surrender all that I have in the hopes of gaining eternal life.

March 10

"How hard it will be for those who have riches to enter the kingdom of God."
— Mark 10:23

How much value do we place on objects? Do we cling to the things of this world, giving them power over ourselves, or our relationships with family and friends? This Gospel passage challenges us to think of everything relative to eternal life. This is what our Blessed Mother did. Because she kept everything in proper perspective, she was able to surrender everything about her earthly life for the sake of what was eternal.

When Mother Mary fled to Elizabeth, with Jesus conceived in her womb, she surrendered everything, even that which was not material possessions, for the love of God. Mary surrendered her fear of being judged, her safety, her reputation, and her attachment to her community. She surrendered her will to the will of God.

— Dr. Barb Jarvis Pauls

WHAT DO YOU VALUE most in life? How important is your relationship with the Lord? Are you willing to surrender your pride, your prejudices, and your possessions as you carry on your mission in the world?

Prayer: Mother Mary, pray for us to be generous and self-giving, surrendering our giftedness for the greater good of all who need us.

March 11

*"Trust in the LORD with all your heart, / and do not rely
on your own insight." — Proverbs 3:5*

Is there a greater example of trusting in the Lord than Mary, a young girl from Nazareth? Although we are people of faith, we often feel we know what's best for us. We pray for a certain outcome and even get upset if our prayers are not answered to our liking.

Mary's life invites us to keep the prayer of surrender at the forefront of our hearts. Mary did not stand before the angel Gabriel and say, "I'm not sure how this is going to work." Mary simply surrendered her free will and trusted that God would make her path straight. God put his plan of salvation into Mary's hands, and Mary put her whole life into the hands of God.

— Lauren Nelson

CALL TO MIND a particular situation or event that you have not yet totally surrendered over to the Lord. Ask Mary to help you trust that God will make your path straight as he did hers.

Prayer: Mary, help me to surrender my life over to the Lord as you did. Be with me as I walk the path that God sets forth before me.

March 12

*"When the wine failed, the mother of Jesus said to him,
'They have no wine.'"* — John 2:3

Mary is an inspiration for all of us, especially when we run out of wine. When life is difficult and we are depleted, we can learn from Mary's unwavering faith in Jesus. This is not always easy, because we like to be in control. We like to tell God what to do. We bring God our prayers and petitions, but most often we also give him a suggestion about how things should work out.

At the wedding feast at Cana, Mary simply stated the problem; she didn't tell Jesus how he should solve it. Our Blessed Mother shows us how to place our complete trust in God, to live with the reality that the Lord knows what is best and that we can — and should — trust him. This calls us to cultivate a spirit of surrender, a willingness to let go of our own agendas and place our entire lives into the hands of our God, who fashioned us from the beginning.

— Dr. Mary Amore

GIVE ONE SITUATION in your life totally over to God. What can you do to avoid taking it back again?

Prayer: Mary, help me to have your faith. Teach me to trust in the Lord every moment of every day.

March 13

"Behold, I am the handmaid of the Lord; let it be to me according to your word." — Luke 1:38

From a worldly perspective, surrender can seem a lot like weakness. Whenever someone is giving up, we tend to see it as a failure. But surrendering to God is a completely different experience. It is anything but weakness and failure.

We see that Mary's visit with the angel Gabriel begins with fear and concern. But because Mary had already resolved to be the handmaid of the Lord, she surrenders to God's will. What comes from this surrender is nothing short of miraculous.

Surrendering to God is not an act of weakness. In fact, it is one of the most courageous things we can do. The world's message is to depend on ourselves; but God's continual message is to fear not and trust him. When we surrender our lives to the Lord, we can fully live in God's peace and joy. Our lives are transformed when we surrender to God.

— Suzette Horyza

THINK OF SOMETHING you once surrendered to God. What did God do with what you entrusted to him?

Prayer: Mary, teach me how to surrender the things in my life, especially those I cannot change; help me to follow in your footsteps by doing the will of God.

March 14

"The LORD is my strength and my shield; / in him my heart trusts."
— *Psalms 28:7*

My friend asked me to be her confirmation sponsor. We met frequently to discuss faith topics that interested her. The year of preparation went well. It concluded with a powerful retreat experience. When confirmation was two weeks away, we decided to go shopping for her dress. In between trying on dresses, she asked me, "Will God's Spirit always be with me?"

I was beside myself. For months, we had talked endlessly about the presence of the Holy Spirit in her life. In that moment, I realized I had neglected to include Mary in our discussions. Like Mary, each one of us is asked to surrender to the Holy Spirit. I invited her to be open to the new life God was calling her to, like Mary was so long ago.

— Sharon A. Abel, PhD

BE SILENT. Close your eyes and surrender to the Spirit.

Prayer: Mary, help me surrender to the Spirit and let God's grace flow in my mind. Show me how surrender to the Spirit can be my dawn. Lord, send a gentle breeze of graces flowing by. Stir within my mind your vision for my life. Lord, set a flame in me to light my darkened way. Gently guide my steps down pathways left unknown.

March 15

*"'My hour has not yet come.' His mother said to the servants,
'Do whatever he tells you.'"* — John 2:4-5

As children, our mothers can seem infallible. As we mature, we grow to understand that our mothers are just people, too, who need the same love and devotion they are called to give us.

At the wedding feast at Cana, we see a pivotal reversal of roles. The giving and benevolent mother now makes a request from her Son. Jesus fulfills his mother's request in the first miracle of his public ministry by changing water into wine. Just as Mary surrendered her will to the Lord years before, Jesus now surrenders himself to the request of his mother. All flows from mutual love and trust.

Perhaps we did not all grow up with a loving mother, or even an image of a perfect mother, but most of us can probably recall a person who was always there for us; someone who surrendered himself or herself to be there for us. In this person, we see a glimpse of our mother, Mary.

— Dr. Mary Amore

REMEMBER A PERSON who surrendered to you. Now, recall a time you surrendered to someone else.

Prayer: Mary, help soften our hearts, and guide us toward the love you shared with your Son, Jesus.

March 16

"Behold, like the clay in the potter's hand, so are you in my hand,
O house of Israel." — Jeremiah 18:6

Mary is the perfect example of clay in the hands of the potter. Mary allowed God to shape and form her life into what God desired her to be. She trusted that the Lord would gently mold her to perfection.

Even as her beloved Son hung on the cross, Mary accepted whatever she encountered as another movement of the potter's hands. She trusted that, just as the potter reveals the beauty of his creations, the beauty of her life would be revealed in God's handiwork.

We, too, are clay in the hands of our divine potter, and we are being shaped and molded by God. In this divine process of creation we are invited to bend to God's will as the Lord makes of us what he intends. In the end, the beauty of our lives as fashioned by the hands of our creator will be revealed, just as it was in Mary's life.

— Lauren Nelson

How is the Lord fashioning your life? In what ways can you surrender to the creative forces of God?

Prayer: Mary, your life inspires me to be a moldable piece of clay in the hands of Our Lord. Guide me in surrendering my life to God, that I may become his divine creation.

March 17

"Come to me, all who labor and are heavy laden, and I will give you rest."
— *Matthew 11:28*

Here, the Lord is asking us to surrender our problems into his loving care. He wants us to let go of our desire to control the people and events of our lives and trust in him. This is a difficult task for many people.

Mary's life shows us the pathway to spiritual surrender. As the mother of our Savior, Mary lovingly let go of Jesus when it came time for him to leave her and follow his call to preach, heal, and evangelize. She also surrendered the unspeakable pain of her broken heart as she stood beneath the cross as Jesus gave his life so that we could live with him forever.

So much of what we experience every day can be lifted off of our shoulders simply by giving it to the Lord. We can follow Mary's example and prayerfully surrender our joys and sorrows to the Lord and find rest in his loving arms.

— Dr. Barb Jarvis Pauls

WHAT BURDENS can I hand over to the Lord this day? What joys can I give to God?

Prayer: Mother Mary, help me to trust in the workings of the Lord, that I may have the strength to surrender both the problems and joys of my life into the hands of our loving God.

March 18

"I appeal to you therefore, brethren, by the mercies of God, to present your bodies as a living sacrifice, holy and acceptable to God, which is your spiritual worship. Do not be conformed to this world but be transformed by the renewal of your mind, that you may prove what is the will of God, what is good and acceptable and perfect." — Romans 12:1-2

Paul appealed to his fellow disciples to surrender their bodies as a living sacrifice. This models Christ's sacrificial surrender to death on the cross. Warning believers not to conform to the age, Paul encourages us to renew our minds. Once that happens, we can discern the will of God for us.

Again, we have Mary as an example, giving her all in cooperation with the Holy Spirit to become the mother of our Lord and Savior. While God's will for Mary seems quite straightforward to us, she needed to surrender first in order to see with a renewed mind. Mary gave God her body. Her surrender filled her with grace, the grace necessary to become the Mother of God.

— John Holmes

WHAT RENEWS YOUR MIND? How are you called to offer God your body as a "living sacrifice"?

Prayer: O Virgin Mary, thank you for your surrender and your response to your calling! Help me to be open to a change in my heart and mind.

March 19

"You heard me say to you, 'I go away, and I will come to you.' If you loved me, you would have rejoiced, because I go to the Father; for the Father is greater than I." — John 14:28

Being separated from the people we love hurts. Separation can be experienced through death, a loved one moving far away, a conflict in a relationship with a close friend, a divorce, a loss of employment and colleagues, and more. In times like these examples, I have often sought solace in the arms of our Blessed Mother. Mary knows what we are feeling when we are separated from the ones we love. As Joseph's wife and the mother of Jesus, Mary experienced more than her share of suffering and hardship, and she coped with these events by surrendering her life over to the Lord.

— Dr. Barb Jarvis Pauls

IDENTIFY TIMES IN YOUR LIFE when you have suffered a painful separation from someone or something you loved deeply. Prayerfully invite our mother, Mary, to share your pain and to help you find the courage to give this event over to the Lord.

Prayer: Holy Mary, Mother of God, pray for us as we surrender our losses, our loves, and the painful experience of letting go. We trust in your comfort and hope for your grace in our midst.

March 20

"When Jesus saw his mother, and the disciple whom he loved standing near, he said to his mother, 'Woman, behold, your son!' Then he said to the disciple, 'Behold, your mother!' And from that hour the disciple took her to his own home." — John 19:26-27

Women had no voice in first-century Palestine. Their well-being was dependent upon the men in their family who took care of them. St. John tells us that as Jesus hung on the cross his last thoughts were about his mother. In this poignant moment of self-emptying and self-gift, Mary bravely accepted that her Son, Jesus, was about to die. She also accepted the beloved disciple as her son. This could not have been easy. At this same moment in salvation history, God gave all of us to Mary, too. Mary became our mother, the mother of all who follow Jesus.

Mary's example challenges us to be faithful to God even in the midst of tragedy. With Mary as our heavenly mother, we are never alone to face the perils of life.

— Lauren Nelson

PLACE YOURSELF at the foot of the cross. Consider one way you can welcome Mary into your heart today.

Prayer: Mary, come close to my heart. Be a mother to me; help me to honor you each day.

March 21

"It is no longer I who live, but Christ who lives in me; and the life I now live in the flesh I live by faith in the Son of God, who loved me and gave himself for me." — Galatians 2:20

So many people have a hard time with the topic of surrender. They can't imagine giving themselves up. Who will I be if I give myself over?

Early on in my marriage I struggled with a gripping addiction. Eventually, I had to make a choice between getting help or losing my family. One night I said to God: "Okay, I've been doing this my way, and it's not working. I need your help." The moment I surrendered, I started on the road to recovery.

I'm sure that when Mary's pregnancy began, she had no idea what life would be like. But she knew that she was giving her life over to a loving God. I found out that God has goodness in store. The life of Christ enters us — as it did literally with Mary — and becomes our new identity.

— Christine Grano

WHAT IS GOD ASKING YOU to give over, to surrender to? Can you surrender into the loving arms of God as Mary did?

Prayer: Mary, thank you for your perfect example of surrender. Pray for me that I may do the same.

March 22

"Have this mind among yourselves, which was in Christ Jesus, who, though he was in the form of God, did not count equality with God a thing to be grasped, but emptied himself, taking the form of a servant, being born in the likeness of men. And being found in human form he humbled himself and became obedient unto death, even death on a cross." — Philippians 2:5-8

Paul instructs us to adopt the same attitude Jesus had. This attitude, which is ours in Christ, recognizes the role our ego plays. It warns us that if our egos rule, we are likely not to see God's plan or will for us. We must empty ourselves of our selves.

Mary clearly had this attitude of self-surrender and embraced the art of self-emptying. How else could she possibly have had the courage to willingly surrender her life over to the Lord? What can we do to model this? Let us seek our Blessed Mother's assistance in letting go of our egos and the desire to control, so that we may pattern our lives after Mary's, and become obedient to the Father.

— John Holmes

FROM WHAT do you need detachment? In what ways might you consider self-emptying?

Prayer: Mother Mary, help me let go of attachments. With your help and God's grace may I adopt the attitude of your Son.

March 23

"When the feast was ended, as they were returning, the boy Jesus stayed behind in Jerusalem. His parents did not know it." — Luke 2:43

Where was Jesus? Mary wondered and worried for three days as she and Joseph wandered in search of their twelve-year-old Son. The distress Mary felt shows in her words: "Son, why have you treated us so? Behold, your father and I have been looking for you anxiously" (Lk 2:48).

Like Mary, we can be overwrought in the face of unknowing, ambiguity, and distress. For most of us, being thrust into the unknown, the space of uncertainty, is difficult and frightening. As a human being, Mary must certainly have experienced the feelings of upset, worry, and distress when Jesus was missing. That shared human experience is why Mary can hear our prayers compassionately. But Mary knew that even in the unknown God was with her. That reality gave her the courage to surrender to him.

— Dr. Barb Jarvis Pauls

WHAT ARE YOU ANXIOUS or distressed about today? What are the uncertainties you are facing in your life? Ask Mary to help you find Jesus in the midst of them.

Prayer: Holy Mary, help us surrender with faith and trust in God's presence, even when we lose sight of him.

March 24

"I can do all things in him who strengthens me." — *Philippians 4:13*

Mary became pregnant by the power of the Holy Spirit at a young age, and was told by the angel Gabriel that her childless cousin Elizabeth was also pregnant. Shortly after the birth of Jesus, Mary presented him at the Temple. There Simeon prophesied that a sword would pierce her heart. How did young Mary make sense of these miraculous proclamations in her life?

Mary didn't know everything the future held. It was Mary's great faith that enabled her to surrender her life to God without seeking an explanation. She drew strength from knowing that God can accomplish all things.

Our lives are full of people and events we just don't understand. Many of us seek solutions and explanations in order to gain a sense of control. Instead, we are called to model Mary's life of trust, which invites us to surrender all into the hands of the Lord.

— Lauren Nelson

CALL TO MIND one situation in your life that is beyond your knowledge or understanding. Seek Mary's help to strengthen your faith so that you have the courage to surrender this to God.

Prayer: Mary, help me to accept all the mysteries of my life and be with me as I surrender them to the Lord.

March 25
Solemnity of the Annunciation

"Behold, a virgin shall conceive and bear a son, / and shall call his name Emmanuel / (which means, God with us)." — Matthew 1:23

Mary was a young virgin when the angel Gabriel came to announce that she would bear a son. Upon hearing this news, Mary's only question was, "How can this be?" She didn't interrogate or try to bargain with the angel about what was to take place. Mary simply surrendered her life to the power of the Holy Spirit. Knowing that he was with her, she chose to be with him.

The Annunciation has much to teach us about living in this wounded and broken world. No matter how bleak things appear or how violent the world becomes, God is with us today and always. The Lord did not abandon his people of long ago, and he will not abandon us. As Christians, our call is to follow God as Mary did, and surrender our pressing agendas, our movements, and our fears over to the Lord, trusting that he is with us.

— Dr. Mary Amore

CONSIDER THE WAYS that your life reflects the reality that "God is with us."

Prayer: Mary, help me to have the courage to live each day with the knowledge that God is with us and that I am never alone to face my fears.

March 26

*"You call me Teacher and Lord; and you are right, for so I am.
If I then, your Lord and Teacher, have washed your feet,
you also ought to wash one another's feet.'" — John 13:13-14*

Jesus surrenders in action. He recognizes his relationship with his disciples, but steps out of the role of Lord and teacher to one of servant. This very humble act is an image of surrender.

Mary was always the humble servant; often, simply by being present. She never made things about herself, but always about others, and always focused on Jesus. From the Annunciation, to the wedding in Cana, to her presence at the foot of her Son's cross, Mary was there as a servant. She was always prepared to surrender herself for others.

— John Holmes

How CAN YOU put yourself in service to others?

Prayer: Mother Mary, thank you for your service and your example of service in community. Help me to follow you and your Son in the same way.

March 27

"My grace is sufficient for you, for my power is made perfect in weakness."
— 2 Corinthians 12:9

In our competitive society, it's difficult to resist the pressure to be perfect. We are told that we should strive to be perfect employees, husbands, wives, parents, and neighbors. We like to project that we are in control and tend to become defensive when criticized. We are taught how to accentuate our good qualities and minimize our weaknesses. This often serves us well in gaining approval.

Sometimes, however, our "strengths" can work against us — even sabotage us. If we are generous to others all the time, we may find that we have neglected our family's needs. If we are enthusiastic about our work, we can lose a sense of how to balance how we spend our time. Our strengths can become our weaknesses.

Mother Mary knew the secret of the spiritual life: our weaknesses, given to God, can become his strength. His grace is enough. His power is perfected in what we are unable to do.

— Dr. Barb Jarvis Pauls

HOW CAN YOU SURRENDER your need for perfection, control, and approval? What weakness or frailty can you give to God?

Prayer: Most Holy Mother of God, help us to surrender to the times we are weak, remembering that the power of God's grace will be sufficient for us.

March 28

"Clothe yourselves, all of you, with humility toward one another,
for 'God opposes the proud, but gives grace to the humble.'"
— *1 Peter 5:5*

Humility before God is not a popular concept in today's egotistical and overconfident society. Mary's life is a reminder that the God of grace will exalt us when we do not exalt ourselves. Mary knew how to cast her cares upon God, trusting that he cared about her and would care for her. Her gentle surrender to God encourages us to surrender our concerns to the Lord, too. God rewarded Mary by sharing his kingdom with her, making her queen of heaven and earth. He promises to reward us with eternal life.

— Lauren Nelson

EMULATE MARY TODAY. Embrace the humility she brings and acknowledge that one (or more) of your accomplishments are from his grace. Then surrender something you are concerned about to his care.

Prayer: Mary, help me to put away my pride and to be thankful for all God has done for me.

March 29

*"Jesus said to him, 'If you would be perfect, go, sell what you possess
and give to the poor, and you will have treasure in heaven;
and come, follow me.' When the young man heard this he went away
sorrowful; for he had great possessions." — Matthew 19:21-22*

Mary lived this Scripture passage to the fullest. When asked to become the mother of Jesus, Mary didn't hesitate. Mary acted bravely and without fear, leaving everything she had behind, including her future and her dreams and aspirations, to follow the will of God.

Mary's actions invite us to do some serious soul-searching. How open are we to leaving behind a cushy job, material possessions, and a comfortable lifestyle in order to follow the Lord? The Lord does not usually expect us to literally drop everything; but if he did, what would our response be? Mary willingly gave herself body and soul to the Lord, and she is here to show us how we can leave everything behind and follow Jesus.

— Dr. Mary Amore

WHAT IS THE DRIVING FORCE in your life? Money? Power? Enjoyment? Family? Where does Jesus fit into your priorities?

Prayer: Mary, help me to let go of all that keeps me from following Jesus with my heart and soul.

March 30

"For I know the plans I have for you, says the Lord, plans for welfare and not for evil, to give you a future and a hope." — Jeremiah 29:11

Mary's parents, Joachim and Anne, would have introduced their daughter to the Scriptures so that she might come to know the God of Israel, the Giver of all that is good. The words of the prophets were frequently read by the Jews to give them hope and trust in God, especially during difficult times.

Hearing and discussing the wisdom of the prophets surely inspired Mary to stand firm in her faith. These deep convictions prepared her to say "yes" to God's plan, to surrender her life to him, trusting that God would always be with her. Mary's life inspires us to turn our lives over to the Lord and trust that his plan is one of prosperity and hope.

— Sharon A. Abel, PhD

ARE YOU OPEN to releasing control of your life to God? Seek Mary's help that you may learn to trust in the Lord.

Prayer: Mary, may I come to know my God as abundant love and surrender myself to his plan for me with faithful confidence as you did all during your earthly life. Like you, may I live each day according to his will.

March 31

"If any man would come after me, let him deny himself and take up his cross and follow me. For whoever would save his life will lose it; and whoever loses his life for my sake and the gospel's will save it." — Mark 8:34-35

Mary was the first person to surrender her life in pursuit of discipleship. She gave up the life she anticipated for herself and Joseph when she chose to answer God's call to become the mother of Jesus. Mary freely surrendered her life and her future, and took up her cross. It became the source of her deepest joy.

Mary's life inspires us to take a second look at our own hopes and dreams. Do they align with God's plan for us, or are they rooted in our personal preferences and goals?

— Lauren Nelson

CONSIDER THE WAYS God might direct your dreams and aspirations, if you let him. Ask Mary to guide your steps to the right path for the future, one that leads away from self and toward God.

Prayer: Mary, you surrendered your entire life and all your dreams in order to be God's servant. Pray that God's will becomes my deepest desire, and help me to follow your example.

~ FAITHFULNESS ~

Palm Sunday

*"So they took branches of palm trees and went out to meet him, crying,
'Hosanna! Blessed is he who comes in the name of the Lord,
even the King of Israel.'" — John 12:13*

None of us has any idea of what tomorrow will bring. Joy can turn into sorrow in the blink of an eye. On Palm Sunday, Mary's Son was hailed as King and palm branches paved a peaceful path for Jesus to enter into the city of Jerusalem. Several days later, he was violently executed on a cross. While we may never know what Mary was feeling on Palm Sunday, we can be certain that it was her unwavering faith that sustained her in the days that followed.

Mary's life teaches us that our faith must be strong so that we can endure all that life will bring. She is here to help us deepen our faith in times of joy, so that we can find strength in times of suffering.

— Dr. Mary Amore

TAKE A MOMENT to thank the Lord for all of your blessings. Make a list of three joys that you can look to for strength when life is difficult.

Prayer: Mary, help me to deepen my relationship with Jesus so that I may have the strength and courage to carry my crosses from death to new life.

Monday of Holy Week

"The LORD is my light and my salvation; / whom shall I fear?"
— *Psalms 27:1*

After hearing about Jesus' triumphant entrance into Jerusalem, most assuredly Mary also heard the cries of the mob which were turning against her Son, calling him a blasphemer and seeking to stone him to death. In those last days, Mary found herself unable to protect her Son from the power of those who were seeking to harm him. Rather than fearing what was about to transpire, our Blessed Mother entrusted everything to the Lord.

Like Mary, we have moments in our lives that make us feel powerless. Perhaps a loved one is suffering and it becomes painful to accompany him or her through daily struggles. Perhaps a family member has turned away from God and we feel utterly helpless to change the situation. In moments of fear and anxiety, we can turn to Mother Mary and ask for help to deepen our faith in God and his presence in our lives.

— Dr. Mary Amore

INVITE MARY to help you calm your fears and place your life completely in the hands of the Lord.

Prayer: Mary, help me increase my faith so that I may not fear the events of my life but recognize that the Lord is my light and my salvation.

Tuesday of Holy Week

"When it was evening, he sat at table with the twelve disciples; and as they were eating, he said, 'Truly, I say to you, one of you will betray me.'"
— *Matthew 26:20-21*

The events leading to the passion and death of Jesus include many acts of betrayal. Among the worst were those of Judas Iscariot, one of the Twelve, who turned Jesus over to his enemies for thirty pieces of silver. These deeds of deception pierced Mary's heart with sorrow; yet Mary remained strong in her faith. She did not allow hurt to affect her relationship with God.

We, too, experience disappointment and hurt at the hands of those we love and trust. When a family member, spouse, or close friend betrays us, it can tear our hearts in two and fill us with a desire for revenge. Mary can help us turn away from the inclination to strike back. Her motherly love shows us how to regain our footing and trust God to take care of us when we are wronged.

— Dr. Mary Amore

CALL TO MIND a time when you felt betrayed. Ask Mary for the strength and guidance to pray for all those who have hurt you.

Prayer: Mary, your faith sustained you through many difficult times and kept you from seeking revenge. Help me to follow your example.

Wednesday of Holy Week

"He said to his disciples, 'You know that after two days the Passover is coming, and the Son of man will be delivered up to be crucified.'"
— *Matthew 26:1-2*

What must have been going through Mary's mind as Jesus announced to his disciples that he was about to die? As his mother, her first instinct may have been to save Jesus from this horrible execution. Or perhaps she was tempted to get angry at God for what was about to transpire. Nevertheless, in the midst of unspeakable violence against her Son, Mary remained faithful to the Lord. She trusted that God would not abandon her — or Jesus — in their time of need.

Mary's experience as the mother of Jesus invites us to do some soul-searching. When our lives are difficult and pain is everywhere, many of us tend to blame God for our troubles. We may even question our faith at its most basic level and ask, "Where are you God?" Mary's life invites us to remain faithful in times of suffering — for God is with us always.
— Dr. Mary Amore

INVITE MARY to face today's trials and tribulations with you.

Prayer: Mary, help me to follow your example and to place my pain and distress into the hands of the Lord.

Holy Thursday

"For I have given you an example, that you also should do as I have done to you." — John 13:15

At the Last Supper Jesus washed the feet of the disciples, providing them, and us, an example of humility and loving service. Humble service to others is not common in today's self-centered society as many people do favors for another with the expectation of receiving something in return. Genuine and selfless service is, however, the hallmark of a life of faithful discipleship. Jesus summons us to do for others as he has done for us.

No one demonstrates this better than Mary. Even as the hour of his death approached, Mary's life modeled a faithful response to the Lord's call to humble service. From the cradle to the cross, Mary never wavered in her faith. She lived her life as a humble handmaid of the Lord. Mary is here to help us to recognize and lovingly respond to the needs of those in our lives, without expecting anything in return.

— Dr. Mary Amore

CALL TO MIND a family member or friend who is in need. How can you serve that person today?

Prayer: Mother, your life is one of gentle service to the Lord. Help me to model my life after yours.

Good Friday

"When Jesus saw his mother, and the disciple whom he loved standing near, he said to his mother, 'Woman, behold, your son!' Then he said to the disciple, 'Behold, your mother!'" — John 19:26-27

Mary's deep faith in God did not spare her from suffering. Rather, it brought her to the foot of the cross where she witnessed the brutal crucifixion and death of her beloved Son, Jesus. As he hung there in agony, Jesus did not abandon Mary, but entrusted his mother to the care of his beloved disciple. In that moment, Mary became the mother of that disciple. She also became the mother of all the disciples of Christ in every place and age.

We have all suffered loss, and the deep wounds of grief, anger, guilt, and despair can hinder our spiritual growth. As our heavenly mother, Mary is here to hold us in our darkest moments of grief and sorrow as only a mother can. She is faithful in helping to tend our spiritual wounds.

— Dr. Mary Amore

IS THERE A LOSS IN LIFE you are grieving? Ask Mary to grieve with you and guide you on the path of acceptance and faith.

Prayer: Mother of Mercy, take my hand and lead me through the difficulties of this day.

Holy Saturday

"[The women] saw the tomb, and how his body was laid; then they returned, and prepared spices and ointments. On the Sabbath they rested according to the commandment." — Luke 23:55-56

There is an ancient homily that speaks of the day immediately following the Crucifixion: "Today there is a great silence over the earth, a great silence, and stillness, a great silence because the King sleeps."

Those of us who have lost a loved one know this feeling, the great silence that comes over us; the feeling of a loss so deep that it echoes no sound within us.

Mary surely experienced this kind of profound silence at the death of Jesus. Yet her faith in the Lord did not fail. Faithfulness carried her and all the women who mourned the loss of Jesus through their sorrow. Though overwhelmed by sadness, the women prepared what would be needed to bury Jesus properly, and they rested as the law required them to do. They found the strength to remain faithful because they trusted that God would be faithful, too.

— Dr. Mary Amore

INVITE THE BLESSED MOTHER into your silence. Ask her to show you how to respond to loss with faith.

Prayer: Virgin most sorrowful, help me to live faithfully in the midst of loss and despair.

Easter Sunday

"Why do you seek the living among the dead?
He is not here, but has risen." — Luke 24:5

The Scriptures are filled with stories of Jesus appearing to various disciples after his resurrection, yet there is not a single account that speaks of him appearing to his mother, Mary. Early Christian tradition, however, has suggested an encounter between Mary and the risen Jesus. Perhaps that is why she was not at the tomb with the other women who went to anoint his body. Whatever the case, Mary's heart must have filled with joy and glory on that first Easter morning. Her faith was not in vain.

Today, so many of us are stuck in Good Friday moments of pain, fear, and despair. In our broken world, it is difficult for us to remain faithful and find hope in the midst of darkness. Mary's life invites us to trust in the Lord, so that he can transform our darkness into the glorious light of the Resurrection.

— Dr. Mary Amore

HAVE YOU BEEN SEEKING life "among the dead"? Spend a few minutes asking Mary to help you find the risen Lord in your life today.

Prayer: Mary, your unwavering faith in the Lord inspires me. Help me to live my life in faithfulness with the hope and joy of the Risen Christ.

~ HOPE ~

April 1

"Seize the hope set before us. We have this as a sure and steadfast anchor of the soul." — Hebrews 6:18-19

Epitaphs on Christian tombs in the first century frequently displayed anchors alongside messages of hope. The symbol of the anchor evidently gained popularity during the periods of Roman persecutions. It was a means of affirming how the early Christians felt about Jesus in their anticipation of heaven. The anchor slowly fell out of widespread use in the fourth century as the Roman Empire embraced Christianity.

Today, Mary is a source and symbol of hope for us. Her entire life reflects the amazing works of our faithful God, who lifts up the lowly and remembers his promise of mercy. As our anchor of hope, Mary is here to reassure us that God will not abandon us when the turbulent seas of persecution or injustice threaten.

Mary's hope was in the fidelity of God and his promise of mercy. From this assurance, Mary believed, trusted, and hoped. The source of Mary's hope — and ours — is God's faithfulness.

— Joseph Abel, PhD

SPEND SOME QUIET TIME reflecting on the ways that hope has guided your spiritual journey.

Prayer: O Mary, help us to be people of hope by remembering God's faithfulness to us and his presence with us.

April 2

*"Lead me in your truth, and teach me, / for you are
the God of my salvation; / for you I wait all the day long."*
— *Psalms 25:5*

Hope is such a powerful gift. Relinquishing, trusting, giving up our cares and troubles to someone who is willing to take them on is one of the greatest gifts we will ever receive. We have a God who wants to guide us, teach us, and lead us to hope in him all day long. We are his priority, and his great love and support are there for the taking.

Yet how many of us really take God up on his offer? How often do we put our hope in someone or something else — or even ourselves — instead of putting our hope in God?

— Betty Bentley

MARY IS A BEAUTIFUL EXAMPLE of someone who put her hope in the Lord. Mary is there for us, too, willing to intercede on our behalf. Will we take her up on her offer?

Prayer: Mary, help us to accept the powerful gift of hope. Help us to follow God's lead, to accept his guidance, his teaching, and to hope in him always — all day long.

April 3

"It is he who remembered us in our low estate, / for his mercy endures for ever; / and rescued us from our foes, / for his mercy endures for ever."
— *Psalms 136:23-24*

Spring has always been my favorite season. After months of cold and snowy Midwestern winter days, many without sun, the colors seem to come alive in springtime. The hope I had all winter for the green grass, vibrant flowers, and kids joyfully playing outside comes to fruition.

For me, Mary's life is a lesson in hope. How often do we go through challenging moments and lose hope? How often do we want to cast blame or make excuses? Staring the death of her Son in the face, Mary could have blamed many others. Yet, our Blessed Mother maintained hope for what was to come. Mary invites us to remain hope-filled, as we place our trust in the Lord.

— Meg Bucaro

THINK ABOUT A TIME you have experienced hopelessness; reflect on Mary and how she must have felt through Christ's life and death. By grace, she remained hopeful for you and me.

Prayer: Blessed Mother, please strengthen my sense of hope, especially during moments when I falter. Grant me childlike hope, knowing that when we lean on Christ no lasting harm shall come our way.

April 4

"Honor the Lord with your substance / and with the first fruits of all your produce; / then your barns will be filled with plenty, / and your vats will be bursting with wine." — Proverbs 3:9-10

My community offers garden plots to residents who are eager to till the soil. I enjoy driving by just to see what's growing. In early spring, there are a few spots of green. By midsummer the garden is flourishing, and by September the harvest is ready.

We can envision our relationships with Mary and Jesus in this light. There are times we can't imagine the full harvest. But just as we nourish the plants in a garden, our hearts and souls also need time to grow. Our Blessed Mother shows us how to remain hopeful even when there isn't much to see. While the Lord may prune away all of our lifeless branches, it is the presence of our heavenly mother that encourages us to plant our spiritual roots in the life-giving soil of hope in her Son, Jesus.

— Alice Smith

CONSIDER ONE WAY that you can sow seeds of hope in the soil of your soul and in the lives of those you love.

Prayer: Mary, give to Jesus the fruits of my labor and help me to grow in my love for him all the days of my life.

April 5

"Behold, God is my salvation; / I will trust, and will not be afraid; / for the Lord God *is my strength and my song, / and he has become my salvation."*
— *Isaiah 12:2*

How often do we feel that the mere thought of hope is beyond the realm of possibilities? Mary is a spiritual mother who understands. She can be our source of hope in difficult situations.

The Scriptures recount many painful moments in Mary's life, times when her heart must have been broken with sorrow. Yet, she never lost hope or became discouraged.

Today, during times of world conflict and wars, our hearts are often touched by the images of suffering children. Mary understands this pain.

Like Mary, we, too, cannot avoid suffering; it's a part of life. Yet Mary's response to suffering invites us to live with the hope and promise that Our Lord is with us always, and we have nothing to fear. Mary is the mother of hope.

— Chris Hannighan-Wiehn

RECALL AN EXPERIENCE when you lived with hope in spite of personal difficulties. Do you believe that God will continue to be present during difficulties — both now and in the future?

Prayer: Mary, you are a loving mother and you will not turn me away when I am faced with difficulties. Grant me the gift of hope and peace of heart as I journey through this day.

April 6

"Awesome God, who keep covenant and mercy, let not all the hardship seem little to you that has come upon us." — Nehemiah 9:32

The Shawshank Redemption is the story of Andy Dufresne, a banker convicted of double homicide, who is serving a life sentence in the fictional Shawshank prison. Andy befriends Red, the jaded man inside who can get you anything you want, except a future. Red laments that it wasn't until he was sent to prison that he learned how to be a crook. Despite his circumstance, however, Andy is never without hope. In a memorable scene, he tells Red that hope is a good thing, "the best of things," and that no good thing ever dies.

Mary showed the same undefeatable spirit of hope. In Mary's culture, women were largely without rights. She was entirely dependent on subsistence farming and light trade work. Her land was occupied by a foreign force that disdained her way of life. Her Son suffered unjust execution. Still, Mary knew good things never die and that hardships are passing. Mary placed hope in what does last — the mercy of God from age to age.

— Joseph Abel, PhD

CALL TO MIND a difficult situation you are facing. Bring it to God by praying the Scripture above.

Prayer: O Mary, God's mercy was your hope; may it also be my hope and redemption.

April 7

"For I know the plans I have for you, says the LORD, plans for welfare and not for evil, to give you a future and a hope." — Jeremiah 29:11

Several years ago, I experienced life-altering news that left me feeling hopeless and unsure of myself as a mother.

A few weeks later, still reeling and shaken, I happened upon a plaque with Jeremiah 29:11 on it. It seemed to be calling me not just to read it but to receive its message. It has been on my nightstand ever since, and I pray the verse at the beginning and end of every day.

Until that time in my life, I rarely asked Mary for help. As I reflect back, it seems as if Mary found me, instead of the other way around. I felt her presence without seeking it. Most importantly, I felt her acceptance at a time when I worried about being judged.

— Betty Bentley

DO YOU THINK MARY ever worried about being judged, or had doubts about her role as mother? Has Mary found you yet?

Prayer: Thank you, Mary, for finding me. Thank you for helping me to accept the plans God has for me. Pray that I am able to place my hope in his plans to prosper me, and give me hope for the future.

April 8

"And why is this granted me, that the mother of my Lord should come to me?" — Luke 1:43

I was exhausted as a new mother, especially when my infant cried in the middle of the night. After trying to comfort the restless baby, I would return to bed, hoping that the child would settle into sleep. Not getting much sleep made me desperate for just a little rest so that I could be ready to face the new day.

I remember begging the Blessed Virgin to mother my child in the crib, to comfort him, to hold him in her arms, and to calm him down. Within minutes, the baby's cries turned from screams to gentle whimpers, then to a peaceful sleep.

Why did I have to wait for a screaming infant to learn this lesson? We do not have to wait until times become desperate. We can invite the Blessed Mother to help us with all our struggles.

— Meg Bucaro

WHAT CAN YOU GIVE to Mary today so that she can intercede on your behalf? Can you ask her to help in a relationship? An employment opportunity? Guidance on a financial strain? A health issue?

Prayer: Mary, you are with me always. Pray for me today as my mother, and lead me to your Son.

April 9

"And he went and dwelt in a city called Nazareth, that what was spoken
by the prophets might be fulfilled. 'He shall be called a Nazarene.'"
— *Matthew 2:23*

Mary and Joseph were parents with high hopes for their Son, especially during their life in Nazareth. As a carpenter, Joseph made and repaired things; Mary cared for her family. One of my favorite images of the Holy Family shows our Blessed Mother watching Joseph and Jesus work together. Mary's heart was filled with hope and the promise of a bright future for her family.

Because Mary wanted only the best for her Son, she instilled a deep faith and knowledge of God in Jesus. She taught him to place his hope in the Lord. As our spiritual mother, Mary desires to help us as we endeavor to pass on the Faith to our family and friends. We can turn to Mary for hope and perseverance when we share our faith with the people we love.

— Alice Smith

CONSIDER THE WAYS that you can lead others to know and love Jesus by your example.

Prayer: Mary, Mother of Good Counsel, by your example you give hope to all people who wish to share the Faith with others. Help me to persevere in my efforts, that my friends and family can come to know your Son, Jesus.

April 10

"Whatever you ask in prayer, believe that you receive it, and you will."
— *Mark 11:24*

Two years ago, my grandson was born with a heart condition that required surgery the day after his birth. My daughter held him in her arms amidst the multiple wires that were attached to life-support systems. As the hours passed, doctors and nurses anxiously watched the numbers on the monitors drop; my daughter cradled her newborn infant in her arms, gently stroking his head. I sat next to her silently holding them both in prayer.

In the stillness of that moment, I prayed to Mary, and hope took root and slowly grew. With Mary's help, we surrendered ourselves totally to God, and we were both filled with hope and strength beyond our own. Gradually, my grandson's numbers began to rise. This infant showed us the power of hope and prayer. The doctors were amazed.

Mary invites us to turn to her with our needs and petitions; she will comfort us and give us hope. She will gently remain present with us when we are fearful and show us how to place all our hope in God.
— JoAnne McElroy

How do you experience the power of hope in your prayers?

Prayer: Mary, fill us with your hope, that we may love as you love Jesus.

April 11

"I wait for the Lord, my soul waits, / and in his word I hope."
— Psalms 130:5

One of my favorite television advertisements depicts children offering their perspectives on a variety of life's situations. After they share their detailed, elaborate descriptions, the general conclusion drawn is that it's not complicated. This verse from Psalms 130 brings that very message to us. We must wait for the Lord with our whole being and put our hope in him. It's not complicated.

Clearly this is the way Mary lived her life as mother, wife, and faithful servant. Understanding the Annunciation may be complicated, but Mary's response was not. She waited for the Lord, put her hope in him, and lived her life according to his plan.

— Betty Bentley

DO YOU EVER LET THINGS get overly complicated in your life? Can getting caught up in the pace of life, the demands of work, school, activities, and family distract you from this simple message?

Prayer: Mary, help us to follow your lead of waiting and hoping. Help us to not let our lives get so complicated that we lose the simple message of waiting for the Lord and putting our hope in him.

April 12

"You shall make of these a sacred anointing oil blended as by the perfumer; a holy anointing oil it shall be." — *Exodus 30:25*

"Hmm! Smells good in here." That's what I think when I enter a large department store with a perfume section.

The Scriptures make reference to people anointing one another with perfumes and aromatic fragrances as a way to honor a guest. In her Jewish household, the Blessed Mother surely participated in rituals of anointing, using perfumed mixtures. It is likely she also anointed Jesus and Joseph, reminding them to hope for the fulfillment of God's long-awaited promise.

For me, Mary is the fragrance of the Gospel, and her presence fills the air with hope. Each time I am aware of a beautiful scent, whether I am in a store or in the presence of someone, I think of Mary and how she brought forth God's gift of hope for the world. We can breathe deeply the sweetness of Mary's motherly presence in our lives.

— Alice Smith

DO YOU HAVE a perfume, shaving lotion, or an oil that has a pleasant aroma? Pray a short prayer of gratitude to our Blessed Mother the next time you use it.

Prayer: Holy Mary, you are the sweet cause of my hope. Help me to wear the fragrance of the Gospel on my heart and in my life.

April 13

"Do you not know that you are the God's temple and that God's Spirit dwells in you?" — *1 Corinthians 3:16*

Mary's life beautifully demonstrates the sacredness of our bodies. God chose to become one like us, and when the time for fulfillment came, he was born of a woman. Mary carried Jesus within her holy womb; we, too, carry the presence of God within us, for we are made in the image and likeness of our Creator. Through faith and baptism, our bodies hold the presence of God's Holy Spirit. No matter what happens to our bodies here, they contain God's promise of eternal life in heaven.

How easy is it for us to become distracted with false messages found in today's media telling us that we are not good enough, not thin enough, not pretty enough. Yet, we are God's temple. When we begin to view our bodies as sacred, we can find the hope we need to live our lives to the fullest. God is alive in us!

— Sheila Cusack

WHAT CAN YOU DO TODAY to honor the fact that God's spirit dwells in you? Are you willing to follow Mary on the path of holiness?

Prayer: Mary, help me to see my body as a vessel of hope and a sacred temple of God's spirit.

April 14

"Hope does not disappoint us, because God's love has been poured into our hearts." — Romans 5:5

In 1958, the world-famous Hope Diamond, valued then at one million dollars, was delivered by U.S. mail in a brown paper package to the United States Museum of Natural History, where it resides to this day. What a mail delivery that was! Who would dare send something so valuable through a system with such a great potential to lose it? God would.

Two thousand years ago, God sent his only Son, Jesus, to be born of Mary of Nazareth, a young virgin of little means. In Mary, we see a startling truth: not only do we hope in God, but God hopes, believes, and acts in us. Hope is a two-way street.

As the mother of our Savior, Mary shows us how to place our hope in the Lord, believing that God is with us and that he desires to live and act through us. God powerfully demonstrates, with Mary's assistance, his desire for closeness with us. God hopes in us. Do we hope in him?

— Joseph Abel, PhD

MARY BROUGHT HOPE into the world. How will you share the good news of this hope today?

Prayer: O Mary, ever hopeful, may we fulfill God's hope for the world by willingly accepting your Son in our lives.

April 15

"Now faith is the assurance of things hoped for, the conviction of things not seen." — *Hebrews 11:1*

The apostle Thomas may be considered the poster child for people with doubts, but we have to admit that there is a little "doubting Thomas" in all of us. It is difficult to have strong convictions for things we have not experienced or seen.

This passage from Hebrews teaches us that faith is more than just a belief in God. Faith is belief in the goodness of God. It is this great hope which commands our obedience and forms our spiritual foundation.

Imagine the strength it took for our Blessed Mother to obey her calling. She must have feared being ridiculed, berated — even stoned! — for what would have appeared to be scandalous behavior. And while Mary trusted God completely, she may have had doubts about her own ability to do what God was asking of her.

— Betty Bentley

WHAT DO YOU DOUBT IN LIFE? What aspects of your faith do you struggle with? Seek Mary's help to overcome your doubts with hope in the Lord.

Prayer: Mary, you demonstrated tremendous courage, with great hope, when you accepted God's mission for your life. Pray for me when I lose hope, that God's grace and his promise of eternal life will guide my thoughts and actions as they did yours.

April 16

"Therefore, since we are justified by faith, we have peace with God through our Lord Jesus Christ." — Romans 5:1

An article I read long ago examined whether it was disrespectful to fall asleep during prayer. The author compared drifting off to sleep while trying to pray to a child who falls asleep in his parent's lap. Is the parent offended? Not one bit.

I often pray the Rosary at night before bed. I don't always finish it, but our Blessed Mother is patient. She does not refuse to hear me in the morning when I pick up where I left off.

I started praying the Rosary when headlines of mass shootings and terrorism crowded the news, because I needed hope. I've found that the Rosary allows me restful sleep no matter what troubles surround me. This is because Mary gives me hope.

Turning to our Blessed Mother reminds us that no matter what is blanketing the news we will always find hope in Christ Jesus.

— Meg Bucaro

PRAY THE ROSARY TODAY before you sleep. Rest in the hope that the Lord is in charge.

Prayer: Mary, please strengthen my faith and hope, especially when the world suffers.

April 17

"The eye is the lamp of the body." — Matthew 6:22

While I was praying in a chapel one day, the silence was broken by the crying of a young child. The child cried and cried, and then suddenly the child's eyes met with the mother's eyes. Then there was quiet.

Mary's eyes are a mother's eyes, eyes that penetrate, eyes that bring hope and security even during the most chaotic times. Mary's eyes bring light to those who call upon her. Mary's eyes are loving eyes that can comfort even the deepest of hurts and give us renewed hope.

A mother watches her children to protect them from harm and helps them up when they fall. When we turn to Mary and open our hearts to receive the blessing of her motherly gaze upon us, we feel safe and hopeful.

— Chris Hannighan-Wiehn

WHEN A STORM ARISES within you or around you today, try to imagine the gaze of Mary, assuring you that all will be well.

Prayer: Mary, my mother, cast your eyes upon me today. Protect me from falling into traps that limit my ability to live the day in a spirit of hope. If I fall, help me up so that I may peacefully move forward knowing that I have your love and support.

April 18

"Rejoice in your hope, be patient in tribulation, be constant in prayer."
— *Romans 12:12*

On a normal day, after cleaning, cooking, and doing errands, I like to honor the Blessed Mother with a short prayer of gratitude. On special days like holidays or birthdays, I ask Mary for the gift of hope. As the mother of Jesus, Mary is here to help us experience the joy and hope that will accompany us as we walk with Jesus.

Mary's life continues to inspire Christians of all ages. For, like many of us, she endured hardship, suffering, and loss, yet never lost hope. Mary was not a superhuman being who didn't feel pain or anger. Nevertheless, Mary was a person of deep faith who was committed to loving the Lord no matter what transpired in her life. Her hope came from her relationship with the Lord.

— Alice Smith

DO YOU FIND IT EASY to live in hope, or do you struggle finding light in the darkness? Seek Mary's help through prayer to find hope today.

Prayer: Mary, pray with me as I seek to find hope in the midst of my daily trials. Help me to trust in your Son, Jesus, that he may show me the way to a life of hope and joy.

April 19

"Many are saying of me, / there is not help for him in God. / But you, O LORD, are a shield about me, / my glory, and the lifter of my head. / I cry aloud to the LORD, / and he answers me from his holy mountain."
— *Psalms 3:2-4*

Mary had reason to be afraid as she stood at the foot of the cross. Her beloved Son had been betrayed, arrested, and turned over to the authorities to be executed. The jeers and hatred from the surrounding crowds were frightening, but Mary never left her Son's side. She survived the Crucifixion by placing her hope in the Lord. That hope was not misplaced.

Our Blessed Mother's life inspires us to hope in God when we face trials and difficulties. Mary's heart grieved with sorrow, but she found the courage to walk through her fear and grief by calling out to the Lord in hope.

— Lauren Nelson

WHAT SITUATIONS OR PEOPLE cause you fear and grief? Prayerfully bring these situations to our Blessed Mother, asking her to strengthen your hope in God.

Prayer: Mary, help me to have hope when difficulties arise, and to truly know that the Lord is with me always.

April 20

"And now, Lord, for what do I wait? / My hope is in you."
— *Psalms 39:7*

I recently attended a retreat that offered practical ways to live with mindful compassion. As I sat on the cold, bare shore of Lake Michigan, present only to the ebb and flow of the water, it was as if the waves whispered a message of hope, saying, "I am holding you." As the weekend progressed, this sense of hope grew. In silence, I was able to stop telling God all my needs and just listen. This experience reminded me how powerful sitting in silence can be. By surrendering my heart to the Lord hope wells up in my heart.

Mary is a model of one who waits in hope. Throughout Scripture we hear of Mary pondering, or holding a message in the silence of her heart. She internalized, waited, and listened in silence as Our Lord spoke to her. The hope she received carried her from her encounter with the angel Gabriel all the way to the cross.

— JoAnne McElroy

WHAT ARE YOU WAITING FOR in your life? What could you do today that would help you to experience hope?

Prayer: Mary, Mother of Hope, awaken my heart to listen as you did. Show me how to find hope.

April 21

"They went up to the upper room, where they were staying, Peter and John and James and Andrew, Philip and Thomas, Bartholomew and Matthew, James son of Alphaeus and Simon the Zealot and Judas the son of James. All these with one accord devoted themselves to prayer, together with the women and Mary the mother of Jesus." — Acts 1:13-14

For a couple of years, a dear friend kept inviting me to our parish's Rosary group. Because I didn't know much about Mary then, I wasn't very interested. My friend remained patient, consistently extending her warm invitation. Finally, I went to the group and learned how to pray the Rosary. That is how I met the mother of Jesus.

My relationship with our Blessed Mother has been a long, slow journey. The thing that keeps me going is the hope I feel when I ask for Mary's intercession. Our family now turns to Mary every day to ask for her protection. In a world that can be rank with senseless violence and disregard for human life, Mary gives us hope.

— Meg Bucaro

WHAT ASPECT OF YOUR LIFE could be enriched by placing it in Mary's care?

Prayer: Blessed Mother, we ask you to wrap us all in your mantle of care and protection. Please keep us safe, free from harm, and filled with hope.

April 22

"You will have confidence, because there is hope; / you will be protected and take your rest in safety. / You will lie down, and none will make you afraid; / many will entreat your favor." — Job 11:18-19

Our children are all grown, living independent lives. Like all parents, we look back on our successes as well as the list of things we wish we had done differently. Yet our children assure us that they were always encouraged to be hopeful. They grew up realizing that holding onto hope brings a sense of security, peace, and the strength to forge ahead during the darkest times. The power of hope makes a tangible difference in our spiritual lives.

Mary emerges as a model of hope for all of us. When she listened to the angel, she was hopeful despite her worry and confusion. When she stood at the foot of the cross, she remained hopeful for the promise of everlasting life to be fulfilled. At Pentecost, she became a source of hope for the newly established Church.

— Betty Bentley

WHERE DO YOU FIND HOPE in difficult times? How can you share that hope with someone today?

Prayer: Thank you, Mary, for showing us how to keep hope even on our darkest days. Help us to know what it means to be secure in our hopefulness and to rest in that safety.

April 23

"Let us then with confidence draw near to the throne of grace, that we may receive mercy and find grace to help in time of need." — Hebrews 4:16

It's called the "Hail Mary" pass. Here's how it works.

If a football game is tied or the team with the football is a few points behind as time is running out, the quarterback simply throws the ball high into a knot of players gathered at the goal line, hoping one of his receivers will catch it. If a receiver makes the catch — victory! If not, there's always next time. Why is it called the Hail Mary pass? Maybe it is because the Hail Mary offers us last-minute hope, a chance for victory over death.

Asking Mary to pray for us "now and at the hour of our death" reminds us that we are connected to a community of saints who have gone before us and are urging us on to heaven. The Hail Mary is a prayer of hopeful trust in our destiny where we will join Mary and her Son.

— Joseph Abel, PhD

PRAY THE HAIL MARY with an awareness that you are part of the community of saints. Let your heart be filled with hope for the future.

Prayer: O Mary, you are the source of hope in Christ. Pray that our lives bring us to our eternal home with you and Jesus your Son.

April 24

"Set your hope fully upon the grace that is coming to you at the revelation of Jesus Christ." — 1 Peter 1:13

Years ago, I vowed to accept the weather and stop fussing about weather conditions. Complaining is a hopeless exercise, and no one can control Mother Nature! Praying to the Blessed Mother every day is another promise I made to myself, and it has brought great hope into my life. When Mary is on my mind and in my heart, honor, glory, and hope fill my soul.

As my faith deepens, I ask for greater knowledge of God and his magnificent universe. Mary is a vital part of my prayer life. She teaches me how to live a grace-filled life. As a mother, Mary continually reassures me that Jesus will provide the direction to guide me to make the right choices, embrace a fruitful life, and focus on heaven. With Mary's help my hopes for the future can be faith driven, and all I have to do is be open to the Lord's movement in my life.

— Alice Smith

Do you live with hope every day? In what ways might Mary help to deepen your hope in how God is working in your life?

Prayer: Mary, Mother of Divine Grace, cast away doubt as I dedicate my life to knowing the true meaning of hope.

April 25

*"May the God of hope fill you with all joy and peace in believing,
so that by the power of the Holy Spirit you may abound in hope."*
— *Romans 15:13*

When life is difficult, we turn to God for hope. Hope is the glimmer of light in the darkness that shows us God is in control, and that he will not abandon us. Mary believed this more than anyone. She knew that our God is a God of hope.

Mary's life encourages us to hope and believe that we will find joy and peace again. As the Mother of God, Mary experienced more than her share of suffering and pain. Our lives are no different. And while her unique bond with the Holy Spirit gave her hope that brought her joy and peace even in the midst of trials, the Holy Spirit lives in us, too. That kind of hope is available to us.

— Lauren Nelson

REFLECT ON A DIFFICULT SITUATION in your life. Ask Mary to bring hope to your heart so that you can be filled with joy and peace.

Prayer: Mary, strengthen my hope in the Lord's work in my life. Teach me how to be open to the power of the Holy Spirit alive in me.

April 26

"With God all things are possible." — *Matthew 19:26*

A young mom waits in the hospital for a new heart. She is filled with hope because she believes that all things are possible with God. Her journey — from diagnosis to designated heart-transplant patient — has been a long one. As I walk with her and her family, I am struck by the hope she has radiated each day. Although the path is frightening and results unknown, she approaches it with a smile on her face and laughter in her heart. This is her path, and she chooses to receive it with trust in the Lord and belief in the miracle of life.

Life is often filled with unexpected twists. Mary was a young, innocent, everyday girl when she received the news that she was going to bear the world's greatest miracle. Mary received this life-changing announcement with grace and a heart filled with praise for God and his wonderful works. Like Mary, each day we have the opportunity to choose to live with hope, no matter how difficult life may seem.

— JoAnne McElroy

WHAT UNANTICIPATED TRIALS are you facing in your life? How can you choose to receive them with trust in God's works and live in hope as Mary did?

Prayer: Mary, help me to believe as you did that with God all things are possible.

April 27

"The LORD is in his holy temple, / the LORD's throne is in heaven; / his eyes behold, his eyelids test, the children of men. / The LORD tests the righteous and the wicked, / and his soul hates him that loves violence. / For the LORD is righteous, he loves righteous deeds; / the upright shall behold his face." — Psalms 11:4-5, 7

The psalmist here describes a God of presence: he is in his holy temple. Abiding in this presence gives us hope in the face of the trials we all face. We know when we draw life from the temple of God's Spirit within us that we won't tend to wickedness or violence. Rather, we will be upright and ultimately see God's face.

Mary was filled with the grace of God's spirit, and epitomized someone with great hope. This hope is heard clearly in the Magnificat, when Mary praises God's mercy.

— John Holmes

WHAT IN YOUR RELATIONSHIP with God gives you hope? What can you do to place your trust in the help you can receive from Mary and her Son, Jesus?

Prayer: Holy Lady, help us to recognize the great hope we can gain from our devotion to you. Help us to stay connected to the Spirit within us, so that we may live upright lives.

April 28

"The LORD takes pleasure in those who fear him, / in those who hope in his steadfast love." — *Psalms 147:11*

When our family lost 90 percent of our belongings in a house fire, we were left devastated and shocked. Though we realized how blessed we were to be safe, and knew that things could be replaced, we were still knocked to our knees. We expected God would help us, but Mary's presence was an unanticipated surprise.

The full demolition was some months later. Afterward, the five of us walked through what was left of our home. There were two-by-fours in place of walls. It was empty. Right as I was about to break into tears, again, our children screamed with joy!

The three of them ran to show us what they had found: a miraculous medal given to our oldest at her first Communion, a holy card of the Blessed Virgin Mary, a wooden cross our youngest had received in preschool. How did they survive the fire?

Mary visited us in our devastation to give us hope. She inspired our demolition crew to intentionally save those three items and provided a reminder of God's mercy exactly when we needed it!

— Meg Bucaro

LOOK FOR MARY'S HOPEFUL PRESENCE in the midst of your difficulties.

Prayer: Mary, thank you for being with me. Open my eyes to see you more clearly and my heart to feel your hope.

April 29

"The LORD takes pleasure in those who fear him, / in those who hope in his steadfast love." — Psalms 147:11

This passage may seem contradictory at first. Why would we put our hope in something or someone we must also fear?

It took me a while to be comfortable with the scriptural idea of fearing God. But if we think of the fear of the Lord as awe, and giving God the respect he deserves, we can put our hope in him as well. God does not want us to be afraid, but he does desire that we put him first. He is delighted when we place our hope in him and not in other people or things.

Isn't this what Mary did? While she may have been truly afraid of what was being asked of her, she was never afraid of the Lord. Mary was full of awe and respect for his unfailing love. Her whole life centered on putting God first.

— Betty Bentley

DO YOU SOMETIMES put routines, school, work, family, or life's demands ahead of God? Are there days when you do not pray?

Prayer: Mary, we look to you as a model of how God wants us to live. Help us to always put him first in our lives, to both love and respect him, to take time for prayer, and to put our hope in his unfailing love.

April 30

"Blessed be the God and Father of our Lord Jesus Christ! By his great mercy we have been born anew to a living hope." — *1 Peter 1:3*

Project HOPE (Health Opportunity for People Everywhere) is an international charity launched by the United States in 1958. Project HOPE works in developing countries around the world to eradicate infectious diseases. The SS *Hope*, the first-ever peacetime hospital ship, sailed from 1958 until 1974. On these voyages doctors, nurses, and medical-tech staff provided medical care and training to people in each country visited, and hope to people in need.

In a way, Mary is God's Project HOPE (*Holy* Opportunities for People Everywhere). Like the famed ship, Mary "sailed" with her Son to bring compassion and healing to the world. The rough seas of religious culture and an oppressive foreign power did not stop Mary nor cause her to alter her course. The stormy nights of fear and uncertainty did not hinder Mary, whose life was navigated by her love for God. Mary safely transported God's hope to the world. Mary's life inspires us to stay the course in times of difficulty and to never give up.

— Joseph Abel, PhD

READ PSALMS 131 PRAYERFULLY. Allow its words to fill your heart.

Prayer: O Mary, bringer of God's hope, hear us, and help us to see and accept the holy opportunities your Son gives us.

~ GENTLENESS ~

May 1

"Do not be afraid, Mary, for you have found favor with God. And behold, you will conceive in your womb and bear a son, and you shall call his name Jesus. He will be great, and will be called the Son of the Most High."
— *Luke 1:30-32*

Imagine what went through Mary's mind when the angel Gabriel proclaimed that a child would be born to her and that her son would be called the Son of God! Scripture tells us that Mary was deeply troubled at first and that she wondered what the angel's words meant. Gabriel responded gently and told Mary not to be afraid.

This beautiful exchange between the mother of Jesus and the angel Gabriel reflects God's gentleness toward Mary. It also gives us an example of how we are to be gentle with our responses to others. When we don't understand another's viewpoint or have a difference of opinion, we can choose to be kind and gentle in our response. When we do, we, too, find favor with God.

— Sheila Cusack

MAKE A CONCERTED EFFORT today to be kind and gentle in your conversations with others. Try to diffuse confrontations with gentleness.

Prayer: Mary, help me to be gentle with myself and with all those that God sends my way.

May 2

"Peace I leave with you; my peace I give to you; not as the world gives do I give to you. Let not your hearts be troubled, neither let them be afraid."
— *John 14:27*

Let's face it, sometimes life can just be too hard. The overwhelming need to get so much done in our very busy world can leave us lacking peace. That's when we need gentleness most.

Mary's gentle demeanor was a fruit of her steadfast faith in God. Her life was filled with the peace that flows from gentleness. As our mother, she encourages us to remain peaceful and gentle in our dealings with one another, even when things are difficult or don't go our way.

Mary's gentleness is rooted in the gentleness of God. She shows us how to open ourselves up to the gentle voice of God. Slowing things down enough to listen to the Lord's voice calms us and gives us peace.
— Nanci Lukasik-Smith

TAKE TIME TO BE SILENT, to be still. Listen for the gentle whisper of God to guide you. Seek Mary's help in following the Lord.

Prayer: Mary, help me to open my heart, and calm my spirit. Keep me from rushing to address the challenges I face, and show me how to be gentle with myself and with others.

May 3

"Come to me, all who labor and are heavy laden, and I will give you rest. Take my yoke upon you, and learn from me; for I am gentle and lowly in heart." — Matthew 11:28-29

Several years ago, a loved one suffered a debilitating stroke. For the two months that followed, I visited the rehabilitation facility on a daily basis to lend my support in whatever way was needed. After many long weeks, I was exhausted and anxious of what the future might bring. One night, I spiritually, emotionally, and physically "crashed." My spirit was heavy. I dropped to my knees and tearfully unloaded my burdens and fears to Mary, and asked her to bring them to her Son. Afterward, a gentle calm filled my soul.

Mary understands our worries and concerns. As our heavenly mother, she is here to hold us when we are broken and to comfort us when we are worried. Mary always leads us to Jesus; he takes away our burdens and restores us to gentleness of spirit.

— Sharon A. Abel, PhD

SPEND SOME TIME in prayer today as you reflect upon the people and events in your life that weigh down your spirit. Seek Mary's loving assistance in bringing these burdens to the Lord.

Prayer: Mary, help us come to Jesus with our burdens, trusting that we will be heard.

May 4

"Blessed are the meek, for they shall inherit the earth." — *Matthew 5:5*

Ever since I received my driver's license decades ago, I have prayed a simple prayer to Mary whenever I am in a parking lot: "Hail Mary, full of grace, help me to find a parking space." While this little prayer may sound ridiculous, let me tell you, it has never failed me. I believe that as my mother, Mary watches out for me. Even when I ask for something as simple as a parking space.

As our spiritual mother, Mary watches over all of us and takes great delight when her children turn to her in time of need. Her gentle and compassionate heart is always ready to listen to us, to cry with us, and to lead us to her Son. Mary is our advocate in times of trouble, and she rejoices with us in times of joy. We can turn to Mary with our daily needs, for she is only a prayer away.

— Dr. Mary Amore

WHAT NEED can you turn to Mary with today?

Prayer: Mary, thank you for always being there for me. Help me to cultivate my trust in your motherly goodness, so that I may come to know Jesus more deeply and inherit his everlasting kingdom.

May 5

"Wisdom breathes life into her sons / and gives help to those who seek her. / Whoever loves her loves life, / and those who seek her early / will win the Lord's good favor. / Whoever holds her fast will obtain glory, / and the Lord will bless the place she enters." — Sirach 4:11-13

The Wisdom mentioned here has many interesting characteristics. It is presented as feminine, and an object of love: one whose favor is to be sought and won. But there also emerges a certain maternal gentleness in Wisdom; she "instructs her children."

One of Mary's honorary titles is "Seat of Wisdom." She certainly lived her life in communion with Wisdom and can be counted among Wisdom's children. Mary was accustomed to receiving the "instruction" Wisdom gave her and lived her whole life according to it. This is evident at the Annunciation when Mary responds to the angel's message with acceptance. An instruction given in gentleness, can be gently received. This is how our Blessed Mother instructs us as well.

— John Holmes

WHAT CAN I DO TODAY to be more gentle in giving instruction, and in receiving it?

Prayer: Holy Mother, guide me in your wisdom. Lead me to your gentleness, that I may continue in God's grace.

May 6

*"O LORD, in the morning you hear my voice; / in the morning
I prepare a sacrifice for you, and watch." — Psalms 5:3*

Daylight doesn't come at full force all at once. It grows gently on the horizon, and then spreads across the sky. Here the words of the psalmist offer us a gentle reminder of the stillness of the dawn as we rise to greet a new day. As most of us know, however, life can also be noisy in the morning. Our pets are waiting to be fed, children need to get off to school, and we hurry to get ready for work. The household awakens and the sounds of the television and the hum of the computer can break the quiet, gentle space of morning at sunrise.

Like us, Mary's life also had its noisy moments. Still, Mary remained quietly devoted to God. She carried the gentle dawn of his presence in her heart.

— Sheila Cusack

INVITE MARY to your prayers one morning. Ask her to gently take your hand and to lead you to God.

Prayer: Mary, help me to quiet my heart today, so that I am able to listen to the gentle voice of the Lord speaking to me and to experience the dawn of his presence.

May 7

"With all lowliness and meekness, with patience, forbearing one another in love, eager to maintain the unity of the Spirit in the bond of peace."
— *Ephesians 4:2-3*

Life can be chaotic at times. Frustrating or challenging moments in relationships with family, friends, and associates can make it difficult to remain gentle in our expressions and behaviors. Impulse can take over, and we may want to "speak our minds" rather than "hold our tongues." It is in these occasions that we need to stop, reflect, and invite Mary to be present with us. When we call on her to help us redirect our behaviors, and reflect what is good and pleasing to God, we open ourselves to the graces which are meant for us.

Imagine the gentleness, patience, and love that Mary demonstrated, not only in accepting the call to be the mother of God, but to witness her Son's mission on earth.

— Nanci Lukasik-Smith

HOW CAN YOU TAKE Mary's example of gentleness and patience to heart today? During your most difficult moments, is there a way you can demonstrate gentleness so that others can witness Christ working through you?

Prayer: Mary, please remind me when I am challenged and distracted. Redirect my thoughts and actions to imitate the gentle, loving nature of Christ so I can reflect his holy mission.

May 8

"Rejoice in the Lord always; again, I will say, Rejoice!
Let all men know your forbearance." — Philippians 4:4-5

Curtis Mayfield has been called soul music's "Genius of Gentleness." He is noted for using love and encouragement, rather than anger, to say important things. Only fifteen years old when he recorded his first hit, "For Your Precious Love," Mayfield went on to great acclaim in the 1960s and 1970s, writing a string of hits that became anthems for peaceful change during the civil rights movement. Mayfield always remained low-key and understated in his lyrics and singing style, even as he addressed issues he felt passionate about.

Mary was God's "Genius of Gentleness." For Mary, it was enough to live what God asked of her in the normal daily life of a first-century Palestinian married woman. She cooked, cleaned, drew water from the well, and bartered in the local market. She raised a son and cared for a husband. No one in Nazareth knew of her extraordinary favor with God. She had bragging rights but never used them! In this way she was free to rejoice in the Lord always.

— Joseph Abel, PhD

THROUGHOUT THE BUSINESS of this day, stop and rejoice in the Lord. Fill the day with periods of gentle praise.

Prayer: Mary, may we learn your ways of gentleness and rejoice in the Lord always.

May 9

"Let all men know your forbearance [gentleness]. The Lord is at hand."
— *Philippians 4:5*

When our daughter was in eighth grade, she was chosen to crown Mary at the traditional May crowning held every year in our parish community. This honor touched my daughter's heart in a profound way. Her gentle approach in preparing for this annual ceremony helped to reconnect my daughter and her classmates to the real reason for the crowning; Mary is our heavenly mother and seeks to lead us to her Son, Jesus.

Perhaps we should have more than one "Crowning of Mary" throughout the year. In the midst of our busy days, it would be fruitful for us to stop and prayerfully thank our Blessed Mother for all she did to bring Jesus into the world. Every grotto, church, and shrine dedicated to Mary is there to help us deepen our spiritual bond with this beautiful woman of grace who gave of her life that we might know Jesus. Wherever Mary is, the Lord is near.

— Alice Smith

IN WHAT WAYS can Mary's life reawaken within you a sense that the Lord is near?

Prayer: Mary, Queen of Virgins and Queen of Heaven, infuse your gentleness in all of us that we may come to know and love your Son, Jesus.

May 10

"Love is patient and kind; love is not jealous or boastful; it is not arrogant or rude. Love does not insist on its own way; it is not irritable or resentful."
— *1 Corinthians 13:4-5*

This passage is undoubtedly one of the most familiar readings in sacred Scripture. Often heard at weddings, the powerful meaning of this passage is often missed because most people are preoccupied by the nuptials taking place. When read alone, without a bride or groom present, we have the opportunity to open our ears and our hearts to truly listen; and we can come to the realization that love is gentle in both giving and in receiving.

As the mother of Jesus, Mary modeled love in all of its expressions. Surely, when she found Jesus in the Temple after his being lost for three days, Mary stated her anxiety to him, but she did it in a gentle way and as a concerned parent. Mary inspires all of us to love deeply and to love with gentleness.

— Nanci Lukasik-Smith

As you prepare for or reflect upon your day, ask yourself how you can offer to others the patience and kindness that Mary's life exemplified.

Prayer: Mary, gentle mother, please walk with me and offer encouragement that all my actions and words are reflective of your tender love.

May 11

"The Spirit lifted me up, and brought me into the inner court; and behold, the glory of the LORD filled the temple." — Ezekiel 43:5

These prophetic words remind us that the Lord will gently lift us up and lovingly care for us, that we will be brought to the inner court of his glorious presence. Our God is a loving and gentle God who takes care of us.

Mary's experience of God was also one of gentleness and exaltation. When the angel announced to Mary that she would be the mother of Jesus, he gently reassured this young Jewish girl from Nazareth that she should not be afraid, for she had found favor with God. Mary's experience speaks volumes to us on our spiritual journey. If we love the Lord, then we have nothing to fear, for we, too, will have found favor with God. Though we are lowly, the spirit of the Lord will lift us up and the glory of God will enfold us.

— Sheila Cusack

TAKE A MOMENT to thank God today for lifting you up. Ask Mary to help you to become more aware of her presence in your life.

Prayer: Mary, pray for me that when I am facing conflicts, the Lord will lift me up and bring me into his glorious presence.

May 12

"Do not forget my teaching, / but let your heart keep my commandments; /
for length of days and years of life / and abundant welfare
will they give you. / Let not loyalty and faithfulness forsake you."
— *Proverbs 3:1-3*

As a young Jewish girl, Mary was very familiar with the Hebrew Scriptures. She would have been able to join with the other Jewish women and listen in to the readings and discussions of the men who gathered in a separate room at the synagogue in Nazareth.

I imagine that this passage from Proverbs held a special place in Mary's heart. As a human virtue, kindness is often translated as gentleness and faithfulness, and is compatible with fidelity and devotion. In Mary's life these beautiful virtues were in full bloom.

Mary's fidelity to God played out as a never ending "yes" throughout her entire life. As wife and mother, Mary's gentleness was visible to friends and family alike.

— Sharon A. Abel, PhD

TODAY, ASK YOURSELF whether you have forgotten God's teachings. Are you at peace with yourself and others? Does kindness and fidelity direct your actions as they did for the Blessed Mother?

Prayer: Mary, may God's Word fill me with peace, kindness, and faithfulness. Like you, may I proclaim a never ending "yes" to the Lord's commandments.

May 13
Our Lady of Fátima

"Hear, O daughter, consider; and incline your ear; / forget your people and your father's house; / and the king will desire your beauty. / Since he is your lord, bow to him." — Psalms 45:10-11

Our Lady of Fátima is perhaps the most well-known apparition of Mary in our modern world. In 1917, Mary appeared to three young children in Portugal with a message of peace, conversion, and repentance. While an apparition is an extraordinary event, Mary gently comes to each of us every day. She beckons us to return to her Son, and to make reparation for our sins.

Mary is a gentle mother. She is aware of our daily struggles with good and evil, and she is here to help us, her children, find our way back to God. She takes us by the hand and gently helps us redirect our lives toward loving and serving the Lord Jesus Christ.

— Dr. Mary Amore

AT FÁTIMA, MARY ASKED US to pray the Rosary daily. Honor Mary today by praying at least one decade of the Rosary. Consecrate your daily responsibilities to Jesus and Mary, that you might experience the glory of life eternal.

Prayer: Holy Mother of God, teach me to follow the ways of the Lord, that I may walk in his light and love all the days of my life.

May 14

*"The steadfast love of the L*ORD *never ceases, / his mercies never come to an end; / they are new every morning; / great is your faithfulness."*
— *Lamentations 3:22-23*

I am not a fan of large crowds, because they can get unruly and then people begin to push and shove. On a recent trip to a major Marian pilgrimage site, however, I was deeply impressed by how gracious people were. The people who gathered there for prayer were kind and gentle, willing to help others in need, and were smiling at strangers. Our Blessed Mother's gentle presence was palpable in this sacred place.

As the mother who raised Jesus from infancy into adulthood, Mary surely experienced many of the same difficulties that we encounter raising children. Parenting the Son of God had its moments of difficulty. Yet, in the trials and tribulations that Mary encountered as the mother of Jesus, she remained a gentle soul. Relying on God's inexhaustible mercy, her faithfulness to the Lord was renewed each morning.

— Alice Smith

CONSIDER HOW YOU CAN INFUSE gentleness into your dealings today with family members, coworkers, and strangers that God sends your way.

Prayer: Dear Mary, surround me with special reminders that kindness and gentleness are virtues for life. Lift my intentions to Jesus, who knows and loves me.

May 15

"To speak evil of no one, to avoid quarreling, to be gentle, and to show perfect courtesy toward all men." — *Titus 3:2*

Have you ever been in a situation when your expectations did not align with someone else's? Or, have you ever been so upset with someone that you want to lash out because you are hurt? The quality of gentleness can help us.

As youngsters, my parents encouraged us to behave like "ladies and gentlemen." We were taught to be courteous toward others, respectful of their opinions, and to show others that they were important to us. Scripture reminds us that this is pleasing to God.

Mary's entire life was pleasing to the Lord. Mary spoke against no one; she was kind and gentle, and was hospitable to friends and strangers alike. We have much to learn from Mary's life. Mary invites us to commit ourselves to gentleness in our dealings with other people.

— Nanci Lukasik-Smith

CALL TO MIND a person or situation that is causing you difficulty. Seek the Blessed Mother's counsel and help in being kind and gentle to all persons involved.

Prayer: Mary, there are times when I suffer from my own frustrations and want to lash out. Please guide me as I am relating to others so that I can demonstrate gentleness, respect, and genuine courtesy toward others.

May 16

"But Mary kept all these things, pondering them in her heart."
— *Luke 2:19*

One of the toughest parenting lessons for me has been learning to approach my children with gentleness. My first inclination is to be loud, jovial, and energetic. This approach isn't always the best, especially with kids.

Last week, I was attempting to get our three kids out of the house in a rush. The kids were not cooperating. Stressed and harried, I was scurrying around collecting laundry and yelling at the kids to do what I had asked of them. Suddenly, Mary entered my thoughts: She would not have sounded like me. Just then my five-year-old entered the room that I was cleaning. I whispered my request to him, and he answered me in the most loving and calm manner. Everything changed.

I imagine this is how Mary was in her relationships with all people. Mary inspires me be a better mother, wife, and friend, to live in this world with gentleness and a kind heart.

— Meg Bucaro

DO YOU READILY SPEAK without pondering the consequences? Seek Mary's help to ponder more.

Prayer: Mary, help me to model the manner in which you approached all others. Grant me holy silence and gentleness in my words and actions today.

May 17

"Aim at righteousness, godliness, faith, love, steadfastness, gentleness."
— 1 Timothy 6:11

A homeless man entered my parish church to warm himself. He walked down the center aisle, removed his hat, and gazed at the cross in the sanctuary. He then ambled toward where I was standing — the back corner by a statue of Mary.

The beautiful, life-sized sculpture depicts the Annunciation. Mary has just said "yes" to God. Her hands, face, and eyes are raised toward the heavens in a gentle moment of chosen surrender.

For some time, the man gazed into Mary's eyes. He reverently touched her outreached hand, the hem of her garment, and her foot. Then, he asked me, "Who is this woman?" I responded: "Her name is Mary. She's the mother of Jesus."

He replied: "Her eyes are so gentle and full of love. She reminds me of my mother, who died when I was a boy. No one has looked at me like that for a long time. May I come visit her again?" I responded, "Anytime, sir." He left the church with a broad smile and returned to visit Mary often to receive the gentleness he saw in her.

— Sharon A. Abel, PhD

CONSIDER THE WAYS you can greet the next stranger you meet with gentleness.

Prayer: Mary, help me to be a kind, gentle, and loving person all the days of my life.

May 18

"He has helped his servant Israel, / in remembrance of his mercy, / as he spoke to our fathers, / to Abraham and to his posterity for ever."
— Luke 1:54-55

God remembers the promises he makes, and keeps them. Mary remembers, too. The Memorare is a time-honored prayer that contains a plea to our gentle heavenly mother to remember us, and to intercede on our behalf. No matter where we are on our spiritual journey — steadfast in our faith, or faltering and on the fringes — our Blessed Mother is here to pray with us each and every day. The Mother of God remembers us in her prayers:

Remember, O most gracious Virgin Mary, that never was it known that anyone who fled to thy protection, implored thy help, or sought thy intercession was left unaided. Inspired with this confidence, I fly unto thee, O Virgin of virgins, my Mother. To thee do I come, before thee I stand, sinful and sorrowful. O Mother of the Word Incarnate, despise not my intentions, but in thy mercy hear and answer me. Amen.

— Sheila Cusack

PRAY THE MEMORARE TODAY. Ask Mary to help you to pray with gentle intent rather than demanding desperation.

Prayer: Mary, help me to turn to you with all of my needs so that you can gently take my prayers and petitions to your Son, Jesus.

May 19

"The flowers appear on the earth, / the time of pruning has come, / and the voice of the turtledove / is heard in our land." — *Song of Solomon 2:12*

Watching a group of preschool children walking with their teacher past a rose garden took my breath away. The teacher said: "Don't touch. Be gentle. Just smell them." The little children leaned in, folded their hands, and placed their little faces close to the flowers. It made me want to sing.

Images of our Blessed Mother often show her among roses. These remind us to offer prayers of gratitude to God thanking him for all the lovely things he created. With her gentle spirit, Mary is like a rose in God's spiritual garden. Our spiritual mother is sweet and gentle; her life is fragrant with the perfume of God's presence and grace.

— Alice Smith

TAKE A WALK OUTSIDE TODAY. Make a concerted effort to see the world around you with new eyes. Take in the blankets of beautiful flowers, the budding green trees, and the sapphire-blue sky. Whisper a prayer of gratitude to our creator God.

Prayer: Madonna of the Rose, you are my spiritual flower. Teach me how to be gentle. Awaken me to the love of Jesus and his precious gifts for all humankind.

May 20

"For where your treasure is, there will your heart be also."
— *Matthew 6:21*

Mary's heart belonged to the Lord from the moment of her immaculate conception in the womb of her mother, St. Anne. Her true treasure in life was her relationship with God, and this brought great peace and solace to Mary's gentle heart. Scripture tells us that when Jesus was crucified, Mary stayed by his side. She did not hide or cry out for justice, nor did she turn her back on God. Mary's gentle heart rested in the Lord in her darkest hour.

Mary's life challenges us to stay focused on Jesus, even in the midst of our daily struggles. If we remain close to Jesus, our hearts will be gentle and loving, and our souls will find rest. The same holds true for us. When we treasure Christ, our hearts are with him. When we are close to Jesus, we can be strong and secure enough to act in gentleness rather than in anger or fear.

— Lauren Nelson

WHEN YOU BEGIN TO FEEL fear or anger, ask Mary to bring your heart gently back to Jesus.

Prayer: Mary, your gentle heart remained focused on your greatest treasure, your Son. Help me to treasure Jesus always.

May 21

"Set a guard over my mouth, O LORD, /
keep watch over the door of my lips!" — *Psalms 141:3*

It's hard to be gentle, especially if I've decided that I need to let another person know why I am right. There are many reasons we each encounter this challenge. We may not care for the way someone chooses to live his life, or anguish over the decisions another has made. We bristle when someone else's choices don't meet our expectations, or when we simply disagree about an important matter. When things like this occur, it can be difficult to remember that once hurtful, defensive, or judgmental words cross the threshold of our lips we cannot take them back.

Surely Mary experienced frustration and hurt dealing with people in her village. The Scriptures tell us that the people of Nazareth rejected her Son, Jesus. Some even attempted to throw him over a cliff. How did Mary react? Perhaps she prayed this very psalm.

— Nanci Lukasik-Smith

THE NEXT TIME you feel challenged, hold back long enough to think. Imagine yourself having a conversation with Mary. How would she tell you to respond?

Prayer: Mary, please remind me to have a gentle heart toward others. Place holy words on my lips so that I become a mirror of your gentleness and love.

May 22

"Jesus wept. So the Jews said, 'See how he loved him!'"
— John 11:35-36

The image of Jesus weeping at the death of Lazarus gives us a glimpse into the gentle and compassionate heart of Our Lord. This savior, who cured the sick, gave sight to the blind, and fed thousands with a few loaves of bread, shared this human expression of sorrow when he heard about the death of his friend.

As his mother, Mary taught Jesus the essential life skills of being human. She schooled him in his faith, responsibility, and how to be kind and considerate to others. Most importantly, Mary taught Jesus how to love and express that love abundantly. In his humanity Jesus was formed by the love between Mary and Joseph, and between himself and his parents.

As our spiritual mother, Mary desires that we, too, love abundantly. She is here to help us allow ourselves to be deeply touched and to be gentle in our encounters with others. Mary desires that we come to know and love Jesus as she does.

— Dr. Mary Amore

IN WHAT WAYS can we be gentle with our family members, coworkers, and strangers that God sends our way?

Prayer: Mary, your gentleness invites me to follow in your footsteps, that I may live as a person of love.

May 23

"Let not yours be the outward adorning with braiding of hair, decoration of gold, and wearing of robes, but let it be the hidden person of the heart with the imperishable jewel of a gentle and quiet spirit, which in God's sight is very precious." — 1 Peter 3:3-4

Imagining Mary's ancient world was always a challenge for me, until I visited the home of a weathered Pueblo storyteller woman in Taos, New Mexico. Her lodge was simple: a few hanging baskets, a worn wooden mixing bowl on a table, and a blanketed floor near the kiva, a room used for religious rituals, where the aroma of baking flatbread filled the air. Calmly sharing the precious life stories of her people while we shared bread together, this elder woman was the keeper of her peoples' memory. She wore no jewelry, just a plain dress. With a lovely, gentle demeanor she had an "imperishable" beauty.

In many ways, Mary is the keeper of our memories of Jesus. The gentleness of her calm disposition and inner beauty surely filled her home in Nazareth. Her dress was plain, and her life with Joseph was simple. At her table, Mary gathered with family and neighbors to lovingly share bread and stories.

— Sharon A. Abel, PhD

IS THERE SOMEONE in my life I think of as beautiful? How can I be gentle of heart today?

Prayer: Mary, help us to simplify our lives that we may find imperishable beauty God has placed within us.

May 24

"He will feed his flock like a shepherd, / he will gather the lambs in his arms, / he will carry them in his bosom, / and gently lead those that are with young." — Isaiah 40:11

For centuries, master artists have depicted Jesus as the gentle shepherd carrying the lost sheep. Upon prayerful reflection, we can imagine that Jesus may well have learned gentleness from his mother, Mary. Each day of his life, Mary taught Jesus how to be kind, gentle, and compassionate, as any good mother would do.

When we pray the Hail Mary, the words of this heartfelt prayer remind us that the Lord is with Mary. If we follow her example in life, the Lord will be with us as well. Mary and Jesus are here to tend to our spiritual needs and to carry us home to heaven in their loving arms. May the prayer of our hearts reflect this beautiful spiritual reality.

— Sheila Cusack

CALL TO MIND a difficult situation you are going through. Invite Mary to bring you to the Good Shepherd, that you may not be lost, but cradled and carried by the Lord through difficulty.

Prayer: Mary, help us to hear the voice of your Son, Jesus, the Good Shepherd, that we may never stray from his flock.

May 25

"Let all men know your forbearance [gentleness]. The Lord is at hand."
— Philippians 4:5

Most people think of a gentle person as someone who is kind, but weak. In reality, a gentle person is strong. It takes strength to offer a gentle smile, a soothing word, or a helping hand, to treat everyone with kindness, to forgive, and to be faithful. This is how Mary lived.

Throughout her life, Mary exemplified gentleness through many difficult situations: when the angel Gabriel announced God's plan for her, even though she was terrified; when she and Joseph made the difficult journey to Bethlehem at the end of her pregnancy; as she gave birth to Jesus in a stable; with the child Jesus, even when she did not understand his words or his actions; at the wedding in Cana, when she quietly urged Jesus to perform his first miracle; as she stood at the foot of the cross watching her Son die in agony; in the Upper Room praying with the disciples at Pentecost.

— Mary L. Kostic

AS WE THINK ABOUT THE WORLD we live in today, we can choose to return to the strength of gentleness and treat everyone with kindness, compassion, and love.

Prayer: Mary, help us to grow in gentleness by your example and through your Son, Jesus. Help us find the strength to be compassionate, kind, and patient.

May 26

*"Learn from me; for I am gentle and lowly in heart,
and you will find rest for your souls." —Matthew 11:29*

On a recent trip to the Holy Land, we stopped in Cana, the site of the wedding feast in John's Gospel. I was overjoyed at the thought of renewing our wedding vows there, while my husband approached the event gently. We both began to reflect on Mary's role at Cana.

How beautiful it must have been for Mary to gently nudge her Son into taking on his role as a miracle worker. As his mother, Mary knew the heart of Jesus, and when the time was right, she helped her Son to begin his public ministry. At Cana, Mary gently informed Jesus that the wine had run out, and she trusted Jesus to take care of things. We can learn much from Mary's actions.

— Alice Smith

HOW CAN YOU APPROACH your life with gentleness? Consider the ways that you can change your demeanor from one of confrontation to one of understanding, trusting that the Lord will take care of your problems.

Prayer: Mary, help me to learn from your gentle ways so I may proclaim my love for Jesus in a respectful manner.

May 27

"A soft answer turns away wrath, / but a harsh word stirs up anger."
— Proverbs 15:1

Do you have a family member or friend who is soft-spoken and gentle in their mannerisms? I do. Actually, I have several who qualify with these characteristics. They are firm in their faith, yet they can engage others in a warm and respectful approach. Even with heavy or controversial subjects they come across as calm and confident. They provide a genuine softness that makes one feel at ease, and the conversation is positive for all involved.

I imagine that our Blessed Mother was like this in her dealings with people. Her gentle nature and respectful demeanor helped others to know and love Jesus. Mary's life inspires us to listen to others with respect.

— Nanci Lukasik-Smith

CONSIDER THE WAYS you can exhibit a gentle nature, one of welcome and warmth. What could you do today to make others feel comfortable in your presence?

Prayer: Holy Mary, when I am with others, please help me to represent the kind of character that is pleasing to the Father. Let me be welcoming and gentle in bringing others to Christ. Guide me to speak and act in ways that draw people to your Son.

May 28

"The Lord is gracious and merciful, / slow to anger and abounding in mercy."
— *Psalms 145:8*

Mary is a model of goodness, love, and grace. This is most evident in the early days of Mary's role as the mother of Jesus. As a new mother, Mary was gracious in welcoming the shepherds who came to see her newborn baby boy. She opened her heart to foreigners, too, the Magi from the East who brought gifts. From the moment of his birth, Mary realized that she would have to share Jesus with all those who would seek him.

Mary's life has much to teach us about how to bring gentleness to today's world. So much of our culture seems to relish turmoil. People are quick to argue, and many judge and condemn others simply because they see things differently. Our heavenly mother invites us to graciously welcome the stranger, for we are all children of our heavenly Father.

— Lauren Nelson

REACH OUT TO SOMEONE today, perhaps someone you don't understand well, and encourage that person with gentle and compassionate words.

Prayer: Mary, your heart is gentle and pure. Help me to be welcoming and act with gentleness toward all people.

May 29

*"Fear not, for I have redeemed you; / I have called you by name,
you are mine." — Isaiah 43:1*

Mary's "yes" to God found her betrothed, pregnant, and a candidate for stoning under the law of Moses. Mary had every reason to be afraid, yet her faith helped her to remain calm. She married Joseph and left her home, neighbors, and friends behind. Her baby was born in Bethlehem, a town she would never call home. The family fled to Egypt and remained in exile until it was safe to return to Nazareth.

Our lives get complicated, too. Circumstances often find us in a whirl. How do we cope? How do we hold onto gentleness the way Mary did?

Isaiah's words have the answer. Don't let the fears or pressures of this day take control of you. Have faith in God like Mary did, and trust that he will never abandon you. Remember that God is a gentle and loving Father, always ready to hold you and lift you up.

— Sharon A. Abel, PhD

TAKE TIME to pray today. Ask God to show you his gentleness and to help you experience that you belong to him.

Prayer: Mary, because we share the same heavenly Father, you are my sister in faith. When I am burdened or afraid, lead me to his gentle, loving, and redeeming arms.

May 30

"My mouth will tell of your righteous acts, / of your deeds of salvation all the day / for their number is past my knowledge." — Psalms 71:15

This Scripture passage challenges us to use our words to proclaim the goodness of God. Sadly, however, we often fall to the temptation to become caught up in a whirlwind of verbal conflict. At times, we may even tear down another person just to prove our point.

Actions speak even more clearly and eloquently. When we choose gentleness over power and control, our actions proclaim God's love. No one is a better example of that life-giving choice than Mary. As our heavenly mother, Mary is here to accompany us on our paths of conflict. She invites us to cultivate gentleness in all our relationships, even when we see our circumstances only through the cloudy lens of strife and division. When this happens, we can seek her assistance.

— Sheila Cusack

PRAYERFULLY CALL TO MIND a recent disagreement or argument you had with another person. Invite Mary's gentle presence to help you walk away from this strife and disagreement, to choose gentleness, and to seek reconciliation.

Prayer: Mary, help me remember your Son's strife on earth. Help me to know that the conflicts I experience are opportunities to grow in gentleness.

May 31

"The LORD is merciful and gracious." — Psalms 103:8

Kindness is rare in our wounded and broken world. So many are quick to judge and condemn others simply because of a difference of opinions, appearance, or behavior. Social media is filled with "haters," people who troll the Web looking to instigate arguments against people they will never meet in person. Our world desperately needs the Lord's mercy and kindness.

Mary knew the need for kindness in her life. Her homeland was occupied by the Romans, and the Jewish people were considered inferior. Surely Mary endured much criticism in her daily life as a pious Jewish woman and mother. Yet she remained kind. She allowed the mercy of the Lord to come upon all those she met.

Mary nurtured Jesus in this same manner. Her family life was centered on the knowledge that the Lord is kind and merciful, and this helped to form Jesus in his ministry.

Mary's life has much to teach us about living in today's world. Her gentle motherly manner can help us see the good in all people, and to recognize and respond to the presence of God in our brothers and sisters.

— Dr. Mary Amore

DO ONE KIND and gentle deed today.

Prayer: Mary, help me to be kind and gentle of heart so that others may come to know Jesus through me.

~ JOY ~

June 1

"Blessed are those whose way is blameless, / who walk in the
law of the LORD!" — Psalms 119:1

I grew up in a home where everyone sang. Now, I delight in listening to my children joyfully singing as they play with friends and family. Mary's childhood included singing, too, except that the songs she likely grew up with were what we know as the Psalms. I can picture Mary skipping about her home singing out her faith while her parents listened in delight.

Mary was influenced by her culture and times. Her parents grounded her life in the Lord's teachings. They taught her about God's faithfulness, how he saved them and loved them. Mary learned to live by God's commandments and to pray to God with an open heart. This filled her with much happiness and joy.

We, too, are shaped by our environment. How familiar are you with the Lord's teachings? How often do you study or read the Scriptures?

— Sharon A. Abel, PhD

WHAT CAN YOU DO or change in order to live each day with genuine joy in the Lord?

Prayer: Mary, remind me to read from God's Word each day. Help me to find joy as I seek the Lord with an open heart and follow his ways.

June 2

"Truly, truly, I say to you, you will weep and lament, but the world will re-
joice; you will be sorrowful, but your sorrow will turn into joy.
If you ask anything of the Father, he will give it to you in my name.
Until now you have asked nothing in my name; ask, and you will receive,
that your joy may be full." — John 16:20,23-24

As Jesus prepared his disciples for his death, he also prepared them for the joy of his resurrection. We, too, are called to joy. Our Lord invites us into relationship with him. He also encourages us to pray in his name, so our joy may be complete. At Cana, Mary became the first to ask something of Jesus. We can only imagine the joy she experienced!

The Franciscans have a special devotion to the Seven Joys of Mary called "The Franciscan Crown." In addition to the Rosary's joyful mysteries, the joy of Mary at the adoration of the Magi and meeting Jesus after his resurrection are also prayed.

— John Holmes

RECALL HOW an answered prayer touched you in a joyful way. What can you do to rekindle that joy today?

Prayer: Dearest Mother, lead me to a more joyful life in your Son.

June 3

*"My spirit rejoices in God my savior / for he who is mighty
has done great things for me." — Luke 1:47,49*

Joy is not defined as a cheerful temperament or a sunny disposition, but rather the delighted peace we experience because of what God has done. We see this in what Mary tells her cousin Elizabeth the Lord has done, in the Magnificat. Mary put aside any idea that joy is found in things apart from God, or that God is a gloomy and punitive being who seeks to repay us for our faults and failings. Instead, she proclaimed the greatness of the Lord who desires to restore us to fullness of life.

Joy is the echo of God's footsteps in those freed from sin, brokenness, neglect, and want. Mary, the humble handmaid of the Lord, offers us the proper understanding of our God: the one who powerfully restores, repairs, and renews.

— Joseph Abel, PhD

CALL TO MIND the blessings you have received today. Spend time in prayer thanking God for his joy and blessings.

Prayer: O Mary, your spirit rejoiced in God and proclaimed the Lord who restores. With your help, may we come to share your joy by bringing our wounded hearts to God, who seeks to restore our joy.

June 4

"So you have sorrow now, but I will see you again and your hearts will rejoice, and no one will take your joy from you." — John 16:22

There is no greater pain than that of a parent who buries a child. So incomprehensible and unimaginable, we often find ourselves wondering how God could allow a family to experience such pain. Such has been the case with the loss of our twenty-four-year-old niece, Jillian. Her earthly joyfulness was nourishment for us all, and her passing shattered the faith of many and left her family broken.

In the years following Jill's death, Mary has been a great source of comfort to me. Mary felt a mother's pain, anguish, and heartache as she watched Jesus die on the cross. Yet she never lost sight of God's eternal plan. She grieved the loss of her Son, but always believed she would be joyful again.

— Betty Bentley

WHAT SITUATION in your life is a source of grief and sadness? Bring this to Mary and ask her to help you believe in God's plan for you.

Prayer: Mary, we ask that you help us to understand that our pain is part of life. We look to you as a beacon of faith and as a reminder of God's great love for us. Help us to believe, as you did, that we will rejoice again and that our joy will be eternal.

June 5

"These things I have spoken to you, that my joy may be in you, and that your joy may be full." — John 15:11

One of my greatest joys is cooking and sharing a meal with good wine, conversation, and prayer with friends and family. The ritual of meal sharing and breaking bread connects us in a very intimate way. And I love to do what is necessary to make it happen.

Mary's life inspires me to serve with joy. When I am preparing a meal, I like to imagine that Mary is serving her family at Nazareth. She, too, took great delight in cooking for her loved ones. That is because Mary had a servant's heart. Mary's life was spent in loving service to Jesus and Joseph, and all those who followed Jesus.

Mary invites us to follow her in loving service. The result is "joy," the joy that comes from self-giving love.

— Dr. Barb Jarvis-Pauls

CALL TO MIND a time when you have experienced joy in serving others. Take a moment to thank God for the grace to serve others joyfully. Do something for someone else with joy today.

Prayer: Mother Mary, help me to be a sign of your loving and generous service in my family, community, and world, that others may know your Son, our Lord Jesus Christ.

June 6

"My soul magnifies the Lord." — Luke 1:46

I've prayed the Rosary my entire life. At times, it's as if Mary is leading me through a guided meditation as she opens her heart and reveals her own feelings. A key insight about the Joyful Mysteries is that while they are joyful, they each contain an element of difficulty, fear, or sorrow.

Mary is a young girl, pregnant, and unmarried who travels to visit and care for an older relative. She delivers her baby in a cave after another long journey, and receives surprise visits from shepherds and foreigners. A prophet tells her that a sword will pierce her heart. Finally, the last mystery includes losing her only child for three days.

Through it all, the words of Mary's great prayer — focusing on the greatness of the Lord — resonate in my being. Mary sees the joy in all these events because she knows that God's plan of salvation is unfolding. She joyfully surrenders herself to God's will.

— Bob Frazee

REFLECT ON YOUR OWN joyful mysteries of your life. Praise God for the joy as well as the challenges they may bring.

Prayer: Mary, I pray that you will guide me through difficult times and help me to see the joy in God's work in my life.

June 7

"For he who is mighty has done great things for me, / and holy is his name!"
— Luke 1:49

Beethoven's Ninth Symphony was the first example of a major composer using voices in a symphony. The words are sung during the final movement by four vocal soloists and a chorus. They were taken from the "Ode to Joy," written by Friedrich Schiller in 1785: "Joy! Joy! Beautiful spark of Divinity!"

Mary's "Ode to Joy" is her Magnificat. In it, she proclaims God's love and praises his handiwork of salvation. Mary invites us to be joyful disciples in this world — that is, faith-inspired men and women who are excited about singing and sharing praises to the Lord. Joy sits at the heart of what it means to be a Christian. We can join Mary's hymn of praise as we joyfully proclaim to all the world the great things that God has done for each one of us.

— Joseph Abel, PhD

SELECT A FAVORITE HYMN. Prayerfully call to mind the words and use them as a joyful song of praise. Sing the hymn in the car, at home, or outdoors.

Prayer: O Mary, help us to imitate your joyful hymns of praise to the Lord. May we never take his goodness for granted.

June 8

"Each one must do as he has made up his mind, not reluctantly or under compulsion, for God loves a cheerful giver." — 2 *Corinthians* 9:7

What's in it for me? Many use this question as a means to decide what they will give, what talents they will share, and what time and money they will spend on someone else. It is easy to be motivated more by a sense of self-interest or obligation than from sincere desire. It's easy to find ourselves going through motions, never embracing the joy of selfless giving.

Mary shows us how to make a gift of our lives to God. When she answered God's call and his plan for her life, she decided to give her heart fully — not reluctantly or under compulsion. Mary was a cheerful giver. It is through her "yes" that Mary found complete and perfect joy. Mary's life inspires us to give ourselves to the Lord so that our joy may be complete.

— Betty Bentley

DO YOU FIND JOY in giving? Seek the Blessed Mother's help in giving freely and totally the gift that you are.

Prayer: Mary, help us to say yes to God's plan for us and to serve him as you did, deciding in our hearts to give freely and completely. Thank you for showing us the joy that comes from cheerful giving.

June 9

*"So they departed quickly from the tomb with fear and great joy,
and ran to tell his disciples." — Matthew 28:8*

How excited the disciples must have been to discover Jesus' empty tomb! Imagine the joy in telling Mary that her Son was no longer dead. He had risen.

How quickly emotions can change from fear to joy. Mother Mary experienced deep joy as Jesus was born, grew up, taught in the Temple, and healed the sick. Yet, our Blessed Mother also experienced the terrifying fear of Jesus' arrest, captivity, and crucifixion. That terrible scene, however, gave way to the power of God revealed in the resurrection of Christ.

When we truly love someone, we make ourselves vulnerable. Relationships are a risky business; we expose ourselves to fear and joy. Our Blessed Mother is an inspiration to place our trust in God and in relationships that will help us overcome our fears in life with joy.

— Dr. Barb Jarvis Pauls

WHEN HAVE I EXPERIENCED fear in a relationship or in sharing my passion? When have I also experienced joy as a response to sharing my passion?

Prayer: Blessed Mother Mary, thank you for your inspiration to trust with faith and to share my passion and love in this life.

June 10

"Without having seen him you love him; though you do not now see him you believe in him and rejoice with unutterable and exalted joy. As the outcome of your faith you obtain the salvation of your souls." — 1 Peter 1:8-9

Mary is the perfect personification of these words of St. Peter. As a young woman, accepting and believing in what the angel Gabriel told her, Mary loved the child she conceived. Like many expectant parents, Mary's life was filled with unimaginable joy at the life growing within her. As the years went by, and Jesus grew in grace and age, Mary found joy in his mission work on earth.

If Mary lived today, I imagine she would make every effort to let us see all that Jesus is doing in order to help increase our faith. As a proud and joyful mother, perhaps Mary would be posting photos on social media, sending out tweets about her Son, and joyfully sharing him with the world.

— Lauren Nelson

CONSIDER THE WAYS that you can share the joyful news of your faith with your family and friends.

Prayer: Mary, surround me with the joy you have for your Son. Help me to always be joyful in the knowledge that Jesus gave his life to save me.

June 11

"Let your light so shine before men, that they may see your good works and give glory to your Father who is in heaven." — Matthew 5:16

This passage names the mission of the Church: to spread the light of God. As followers of Christ, we become children of his light, joyfully shining on the darkened corners of our world.

Mary is here to help us. She is ever present to nurture us and to keep the flame of God's love burning within us. Mary is our joyful advocate and is here to raise us up to holiness.

Spending time together allows bonds to develop and the light to be joyfully shared. When we share the Eucharist, those bonds of joyful love develop at the heart of our Christian community of faith. Mary invites us to let our light shine and to joyfully proclaim the good works of her Son, Jesus Christ.

— Nanci Lukasik-Smith

HOW CAN YOU LET the light of Christ shine joyfully through you today?

Prayer: Holy Mother, please fill my heart with the light of Christ. Guide me to share what God has given me, and help me to engage others to enter into your joy.

June 12

*"These things I have spoken to you, that my joy may be in you,
and that your joy may be full." — John 15:11*

Have you noticed the popularity of books that include the word "joy" in its title? In today's world, if we are seeking to find joy in a specific arena of life, there's a book for that! Yet, so few people are joyful. That's because our concept of joy has been downgraded, misinterpreted, and commercialized. Joy has largely lost its meaning because our culture associates it with things rather than with personal relationships.

Our Blessed Mary knew the real meaning of joy because she experienced it in the depths of her being. Chosen to be the mother of our Savior, Mary's joy did not come from leisure-time activities, or from reading pages in a how-to or self-help book. Mary's joy — and ours — comes from the knowledge that we are infinitely loved by God. This is cause for great joy!

— Joseph Abel, PhD

CONSIDER YOUR OWN spiritual life. How can you draw near to God? Choose one joyful "drawing near" activity to do today.

Prayer: O Mary, joyful handmaid of the Lord, your willingness to draw close to God brought joy to all creation. May our lives be filled with the delight of the nearness of God.

June 13

"Count it all joy, my brethren, when you meet various trials, for you know that the testing of your faith produces steadfastness." — James 1:2-3

Devotion to the Pilgrim Virgin Statue was our long-standing family tradition. On Friday nights, it was our turn to welcome the traveling Mary statue into our home and kneel on the hardwood living-room floor for what seemed an eternity to pray the Rosary. I must confess that as children we made the best of it, lest we receive "the look" from a parent, aunt, or uncle.

Of all the adults who participated in the Friday-night Rosary, my mom is the only one still living. Now, when I reflect on that family tradition, sore knees are no longer the predominant memory. Instead, I remember the joy of precious moments shared with loved ones, the joy that comes from family, and the joy that faith can bring.

Isn't that what Mary shows us? She cherished her time with Joseph and Jesus. She persevered through every kind of trial as her faith was tested, finding joy in God's eternal and unconditional love.

— Betty Bentley

DO YOU HAVE a family ritual that brings you joy? Prayerfully reflect on the joy that family and faith can bring into your life.

Prayer: Mary, help us to find joy in each day — joy in our families, and joy in our trials.

June 14

"For the gate is narrow and the way is hard, that leads to life, and those who find it are few." — Matthew 7:14

The manner in which Mary lived her humble life reveals that she was one who walked the narrow road mentioned in Matthew's Gospel. In choosing to follow God, Mary ultimately chose joy in her life — even in difficult times. As our heavenly mother, Mary invites us to follow her on this pathway, that together we may enter the narrow gate to a life of joy.

On any given day, we are presented with numerous choices that can ultimately bring us joy. For example, we have the choice to wave hello to our neighbors as we pass them by on our street. We have the option of helping an elderly person struggling with groceries. And we have the possibility of spending time with God in prayer. All of these situations can bring joy into our lives, the joy of following the narrow road that leads to the gate of eternal life.

— Sheila Cusack

CONSIDER WHAT YOU CAN DO to follow the narrow road today. Is there someone you can take with you?

Prayer: Mary, I pray that you can be my companion on this narrow road that leads to your Son, Jesus.

June 15

"Shout, and sing for joy, O inhabitant of Zion, / for great in your midst is the Holy One of Israel." — Isaiah 12:6

Isaiah's words were of great help to the people of his time, yet his prophecies pointed to an even more glorious time when the savior would come. This verse exhorts us to shout with joy. It doesn't say, perhaps we should think about shouting with joy. It commands us to shout for joy, because God is in our midst.

Mary's family waited expectantly for the fulfillment of these Scriptures. At the same time, they knew God's presence was already and always among them. As a Jew, Mary would have heard the prophets' words and been obedient to them. Her whole life is a shout for joy.

We are called to follow the example of Mary in trusting in the word of God and being obedient to what the Lord says to do.

— Chris Grano

CAN WE SHOUT FOR JOY because God is with us? If not, what gets in the way?

Prayer: Mary, please pray that I may experientially know that God is present in my life and will rejoice with you in his divine presence, even when I don't feel like it.

June 16

"Hail, full of grace, the Lord is with you." — *Luke 1:28*

Each one of us experiences pain in our lifetime, as we are human. Relationships and life experiences have emotional ups and downs. We can be empathetic to others, supporting them during the trials and tribulations of life. We can also seek comfort for ourselves when we are hurting. I think about times as a spiritual director and counselor when I have listened to others' problems and pain and tried to offer hope for healing. It is possible to take the weight of the world on our shoulders and still have joy in our hearts when our relationship with God is strong.

When I feel doubt, loneliness, and sadness, I have been reminded of my stronghold, Mother Mary. The words "Hail Mary, full of grace, the Lord is with you" teach me that indeed, the Lord is with me, too! As Christians, Mary's life reminds us of the grace and joy that is ours, even in the midst of pain, because the presence of the Lord is with us always.

— Dr. Barb Jarvis Pauls

HAVE I EVER experienced joy that is deeper than suffering?

Prayer: Hail Mary, full of grace, continue to help us live in the joy that Jesus is with us.

June 17

"When the day of Pentecost had come, they were all together in one place. And suddenly a sound came from heaven like the rush of a mighty wind, and it filled all the house where they were sitting." — Acts 2:1-2

Scripture tells us that Mary was present with the apostles in the Upper Room at Pentecost. At that moment, her grace-filled being must have resonated with complete joy. Empowered by the Spirit, the apostles took the Gospel message to the corners of the globe. Mary remained with John, joyfully accepting her mission in life as a disciple of her Son and mother of the Church.

As followers of Jesus, we carry the joy of the Spirit within us. Like Mary, it is not necessary for us to go to the ends of the earth to preach the Good News. We can share our joy of Christ on a daily basis where we are. Mary's life inspires us to be disciples, joyfully sharing the good news of salvation with our friends and family, coworkers and colleagues, and all who God sends our way.

— Lauren Nelson

SELECT ONE PERSON you can joyfully share the good news of Jesus with this day.

Prayer: Mary, help me to find the courage to joyfully proclaim the good news of Jesus to the world.

June 18

"'He has risen from the dead ... you will see him.' So they departed quickly from the tomb with fear and great joy." — *Matthew 28:7,8*

A parish was preparing children for an Easter play about the Resurrection. Each child had a part. One little boy was given the role of the rock that was placed in front of Jesus' tomb. The boy relished the part and would roll away from the tomb with great gusto, knocking down other children on the stage. The catechist intervened, "Must you roll so recklessly?" "I can't help it," the child exclaimed. "I have the best part. I get to let Jesus out!"

Imagine the joy Mary felt when she heard that Jesus had risen from the dead. This moment in salvation history and in the life of Mary challenges us to believe with great joy that God is alive and will lead us out of our spiritual tombs and into new life.

— Joseph Abel, PhD

IMAGINE YOU ARE with Mary and the frightened apostles in the Upper Room. Then you hear the joyful news of the Resurrection. How does this event change your life? Allow the joy of that moment to enter your heart.

Prayer: O Mary, joyful mother, may we, too, experience the joy of rolling back the stone in our lives to free your Son from all that entombs him in our hearts.

June 19

"Just so, I tell you, there will be more joy in heaven over one sinner who repents than over ninety-nine righteous persons who need no repentance."
— *Luke 15:7*

Jesus is the Good Shepherd. Even though we might stray from his flock, Jesus will come for us, like a shepherd searching for lost sheep. Mary witnessed Jesus seeking the lost: from tax collectors Matthew and Zacchaeus to the forgiveness Jesus offered to the good thief crucified beside him. Each repentant sinner brought joy.

When we learn from our mistakes and turn to God for mercy and forgiveness, joy fills the heavens and fills our hearts. Mary is our mother, teacher, and advocate. She understands our human nature, our failings, our mistakes, and our shortcomings. She invites us to take refuge in her sweet embrace. There, surrounded by her love, we find the strength to change our ways; we find that turning our hearts to God brings us joy.
— Gina Sannasardo

INVITE MARY to stand by your side as you look for ways to change your attitude, convert your heart, and transform your deeds. Choose one change to begin today.

Prayer: Blessed Mother, we thank you for always interceding on our behalf. Help us to know that God's mercy is our joy.

June 20

"Rejoice always, pray constantly, give thanks in all circumstances; for this is the will of God in Christ Jesus for you." — 1 Thessalonians 5:16-18

Have you ever felt pulled in a direction that you did not want to go? Have you ever complained about your circumstances and felt they were unfair? Are there times when praying is difficult and blessings seem to be for others, not you?

Mary could have wondered, "Why me?" She could have seen herself as a victim, or become resentful of being called away from the quiet life she had anticipated. Instead, Mary gave herself fully to the will of God for her with joy. She rejoiced always and gracefully lived her life with an open heart and good intentions. Mary prayed constantly, remaining in God's presence. And the Mother of Jesus gave thanks, living in gratitude for God's blessings. Her life inspires us to seek the joy that can be found in every situation and circumstance.

— Betty Bentley

CALL TO MIND something you struggle with. Seek Mary's help to rejoice, pray, and be grateful today.

Prayer: Mary, help us to see the joy in God's plan as you did. Help us to remain in his presence and open to the flow of blessings we will receive when we are one with him.

June 21

*"Even the sparrow finds a home, / and the swallow a nest for herself, /
where she may lay her young, / at your altars, O LORD of hosts, /
my King and my God." — Psalms 84:3*

It's a joy to watch how a mother bird seeks out twigs and leaves to build a nest where her babies can be safe and well cared for. As a young mother, Mary, too, knew the importance of making a home for Jesus, a place where he could feel safe and well cared for.

Like any mother, Mary wanted her house to be filled with joy, and she took great delight in teaching Jesus the prayers, rituals, and Scriptures of his Jewish faith. Mary chose to place the Lord God at the center of their home life.

Mary's life in Nazareth inspires us to reexamine our priorities. What is the source of joy in your home? Is your faith a light that burns brightly each day, or has the flame faded through the years?

— Sheila Cusack

TODAY, ASK THE BLESSED MOTHER to help you make God the head of your household and the source of your joy. What one thing could you do to restore the joy of faith in the life of your family?

Prayer: Mary, help me to make my home in the heart of Jesus.

June 22

"Go, eat your bread with enjoyment." — *Ecclesiastes 9:7*

Eating freshly baked and buttered bread, hot from the oven, was the way we celebrated the joy of new life in the family I grew up in. With the addition of every new sibling, my aunt would come from the city to watch us and to bake homemade bread with us. We ate it in great celebration as soon as it came out of the oven.

What my aunt did reminds me of how our Blessed Mother would have baked fresh bread for every Sabbath and Passover. Mary's ritual bread baking was also in joyful celebration of new life — the new life of God's covenant with Israel. Remembered and renewed weekly with freshly baked bread at the family table, Jesus would have experienced the joy of God's covenant from his mother, Mary.

As our spiritual mother, Mary invites us to join her at the Eucharistic table — a heavenly banquet where we find joy in Christ as we receive him in the living bread from heaven.

— Joseph Abel, PhD

IF YOUR HEALTH ALLOWS, slice yourself a piece of freshly baked bread. Pray the Our Father, paying special attention to the phrase, "give us this day our daily bread." Enjoy!

Prayer: Mary, teach us to love Jesus as you do. Help us to receive the holy Eucharist with joy.

June 23

"Without having seen him you love him; though you do not now see him you believe in him and rejoice with unutterable and exalted joy. As the outcome of your faith you obtain the salvation of your souls." — 1 Peter 1:8-9

Like us, many early Christians had never seen Jesus. But they still found indescribable joy in their salvation. All of us have relatives who passed on before we could know them personally. But as we listen to the stories from others who did, we can feel close to them through others.

Jesus was Mary's son — she knew him intimately. She had the deepest personal experience of Jesus. There is no better person to help us know Jesus more personally.

In the second verse of this passage, the writer says that we rejoice when we reach the goal of our faith — salvation. Though she was uniquely chosen by God, Mary didn't take her salvation for granted — she rejoiced greatly in what God had done for her.

— Christine Grano

ASK MARY TO SHARE her Son with you. Ask God to fill your heart with the joy of your salvation.

Prayer: Mary, pray that I may come to know Jesus more personally. Show me how to experience the joy of my salvation more fully.

June 24

"For you shall go out in joy, / and be led forth in peace; / the mountains and the hills before you / shall break forth into singing, / and all the trees of the field shall clap their hands." — Isaiah 55:12

The fact that Mary is our spiritual mother is cause for great joy. The salvation of everyone depended on her willingness to turn over her life to God and become the mother of Jesus. Mary was instrumental in the fulfillment of the Lord's promise of salvation, a promise he made in the Garden of Eden, to Noah, to Abraham, and to the people of Israel.

Mary's joy in mothering Jesus gives us an opportunity to know and love the Lord intimately, and to have the joy of Jesus in our own hearts. As our heavenly mother, Mary desires that we pattern our lives after hers so that we can bring the joy of the Gospel into our homes, workplaces, and the world.

— Lauren Nelson

CONSIDER HOW you can bring joy into the world. Select one person or a group of people and do something that makes this day joyful for them.

Prayer: Mary, make my soul truly joyful. Help me to share this joy today and always.

June 25

"Be glad in the LORD, and rejoice, O righteous, / and shout for joy, all you upright in heart!" — *Psalms 32:11*

This prayerful psalm is a reminder for us to rejoice by staying upright in heart and mind. Neuropsychologists are discovering that joyful and positive thoughts change the chemistry in our brains, increasing processes that promote good health and positive emotions.

Mary's life has much to teach us about living with joy. In light of all the rejection she may have faced from the culture of the time, she chose to rejoice, overcoming her fears and opening herself to the will of God in spite of all the obstacles, judgments, and negative consequences that might have come from doing so.

By modeling our lives after that of our Blessed Mother, we can be transformed to be more hopeful and positive by choosing to be open and flexible in our encounters with others as we let God lead and guide us.

— Dr. Barb Jarvis Pauls

WHAT ONE THING can I do to have a more positive outlook or become more upright in heart during times of stress today?

Prayer: Mother Mary, you shouted for joy and rejoiced in God, your Savior, as you did his will. Pray for us to follow God's will with joy and upright hearts.

June 26

"The LORD is my strength and my shield; / in him my heart trusts; / so I am helped, and my heart exults, / and with my song I give thanks to him."
— *Psalms 28:7*

Joy from trusting in God's help? Clearly this is easier said than done. We live in a world where we are bombarded with reasons to doubt, question, and take a cynical view, needing proof or outward signs of God's existence. Yet those who can trust find joy. Those who can admit their own weakness and make God their strength are helped. Believers are filled with joy.

Imagine how filled with doubt, fear, and confusion Mary must have been when first approached by the angel Gabriel, not knowing what to expect. Yet Mary knew in her heart that God would be her strength. She trusted him with her whole being. And, as a result, Mary was helped and filled with an inexpressible and glorious joy.

— Betty Bentley

THINK OF A TIME when God was your strength. Remember the joy you experienced knowing that God had helped you. Decide to trust God more, just for today.

Prayer: Mary, help me to have a faith as strong as yours so that I, too, can experience the inexpressible joy, the end result of our faith, the salvation of my soul.

June 27

"You show me the path of life; / in your presence there is fulness of joy, / in your right hand are pleasures for evermore." — Psalms 16:11

Joy is a state of mind and an orientation of the heart. It is not the result of something that happens to me, but rather my choosing to connect deeply with another, with nature, or with God. Joy rises from my surrender to that which I know is profoundly good. It is in those moments of connectedness, goodness, and loving surrender that I experience joy. I choose those moments. I choose what to hold in my mind and heart. I choose what to say and do. Joy is a choice.

The Bible often connects joy with salvation, a right heart, or surrender. Thus joy can be experienced even in a time of great suffering. Could Mary have accepted her calling in the face of social disgrace and an unknown path if she did not have joy in her soul? Mary chose joy by answering God's call. Choosing joy opens the path to fulfilling my calling and destiny, no matter the cost.

— Jane Zimmerman

How DIFFICULT IS IT for you to keep joy at the center of your heart?

Prayer: Dear Mary, please help me approach all my life's experiences from the very center of my heart and mind, with joy.

June 28

"Shout, and sing for joy, O inhabitant of Zion, / for great in your midst is the Holy One of Israel." — Isaiah 12:6

Mary lived a happy life, content in all her doings, and joyfully followed Our Lord. Although she experienced great losses and difficulties, Mary was able to keep joy in her heart. Her life reminds us that we were not created for suffering and pain. We, too, can be people filled with joy.

Mary invites us to find joy by praising God, not only for what he has done, but for who he is. Our God does not leave us to our own devices. He brings us out of sin and shame and into the light of his presence. That's something to shout and sing about! As our spiritual mother, Mary desires that we join in her hymn of praise proclaiming the amazing truth that God is among us. Holy is his name.

— Gina Sannasardo

HOW CAN YOU RESPOND with joy to life's surprises and difficulties? Invite Mary to fill your heart with joy today as you approach all that life has to offer, and all that it requires of you.

Prayer: Blessed Mother, thank you for loving me. Pray that I may experience the joy that only your Son can give.

June 29

"Ask, and you will receive, that your joy may be full." — *John 16:24*

The Museum of Joy in San Francisco is dedicated to celebrating the wide range of joyous experiences. It bills itself as an "inside-out" museum, exploring joy through performances, installations, artworks, and immersive experiences. The inspiration for the museum is the belief that joy is the flame that lights our way in times of darkness.

Mary knew the joy that lights the way, but she didn't find it in a museum. Joy is one of the fruits of the Holy Spirit at work in our lives. It is the evidence that we belong to the kingdom of God and that the Lord is at work within us. Mary is truly a model for Christian joy. As our heavenly mother, Mary desires that we, too, come to know the source of her joy, and that is a relationship with Jesus Christ.

— Joseph Abel, PhD

SIT COMFORTABLY and quietly. Spend a few minutes inviting the Holy Spirit to come to you by saying, "Come, Holy Spirit, come!" Try to repeat this invitation at various times throughout the day.

Prayer: O Mary, ever-joyful handmaiden of the Lord, your willing acceptance of the Holy Spirit helped establish God's kingdom on earth. May we continually welcome the Holy Spirit so that God's kingdom will be furthered through our lives.

June 30

"No greater joy can I have than this, to hear that my children
follow the truth." — 3 John 1:4

What a simple but profound joy it is when those in our care follow God's plan and walk with him. For many of us, that is the most important hope we have for the people we love.

Easier said than done? Yes, it certainly can be. No matter our age or stage in life, we have challenges, struggles, and outside forces that make it difficult to walk in the truth. We may lose our way physically, emotionally, or spiritually and cause pain not just for ourselves, but also for others.

Even Mary had her challenges. She worried about Jesus just as we worry about our loved ones. Yet what joy she must have felt watching Jesus grow and learn throughout his childhood. What joy she must have felt seeing him become an adult and walk in the light of God's truth.

— Betty Bentley

PRAYERFULLY CALL TO MIND those who struggle with their faith in your circle of family and friends. Pray for them to experience the joy of walking with Jesus.

Prayer: Mary, help our loved ones to know the joy of walking in the light of God's love.

~ SERENITY ~

July 1

"Have no anxiety about anything, but in everything by prayer and supplication with thanksgiving let your requests be made known to God."
— *Philippians 4:6*

The Bible often advises us to bring our needs and worries to God. Some days it is difficult for us to let go of our worries and offer our needs in prayer. From personal experience, I know how easy it can be to allow daily distractions and an over-connected culture steal my calm and push prayer time further down my list of priorities.

In Mary, we have a mother who can gently lead us to a renewed prayer life that will restore peace and serenity to our hectic lives. It was Mary who taught her Son, Jesus, to pray to the God of Abraham and Isaac. Mary can show us, too, how to lay our worries and needs before God.

— Deb Kelsey-Davis

INVITE MARY to guide you in prayer, to meditate upon God's love in your life. Ask Mary to bring your needs to her Son and help you find serenity.

Prayer: Mary, open my heart to the serenity that comes from prayer, that I might truly let go of my worries and trust in your Son, Jesus.

July 2

"He said to me, 'My grace is sufficient for you, for my power
is made perfect in weakness.'" — *2 Corinthians 12:9*

The story line is intriguing: an engaged teenager pregnant with a baby that is not her fiancé's. Her parents are shocked; friends and neighbors would rather stone her than help. She has no job, no money, and her future is uncertain. Yet, this young woman is unusually serene. Interesting.

This is Mary's story. It is an account of an extraordinary young woman whose life was graced with an unshakable faith in God. The gift of grace filled Mary's soul with serenity and calm even in the midst of life's most daunting trials. Mary's serenity came from the knowledge that God was with her and she would not face life alone. As our spiritual mother, Mary desires that we live a graced life and encourages us to place our complete trust in the Lord, knowing his grace is sufficient. Are we up to the challenge?

— Josesph Abel, PhD

SIT COMFORTABLY and quietly. As you breathe, meditate on the phrase, "My grace is sufficient for you." Do you believe this?

Prayer: O Mary, full of grace, you trusted that God's promises to you would be fulfilled. May we experience serenity by trusting that God's grace is indeed sufficient.

July 3

"The doors were shut, but Jesus came and stood among them, and said, 'Peace be with you.'" — John 20:26

Mary lived with this very special peace of Christ. From the moment she gave her fiat, serenity filled every fiber of Mary's being. What a magnificent gift!

In my chaotic life, there are certain people I turn to for serenity, those who, like the Blessed Mother, are visible signs of Christ's peace. No matter what cross I face, one friend in particular knows how to bring Christ's peace to the situation by turning my face toward Jesus so I may be strengthened. I imagine Mary brought serenity to many in her daily life in just this way. As she listened to the cares and concerns of her friends and relatives, I imagine her pointing them toward her Son and, like at the wedding at Cana, telling them with the greatest confidence, "Do whatever he tells you."

— Katie Choudhary

WHO DO YOU TURN TO for serenity in your daily life?

Our Lady, please lift up (insert name from above) to your Son's care today. I am thankful for the example of serenity you and he/she bring to my life. Help me to be open to receiving the peace of your Son so I may also bring it to others.

July 4

"Jesus Christ is the same yesterday and today and for ever."
— *Hebrews 13:8*

Every Fourth of July, my dog seeks a place of shelter and serenity away from the sounds of firecrackers and fireworks that fill this festive holiday. Without human understanding, he instinctively knows that there is something disturbing about these loud noises and withdraws from the experience.

Our lives, too, are filled with noise. Our serenity is always at risk. But we can turn to Mary and Jesus for comfort and consolation. Mary lived a life of serenity in spite of the turmoil and trials she endured. Her human heart was pierced by swords of betrayal and yet her interior soul remained serenely calm because she placed her entire life in the hands of her Son, Jesus Christ. Mary's life inspires us to place Jesus at the center of our lives, knowing that he is the same yesterday, today, and forever.
— Alice Smith

WHAT ARE THE THINGS that are likely to make you feel stress today? Choose three things that you can reach for to help you restore serenity to your soul.

Prayer: Mary, Mother Most Amiable, invite me to open my heart to you that I may embrace your Son, Jesus Christ, in my life.

July 5

"Be still, and know that I am God." — *Psalms 46:10*

Mary offers us an example on how to live in stillness with God. Through a quiet and humble life of prayer, Mary was able to contemplate the workings of the Lord in her life. In spite of the difficulties and hardships that Mary encountered, her faith never wavered and she was able to remain calm and serene before the Lord God Almighty. Mary's serenity came from her act of spiritual surrender to God. Freely and without hesitation, Mary gave herself over to the Lord not only when asked to be the mother of Jesus but every day of her life.

As our heavenly mother, Mary invites us to follow her example. When we are stressed, fearful, or anxious, let us turn to our Blessed Mother for the reassurance we need to be still. Let us seek Mary's help to surrender these difficult events into the hands of the Lord, so that we may know that God is with us.

— Gina Sannasardo

HOW CAN THE KNOWLEDGE that God is with you bring serenity to your family life? Work life? Spiritual life? Ask Mary to help you be still today so that you can see God at work in your life.

Prayer: Blessed Mother, strengthen us so that we can experience God's presence all around us.

July 6

"Trust in the LORD with all your heart, / and do not rely on your own insight. / In all your ways acknowledge him, / and he will make straight your paths." — Proverbs 3:5-6

When I was without work for nearly a year, doubt and fear crept into my days. "How are we going to make ends meet?" is a question my husband and I revisited often. Nightly, I prayed for answers. In the morning, I would wake up to find that the anxiety and dread had returned. Truly, in the darkness of those days, I desperately wanted to do nothing more than to get off the emotional roller coaster. And, I wanted to know where God was in all that was happening.

Mary's life was unsettled, too, but she believed that the Lord was with her. Mary is with us, inviting us to trust in the Lord like she did. We can turn to Mary for help to experience the serenity that comes from trusting in the Lord.

— Deb Kelsey-Davis

How MIGHT Mary's example help you today? What can you do to "remember the Lord"?

Prayer: Mary, help me to let go of the doubts that cause me such great anxiety so that, like you, I can find serenity by trusting that Jesus will show me the way.

July 7

"In returning and rest you shall be saved." — Isaiah 30:15

Friends can have positive or negative influences over our behaviors and choices throughout our lifetime. My father used to say, "Tell me who your friends are, and I'll tell you who you are." For years, I watched my mother gently tuck her rosary into her pocket every morning. She then cheerfully went about her daily housekeeping chores for our family of five. Mary was with my mother; they were best friends.

Praying daily to Mary for decades deepened the loving relationship between the Mother of God and my mother. Like Mary, my mother was sweet and gentle of heart, a loving wife and mother, a good cook, a hospitable hostess, serene, and she had the "patience of a saint." There is no doubt that Mary's beautiful and serene presence transformed my mother's life. Mom passed away at fifty-seven from breast cancer; her rosary was found in her hand the day she died. I'm sure she is thrilled to be spending eternity with her best friend, Mary.

— Sharon A. Abel, PhD

WHAT CAN YOU DO today to cultivate a friendship with Mary?

Prayer: Mother, most serene, may we choose you as our best friend and role model this day. Help us to become more like you.

July 8

"Jesus then said to the Jews who had believed in him, 'If you continue in my word, you are truly my disciples, and you will know the truth, and the truth will set you free.'" — John 8:31-32

In a world of many competing voices and agendas, it is difficult to know which ones are telling the truth. What could give us more serenity than being set free from the falsehoods that permeate our lives in today's world? Knowing what is true enables us to dismiss what is false.

When the angel Gabriel came to her and asked her to be the mother of Jesus, Mary was not shy. She questioned how this could occur and told him the truth: she was a virgin. Through Mary, truth came into the world in the person of her Son, Jesus. Mary can also bring the truth of Jesus Christ to us. He is the truth that will set us free from the falsehoods that tempt us to stray from God.

— Dr. Mary Amore

How OFTEN do you find yourself listening to voices other than Jesus'? Seek Mary's help today in hearing and following the truth as Jesus proclaimed it.

Prayer: Mary, you are the first of all disciples. Help me to follow your Son, Jesus, so that I may be set free by the truth.

July 9

"But as for you, continue in what you have learned and have firmly believed, knowing from whom you learned it and how from childhood you have been acquainted with the Sacred Writings which are able to instruct you for salvation through faith in Christ Jesus." — *2 Timothy 3:14-15*

My maternal grandfather died of a sudden heart attack when I was a senior in high school. The following summer, before I went away to college, Grandma and I spent a lot of time together on her back-porch swing. The squeaking sound of the swinging bench still reminds me of the serenity of those summer nights. She shared her deep faith with me. We sat talking about how it must have been for Our Lady to carry Jesus in her womb for nine months. My grandmother prayed that someday I, too, would be a mom and have serenity of the Blessed Mother.

Serenity is a great gift from God. My grandmother discovered this gift in her relationship with Mary, and she passed it on to me. I hope someday to pass on the serenity that comes from loving our Blessed Mother to my children, family, and friends.

— Katie Choudhary

TURN TO MARY today and seek her serenity for your life.

Prayer: Queen of Peace, rock me gently in your arms so I may find peaceful rest in your Son, Jesus.

July 10

"Let not your hearts be troubled, neither let them be afraid."
— *John 14:27*

Mary is often referred to as the Queen of Peace. Although Mary knew difficulty and experienced tremendous tragedy, she never lost serenity because she loved and trusted in the Lord.

It is very easy for us to have peace when everything is going our way. But the peace that Jesus brings to us is different from what the world can bring. His is a serenity that surpasses all our understanding. It enables us to find peace in our souls even when life is burdensome.

Mary chose to live in God's security each day. As our heavenly mother, Mary invites us to follow her example and to trust in the Lord on a daily basis. If we give our concerns and all our needs to Jesus the way Mary did, he will help us find the pathway to serenity. Mary is there to help us walk that path.

— Deborah O'Donnell

WHAT CAN YOU DO to find serenity in your daily life? How might you share that gift with others?

Prayer: Mary, let peace come into my mind, body, and soul. Let me walk in your footsteps of peace and serenity.

July 11

"Cast your burden on the LORD, / and he will sustain you; / he will never permit / the righteous to be moved." — *Psalms 55:22*

The psalmist assures us that when we totally surrender to the Father's will, everything will work according to God's will. Mary believed this with all her heart and invites us to live in this sacred place of knowing that God is all we need. The Lord will never leave us alone, nor will he ever forget us. Jesus gave Mary to us as a heavenly mother because he knows we need to be nurtured, protected, and cared for.

On earth, Mary trusted in the Lord's plan for her and cast her fears aside, calmly awaiting guidance for her life without fear or anxiety. In heaven, with perfection and grace, Mary is seeking to help us obtain the favors we ask of the Lord.

— Gina Sannasardo

How CAN YOU quietly wait for God's call and message to live your life? Ask Mary to sit patiently with you so that no fear may arise.

Prayer: Blessed Mother, I humbly ask that you provide me the strength to let go and let God. Help me to find rest and serenity in Christ so that I, too, may not fall.

July 12

"Peace I leave you; my peace I give to you; not as the world gives do I give to you. Let not your hearts be troubled, neither let them be afraid."
— *John 14:27*

The phrase "Do not be afraid" is found more often in the pages of the Bible than any other, and for good reason. Mary first heard these words when the angel Gabriel came to ask if she would be the mother of Jesus. Surely, as young Mary heard these words, a feeling of peace and serenity washed over her being.

The Lord does not intend for us to be anxious or fearful, and his presence brings serenity to our souls. God gives us the serenity to live our lives. When Mary said yes to God's will, God gave her the serenity to accept whatever would happen in her life. Mary's life shows us how to accept things in life we cannot change. She teaches us how we can live in serenity with God's will.

— Lauren Nelson

WHAT TROUBLES YOUR HEART? What situations do you find difficult to accept? Ask God for his gift of serenity.

Prayer: Mary, help me to follow your example of serenity and love. Be with me as I let go of things that make me afraid and anxious.

July 13

"Trust in the LORD with all your heart, / and do not rely on your own insight. / In all your ways acknowledge him, / and he will make straight your paths." — Proverbs 3:5-6

Mary lived this wisdom. She did not rely on her own understanding. Instead, she trusted in the Lord in all things. Mary embraced God's will for her life with serene understanding. She didn't have to know all the details. It was enough for Mary to know in her heart that she would bring glory to God. This knowledge did not give her control; it gave her serenity.

How can you trust God more today? How can you feel serenity in knowing God will make all things possible, even those you don't understand?

— Gina Sannasardo

INVITE MARY into your heart and ask her to help you accept the serenity that comes with saying "yes" to God. Look to her with confidence, knowing your mother Mary will guide you all the way!

Prayer: Blessed Mother, I honor you for how you trusted in God so completely. Teach me how to grow in willingness and joy as I serve God and follow his plan for me.

July 14

"But as servants of God we commend ourselves in every way:
through great endurance, in afflictions, hardships, calamities."
— *2 Corinthians 6:4*

Families are not perfect! No doubt about it. Some of our greatest frustrations and toughest trials are due to the choices, limitations, or events that happen in the context of family life. When a situation becomes unsettling, how can we trust in God and patiently work through it?

Our church has a beautiful statue of the Holy Family, situated in a lit alcove. I am struck by the bond that is represented in Mary's cradling of Jesus in her arms, and Joseph's protective embrace of them both. They, too, as a family, endured trials and hardships, yet their love for God and one another helped them find and keep serenity.

— Deb Kelsey-Davis

PRAYERFULLY REFLECT upon the life of the Holy Family and the way they modeled serenity. Turn to Mary today and seek her assistance in restoring peace and harmony to your life.

Prayer: Mary, pray for us, that we may be able to walk in your footsteps and find peace and tranquility in the midst of the trials we face in family life.

July 15

"To him who conquers I will grant to eat of the tree of life, which is in the paradise of God." — Revelation 2:7

There's a beautiful Japanese garden at the Chicago Botanic Garden named *Sansho-En*, lush with bonsai trees, evergreens, flowers, and limestone pathways. Basins of water are placed throughout the garden in special locations to allow visitors to purify themselves, both physically (by washing their hands and drinking water) and spiritually (by symbolically washing away one's cares). *Sansho-En's* design was intended to present natural serenity.

For me, Mary's life exemplifies a natural serenity — a serenity that is real, tangible, and human. Our Blessed Mother's tranquility stems from her close relationship with God. As our spiritual mother, Mary hopes that all of her children will draw near to the Lord so that we, too, may experience serenity as our natural state. We were created to be at peace with God and one another; this is not something extraordinary and elusive, but is within reach.

— Joseph Abel, PhD

FIND A DESIGNATED walking path in a nearby park, garden, or hiking trail. Spend time walking on the path or trail. Invite God to walk with you. Allow beauty and natural serenity to fill your heart.

Prayer: Mary, help me to discover the serenity that comes from being one with God. Take my hand and lead me to the path where God awaits me.

July 16
Feast of Our Lady of Mount Carmel

"But when the time had fully come, God sent forth his Son, born of woman, born under the law, to redeem those who were under the law, so that we might receive adoption as sons." — Galatians 4:4-5

Our Lady of Mount Carmel is the title given to the Blessed Virgin Mary as patroness of the Carmelite order. Popular devotion to Our Lady of Mount Carmel has centered on wearing the brown scapular, which tradition says Mary gave to St. Simon Stock in the thirteenth century. The brown scapular signifies humility, chastity, and a spirit of prayer.

The three elements associated with the brown scapular reflect Mary's life. Chosen by God, Mary, virgin most chaste, gave birth to Jesus at the appointed time. As the mother of Jesus, Mary did not boast but remained the humble handmaid of the Lord, spending her days in a spirit of prayerful serenity. Our Lady of Mount Carmel invites us to practice the virtues of humility, chastity, and prayer in our own lives.

— Dr. Mary Amore

CONSIDER THE WAYS that practicing the virtues of humility, chastity, and prayer might bring you more serenity.

Prayer: Blessed Mary, Our Lady of Mount Carmel, help me to turn away from the temptations of this world and live a life worthy of my inheritance as a beloved son or daughter of God.

July 17

"But I have calmed and quieted my soul, / like a child quieted at its mother's breast; / like a child that is quieted is my soul." — Psalms 131:2

We have a family photo of our teenage son napping in a recliner with his arms wrapped around our infant granddaughter asleep on his chest. One of the simple treasures in life is to feel the dead weight of a baby that has fallen asleep in your arms.

Both the psalm above and the photo mentioned effectively capture the essence of a loving relationship. The one who holds a sleeping baby provides the comfort, love, warmth, protection, and strength the infant requires to rest. The baby is totally at ease, fully surrendered and vulnerable, yet trusting — no fear, only the innocence of feeling absolutely safe and loved.

The familiar images of Mary holding Jesus remind us that she provided a serene, nurturing, and loving environment for him. Mary, as mothers do, taught her baby what love is. As our mother, Mary wants to do the same for us. Can we trust her enough to make ourselves vulnerable and fully surrender to her loving care?

— Bob Frazee

TAKE A MOMENT today to place yourself in the loving embrace of our mother Mary. Rest in her serene presence.

Prayer: Holy Mary, Mother of God, hold me in your arms and pray for me.

July 18

May the LORD give strength to his people! / May the LORD bless his people with peace!" — *Psalms 29:11*

At an early age, my mother taught my brothers and me her favorite prayers. The one that resonated most was about serenity. My mother often reminded us that many things in life are not in our control and that the key is to be calm and trust in Our Lord — just as Mary did.

Because so much is immediately available at our fingertips today, we are trained to be instantly gratified. That doesn't help us to relax and put our needs prayerfully in the Lord's hands. Prayer is not a means for instant satisfaction. Instead, we need to stop, slow down, and learn to live each moment with thoughtful attention.

Mary's life of faith offers us a model for remaining calm in the midst of daily pressures. Difficult as it may be to change our pace, we can choose to surrender to God's plan for us and trust that our paths are being guided in the right direction.

— Mary L. Kostic

CALL TO MIND one particular situation that is causing you anxiety or a desire for instant resolution. Seek Mary's help in giving this over to the Lord.

Prayer: Mary, thank you for giving us the example of remaining calm amidst turmoil in our lives.

July 19

"Finally, all of you, have unity of spirit, sympathy, love of the brethren, a tender heart and a humble mind." — 1 Peter 3:8

When I have an argument with someone, I almost always feel an immediate coldness and distance between myself and the other person. I often regret my words, which can sometimes be insensitive and harsh. We all sin; we do things that we regret. And it's our sins that separate us not only from others, but also from God. Sin destroys the inner peace and serenity we have when we are of one mind and heart with God.

Mary, with her sinless immaculate heart, can help restore serenity to our lives. From the moment of Jesus' birth, Mary took on the responsibility of bringing all of us closer to her Son. As our spiritual mother, Mary directs us to be loving and compassionate toward one another, and she can help us heal our relationships with others by drawing us nearer to Jesus.

— Deb Kelsey-Davis

CALL TO MIND a relationship, personal or at work or school, that is tenuous. In an effort to bring serenity back into your life, seek the Blessed Mother's help in reconciling with this person.

Prayer: Heavenly Mother, show me how to open my heart more fully to your Son, that I may find and keep serenity in all my relationships.

July 20

"And the peace of God, which passes all understanding, will keep your hearts and your minds in Christ Jesus" — Philippians 4:7

Serenity means peace within. Even the word itself has a peaceful tone. If we are living in serenity, we are obtaining and maintaining inner peace on a daily basis. As disciples of Christ, this is what we are called to do every day of our lives.

Mary experienced interior peace in the depths of her soul, and this serenity flowed from her trust in God. Mary freely accepted the Lord's will for her, even though she had no idea what tomorrow would bring. Wouldn't it be wonderful to live in that peaceful state and be able to truly trust in the Lord? We can seek our heavenly mother's assistance in helping us to deepen our trust in God so that we, too, experience the peace which transcends all understanding.

— Deborah O'Donnell

WHAT CAN YOU DO today to find serenity and peace? How will you keep it? How will you spread that peace to those you encounter throughout the day?

Prayer: Mary, allow serenity and peace to come into my heart so that I may live in peace and show others how to do the same.

July 21

"The LORD said to him, 'Peace be to you; do not fear.'" — *Judges 6:23*

We tend to think that the ancient world in which Mary lived was stress-free and less hectic then our current world. But Nazareth would have been a crowded and busy town. Tradesmen and officials would be up early tending their businesses. The market and square would be bustling with social announcements, gatherings, merchants, and animals. Women would travel back and forth to the town well for water as needed. Their days were spent preparing meals, baking bread, and cleaning their homes. They also mended garments, washed clothes, filled oil lamps, and, of course, watched the children. There wasn't much time for recreation or leisure.

Life's struggles of that time certainly fed fears and accentuated anxieties; Mary was not spared from them. Still, her faith in God kept her calm and drove her fears away. Mary seeks to help us de-stress our lives and restore serenity within us. We can turn to the Blessed Mother for help when we are fearful, and for hope when we despair.

— Sharon A. Abel, PhD

FEELING ANY STRESS TODAY? Ask Mary to walk with you as you seek to restore balance and serenity.

Prayer: Mary, grace me with your calm and serene temperament during stressful times. Help me to remember that the Lord never abandons me, that he is always near.

July 22

"Trust in the LORD with all your heart, / and do not rely on your own insight. / In all your ways acknowledge him, / and he will make straight your paths." — *Proverbs 3:5-6*

We all encounter difficult people and circumstances. Sometimes we are able to respond calmly, remain content, and be present. Other times we react violently, grow angry, and become distracted. Overwhelmed, we can feel pulled in many directions, even torn apart.

Jesus would tell us, "Don't be afraid"; and Mary would help us recognize that we make ourselves upset over circumstances outside ourselves, worried over things we cannot control, frustrated by situations we cannot change. Mary would encourage us to let go of the belief that we can fix everything or make things better by rehashing them. Mary would remind us that trusting just in our own efforts is ineffective. She would encourage us to stay on the path — that is, keep goodness in our minds, hold love in our hearts, and act and speak with integrity. Mary would instruct us that we are not called to be perfect, but whole.

— Jane Zimmerman

THE WHOLE PERSON acknowledges both light and dark and trusts God's grace to transform all things in Christ. Focus on that.

Prayer: Mary, please nudge me when I am being pulled away from God's grace — and remind me to stay on the path and trust in God.

July 23

"The sum of your word is truth; / and every one of your righteous ordinances endures for ever." — *Psalms 119:160*

The impression the Virgin Mary creates is one of peace and serenity. My favorite image of Mary is Our Lady of Grace, in which she wears a white tunic and a blue mantle. Serene in appearance, Mary encourages us to look within, to focus our attention on her Son, Jesus.

Mary knows how easy it is for me to fill my life with things that really don't matter. Her presence here to guide me to the truth and to help me deepen my relationship with Jesus often leads me to spend less time on the material aspects of my life and more time on the deeper spiritual components of my life.

— Alice Smith

TAKE A TEN-MINUTE BREAK with Mary and Jesus to look deeper within yourself. Claim the pure heart and serenity that belongs to every Christian. Let the Blessed Mother guide you in prayer and the ability to slow down.

Prayer: Mary, Lady of Grace and Vessel of Honor, lift my heart with your powerful intercession. Lead me to follow the ways that are pleasing to God. Spread your mantle over me so I can live serenely on earth.

July 24

"Blessed are you among women." — Luke 1:42

The dictionary defines serenity as the state of being calm, peaceful, and untroubled. When I think of Mary, the thought of serenity comes to mind. Scripture tells us that there were many circumstances in Mary's life that involved every human emotion, ranging from sadness and grief to joy and happiness. But beyond those feelings, Mary possessed a deeper serenity and peacefulness.

The famous Serenity Prayer begins, "God, grant me the serenity to accept the things I cannot change." That is no small order. But serenity comes from being able to let go. We often hear the phrase "let go and let God." Those are just words until we put them into practice. When we can truly open our hearts and minds and allow God to do whatever brings us closest to him, we can experience serenity.

Mary is blessed among women because this is precisely what she did. We can ask her to help us to let go and let God bring us blessing, too.

— Suzette Horyza

WHAT ONE THING can I let go of today and instead trust God to bring me serenity?

Prayer: Mary, help me to trust in the workings of the Lord, that I may have true serenity in my life.

July 25

"Do not return evil for evil or reviling for reviling;
but on the contrary bless, for to this you have been called,
that you may obtain a blessing." — *1 Peter 3:9*

Mary is a model of serenity and calm. Despite the difficulties and challenges she encountered in her life, Mary's loving presence brought tranquility to the people around her, including Jesus and his disciples.

Throughout the centuries, Mary's apparitions have brought a peaceful presence to our wounded and broken world. At places such as Guadalupe, Lourdes, and Fátima, Mary called the people of those places and times to turn away from evil and to do good. She calls us to do the same. Mary's message to the world is always simple and pure: come home to Jesus. Mary desires that all of her children pursue avenues to peace and tranquility, pathways to rediscovering our relationship with Jesus.

— Lauren Nelson

How can you bring Mary's peaceful presence into your home? Consider the ways you can repay insults with blessings.

Prayer: Mary, embrace me and give me your peace. Be with me through my stress and surround me with your calm and motherly presence.

July 26

*"He has showed you, O man, what is good; / and what does the
LORD require of you / but to do justice, and to love kindness, /
and to walk humbly with your God?"* — *Micah 6:8*

Not knowing all the details, or wanting to know the why and how of things, steals my serenity more than I care to admit. I have struggled at times with wanting to know God's plan for me and then trying to figure out how to carry it out. It's exhausting.

Mary's spirit is serenely calm. Her life inspires me to let go of details that can destroy my inner peace and to refocus my attention to trusting in the Lord. Mary did not know God's whole plan for her, but she trusted him. Her faith-filled heart allowed her to step back without worry and to let him handle every situation. Mary's life reminds us that if we desire serenity, all that is required of us is to trust in the Lord, to do what he commands, and to walk humbly with God.

— Deb Kelsey-Davis

HAVE YOU HAD MOMENTS of doubt or anxiety about turning your problems over to the Lord? How might Mary's example illuminate a path of peace and serenity in letting go?

Prayer: Mary, fill my heart with the same faith you have in order that I might step aside and let Jesus guide me in all matters.

July 27

"For he will hide me in his shelter / in the day of trouble." — *Psalms 27:5*

In Nazareth, a roof was of real importance in everyday life. Mary's home likely had a flat roof with just enough slope to drain off the rainwater. Rainwater was carefully collected into cisterns or large containers, for in the arid climate of Galilee every drop of water was precious.

Roofs were flat, sturdy, and used as an open second floor. On the roof, Joseph's tools were stored, Mary hung the laundry out to dry. On cool evenings, she, Joseph, and Jesus sat on the roof and talked. In better weather, Mary and her family would often sleep there. It was also a place to pray.

The Hebrew people referred to their dwellings as "shelters" because they always considered themselves "travelers on the earth." For Mary, a little house was a sufficient shelter for her family during their earthly pilgrimage. Mary knew serenity was dwelling within God's shelter. The very structure of Mary's house, with its emphasis on living in the open air, highlighted the proclamation of the psalms: God was her shelter and refuge in times of trouble.

— Joseph Abel, PhD

LOOK AT THE ROOF you live under. Ask God to shelter you from evil today.

Prayer: Mary, help us in our pilgrim journey to find and take shelter and refuge in God's saving presence.

July 28

"Cast all your anxieties on him, for he cares about you."
— *1 Peter 5:7*

When I was a little girl, I was terrified of thunderstorms. Whenever a storm came up, I hid under my bed. My mother would gently coax me to come out, assuring me that the thunder was only the angels bowling. Then she would light a candle and tell me that Jesus was with us. Her gentle motherly care made me feel peaceful and not afraid. As I look back on those moments of endearment, I realize that my mother was teaching me to trust in the Lord, to find peace and serenity.

Like my mother, Mary is here to help us find serenity in the midst of our daily trials by placing our trust in her Son, Jesus. She seeks to wrap her arms around us when we are afraid and reassure us that we are never alone. Mary invites us to cast all of our worries upon Jesus because he loves and cares for us.

— Dr. Mary Amore

REFLECT ON A SITUATION that makes you worried or afraid and prayerfully give this to the Lord today. Ask that you may have peace and serenity restored.

Prayer: Mary, you are my refuge. Lead me to your Son, Jesus, where I may find peace and serenity all the days of my life.

July 29

"The Lord is my shepherd, I shall not want; / he makes me lie down in green pastures. / He leads me beside still waters." — Psalms 23:1-2

Have you ever heard the sound of bubbling water coming from a baptismal font? The gentle sound of the font at my parish is what "still waters" sounds like to me. Life. Serenity. In the stillness before daily Mass, the sound of the bubbling water fills the air. As I sit in prayer, with each breath I take in through the sound of these "still waters," my soul reclaims the serenity I own through baptism.

As our spiritual mother, Mary is here to lead us by the hand and bring us to Jesus. He leads me to "still waters." Mary is such a perfect guide for us. As only a mother can, she walks beside us on our path, leading us closer to Christ.

— Katie Choudhary

SIT IN MARY's holy and prayerful presence and allow the still waters that run deep within you to quiet the noise inside and draw you into a place of serenity and grace.

Prayer: Queen of Peace, thank you for being here beside me. Your presence means so much to me and fills me with serenity.

July 30

"With all lowliness and meekness, with patience, forbearing one another in love, eager to maintain the unity of the Spirit in the bond of peace."
— *Ephesians 4:2-3*

In this wounded and turbulent world, we are surrounded by people whose behavior is offensive, distasteful, and sometimes downright vicious. These disturbing behaviors even occur in those closest to us. When I experience negative actions, choices, or offensive language, my serenity seems all but lost. Then I think of Mary.

Mary lived in a time and place in which violence and oppression ruled. Those who wished to do harm were almost always present. She even became a refugee to protect the life of her Son, Jesus. Yet, her heart remained patient, gentle, and full of love. Mary shows us that it is possible to find serenity, even in a world of injustices, when we place our faith and trust in God.

— Deb Kelsey-Davis

CONSIDER THOSE TIMES when, at the hands of others, you lost the precious gifts of patience and serenity. Turn to Our Lady in prayer.

Prayer: Mary, calm my heart and restore peace in my soul with the same gentle strength and faith you have in God.

July 31

"Blessed are the poor in spirit, for theirs is the kingdom of heaven."
— Matthew 5:3

Mary was greeted with startling words from the angel, which amazed and surprised her. Did she understand the fullness of the message that was delivered to her? Surely, Mary had some fear in her heart when the stranger explained that she was a favored daughter and blessed among women. This message of Mary being blessed echoed when she visited Elizabeth.

Mary chose to serenely embrace the graces that were present to her. In the difficulties and joys of raising Jesus, Mary never wavered in her receptivity to God's grace and serenity. Her conscious decision to remain at peace enabled Mary to embrace God's kingdom.

— Larry Dreffein

REFLECT ON YOUR BLESSINGS today and how some of the challenges in your life may be yet another revelation of God's kingdom in your world. Allow for the possibility that blessings will continue to be revealed.

Prayer: Mary, may I serenely embrace with a pure heart my situations in life. May I come to realize that a pure heart sees God's goodness and that the Kingdom created by the Almighty is made available to me in my life now.

~ ABUNDANCE ~

August 1

"For in a severe test of affliction, their abundance of joy and their extreme poverty have overflowed in a wealth of liberality on their part."
— *2 Corinthians 8:2*

St. Paul's words powerfully describe the individuals I've worked with who are homeless and in recovery from addiction. Having been stripped of their job, family, and home, they are experiencing extreme poverty. And yet because of their faith and dependence on God, they often possess an abundance of joy. It's not uncommon to hear them talk about how blessed they are. I've been quite moved by their positivity and profound trust in the grace of God.

This reminds me of the incredible trust of Mary, as she experienced uncertainty in her life. In her Magnificat, in Luke 1, Mary praises God abundantly. Her great trust opened her heart to great joy. Even though she herself would experience poverty and homelessness when delivering her child, Jesus, Mary's generosity with God never waned.

— Gail Krema

THINK OF THE MANY BLESSINGS in your life. What can you do today to allow your abundant joy to overflow generously to others?

Prayer: Mary, full of grace, continue to inspire us to trust and praise God for all that he has given us.

August 2

"The thief comes only to steal and kill and destroy; I came that they may have life, and have it abundantly." — John 10:10

Jesus warns us about the thieves that surround us. Fame, pleasure, material possessions, and self-fulfillment are the allurements of our passing world, and they have the potential to kill and destroy our souls and steal our love for God.

As the mother of Jesus, Mary understands our earthly temptations to seek happiness though the avenues of greed, wealth, and power. But our heavenly mother is ready to take us by the hand and keep us on the right road. She is here to show us the true and everlasting abundance of grace that comes from building a relationship with Jesus. The next time you are tempted to find fulfillment in things that do not last, invite Mary into your decision making and ask her to bring you to Jesus.

— Gina Sannasardo

TODAY, CONSIDER HOW YOU LOOK for abundance in life. Is there anything or anyone that is stealing, killing, or destroying the abundance God wants to offer you?

Prayer: Mother Mary, we ask you to hold us in your heart, to be our safeguard so that we are protected from the thief and given over fully to the Lord.

August 3

"And my God will supply every need of yours according to his riches in glory in Christ Jesus." — Philippians 4:19

In the summer months, I enjoy driving down country roads and seeing rows of beautiful green cornstalks. They are a visual reminder of the abundance of God's presence in this world.

I like to imagine that Mary, as she looked out from her home, saw beautiful spring flowers dotting the desert fields and setting them on fire with color. Surely her beautiful spirit was moved by God's creative handiwork, and no doubt she was filled with gratitude and praise.

How often do we stop and take time out of our frantic days to take in all that's around us? The glory of creation in all its variety is a daily invitation to stop, look, listen, touch, and smell — and say thank you. It is God saying "I love you" and "I want you to see and know beauty and abundance."

— Linda Brinkman

STEP OUTSIDE and take a moment to really experience the abundance that surrounds you.

Prayer: Mary, please help us to grasp the abundance in our world. Help us to stop and focus on what is right in front of us. Let us be mindful as we look, listen, and behold, and help us to be grateful.

August 4

"Thanks be to God for his inexpressible gift!" — *2 Corinthians 9:15*

I was in junior high school when my grandma passed away. I have very fond memories of her, even though she has been gone for decades. She always had candy reserved for her grandchildren for when we visited and made sure we always enjoyed a few scoops of ice cream at her house. She was generous with her time and attention, too. One Sunday afternoon, when I was about eight years old, just the two of us sat at the base of the staircase. That day, she taught me how to pray the Rosary.

Years after her passing, I learned what limited means my grandmother had. She had started cleaning houses to be able to afford Christmas presents for her grandchildren. I never knew that. She was always so generous; I could not imagine that she didn't have much. That's because her spiritual abundance shone through to all who knew her.

Mary's simple life shows us that abundance has nothing to do with large house, nice cars, expensive clothes, or plenty of belongings. We have nothing if material things comprise our abundance. Seek Christ. Seek Mary. And you will have everything!

— Meg Bucaro

How can I give my time and attention to someone today?

Prayer: Mary, help me to focus my time and energy on seeking spiritual abundance more than anything else.

August 5

"Fill the jars with water." — John 2:7

Abundance is a recurring theme in John's Gospel. There was an abundance of water where John was baptizing, and an abundance of perfume when Mary, the sister of Lazarus, anointed Jesus. After Jesus multiplied the loaves and fishes there was an abundance of leftovers. The disciples caught an abundance of fish when the risen Jesus met them in Galilee. Jesus himself said he came so we may have life in abundance.

Mary is not only present at the first scene of abundance, the wedding at Cana, but she plays a pivotal role. It was in response to Mary that Jesus changed more than one hundred gallons of water into an abundance of fine wine. The dialogue between Mary and Jesus is interesting. It delicately reveals something of their relationship as well as Mary's role in God's plan. In Jewish culture, one of the strongest family bonds was between mother and son. Sons advocated for their mothers, so, of course, Jesus did what he knew Mary wanted. The key is that what Mary wanted most was the will of God. That always results in abundance.

— Bob Frazee

ARE YOU WILLING to do the work of filling the empty jars of your life with water? What can you do today to prepare for the possibility of abundance?

Prayer: Mary, I pray for the wisdom to let you lead me to your Son.

August 6

*"You prepare a table before me / in the presence of my enemies; /
you anoint my head with oil, / my cup overflows."* — *Psalms 23:5*

As the mother of Jesus, Mary's cup surely overflowed with an abundance of blessings in her life, whether big or small, planned or unplanned. We can only surmise the abundance of joy that Mary experienced at seeing Jesus grow from the baby steps he took as an infant to his life as an adult. Abundant blessings of a different nature enfolded Mary's heart as she stood at the foot of the cross.

Scripture tells us that Mary pondered all of God's abundant blessings in her heart, filling her days with prayerful reflection. Do we ponder our own blessings in our hearts? Imagine a woman like Mary, who counted even her difficulties as an abundance of blessings. What can we be grateful for? Mary's cup overflowed with an everyday abundance, and we can choose to rejoice simply because our cups overflow as well.

— Lauren Nelson

WHAT HAS GOD poured into your cup? Is this enough, or do you think or feel as if you need more?

Prayer: Mary, your life is anything but ordinary, yet you find joy and abundance in the smallest of gifts from God. Help me to be like you and to find abundance wherever and however God chooses to bestow it upon me.

August 7

"Honor the LORD with your substance / and with the first fruits of all your produce; / then your barns will be filled with plenty, / and your vats will be bursting with wine." — *Proverbs 3:9-10*

As Christians, we are invited to give our lives totally to the Lord and trust completely in him. To the extent we do this, our lives will be overwhelmingly graced. We will live in spiritual abundance and see his love flowing into us in ways we could never imagine.

In a real way, Mary's fiat was a gift of her first fruits to the Lord. As the mother of Jesus, Mary witnessed firsthand the miracles of Jesus, and she knew his heart and his ministry was overflowing with life, love, forgiveness, and mercy. Mary now invites us to do the same and is here to help us discover abundance by drawing us closer to her Son, Jesus.

— Gina Sannasardo

WHAT FIRST FRUITS could you give to God today? Invite Mary to help you receive the grace to identify them.

Prayer: Mother Mary, please unite us today with the heart of your Son, Jesus, so that we might enjoy the spiritual riches promised us.

August 8

"May grace and peace be multiplied to you in the knowledge of God and of Jesus our Lord." — 2 Peter 1:2

Every one of us is offered an abundance of grace and peace as a pure gift from the God who loves us abundantly. Sadly, many of us are unaware of the spiritual treasures that faith in God can provide us each day.

Mary lived according to a deep faith in God. In turn, she was abundantly blessed and full of grace. If we really consider Mary's example, we begin to notice how often we look for abundance in all the wrong places. We cannot look to this world to bring us a deep sense of peace, nor can we expect things such as great wealth or amassing material possessions to make us happy. We will only discover abundant grace and peace when we enter into a relationship with the Lord. We can take heart and follow the example of our Blessed Mother and place our trust in God so that grace and peace may reign in us.

— Gail Krema

WHAT TYPE OF ABUNDANCE are you seeking? What is it that you truly need?

Prayer: Mary, mother of all, guide us to ever deepen our knowledge of and relationship with your Son, Jesus.

August 9

"There was not any one needy among them, for as many as were possessors of lands or houses sold them, and brought the proceeds of what was sold and laid it at the apostles' feet; and distribution was made to each as any had need."
— *Acts 4:34-35*

As a young mom with a baby son, I remember feeling so blessed that I wanted to share my abundant joy with those less fortunate than myself. At Christmastime, my friends and I got together and purchased presents for a needy family with many children. I will never forget how wonderful it felt to help someone else. Sharing my abundance made me feel even more blessed.

Surely Mary experienced similar blessings when the three visitors from the East showered her newborn Son, Jesus, with precious gifts. Mary's heart must have overflowed with gratitude, not only at the kindness of these strangers, but at the extravagance of their gifts. Everything we have comes from God. We should never take his generosity for granted, but should share it freely.

— Linda Brinkman

TAKE A MOMENT to reflect upon your abundant blessings. Seek Mary's help in seeing all of life as a gift from God to be shared.

Prayer: Mary, your life was filled with simple yet abundant blessings from God. Help me to use my bountiful blessings in service to others.

August 10

"I came that they may have life, and have it abundantly." — John 10:10

Life is hard, and so often we feel as though we don't have "enough." This sense of wanting or desiring more can be debilitating to our spiritual growth.

Mary lived a simple and humble life. Measured against our modern standards, she owned virtually nothing, yet she possessed more than we could imagine. Mary was rich in what matters most: her relationship with God. As a result, her life was abundant and full.

Our Blessed Mother's life challenges us to place our priorities on God, and not the passing things of this passing world. As the mother of Jesus, Mary invites us to push away the distraction of material goods and the desire to acquire more and more so that we can have an opportunity to love Jesus with our entire being. This is what will bring true abundance to our lives.

— Jill Bates, DMin

CONSIDER ONE THING you can do today to refocus your priorities so that you may have life and have it abundantly.

Prayer: Mother Mary, help me let go of things that interfere with my ability to live a simple yet abundantly rich life.

August 11

"For you formed my inward parts, / you knitted me together in my mother's womb. / I praise you, for I am wondrously made. / Wonderful are your works!" — *Psalms 139:13-14*

Indeed, every part of my being is a wonder: my physical body, my conscious mind, my ever-seeking spirit. The world and everything in it is a marvel: each plant, each animal, each drop of water. The overflowing grace of wisdom and love is amazing. "How hard for me to grasp your thoughts, God; there are so many!" As a Chinese proverb states so well, "To know you have enough is to be rich."

Living in abundance is living fully. It is living as Mary lived, with gratitude, awareness, and openness to life's challenges. It is seeing the beauty all around with gladness and appreciation. It is acknowledging and sharing the light within. It is giving and accepting kindness and compassion. It is being in right relationship with everything and everyone. It is recognizing that everything is God's gift and that without the fruits of the earth, the love of my neighbor, I would have nothing.

— Jane Zimmerman

TODAY, STOP SEEKING abundance so that you can simply recognize it.

Prayer: Mary, remind me to behold all the abundance that surrounds me and to be grateful for it.

August 12

"For to him who has will more be given, and he will have abundance;
but from him who has not, even what he has will be taken away."
— *Matthew 13:12*

Jesus teaches us that in sharing what we have with those in need we will get back more than we imagined. Those who hoard God's blessings will lose the abundance of his grace. Life with Jesus invites us to share our bountiful gifts, both material and personal, with those around us.

Mary's life offers us a beautiful example of how to love, to share, and to serve others. Our Blessed Mother dedicated her entire life in service to the Lord as his humble handmaid. She invites us to follow in her footsteps by being attentive to what God asks of us day by day and moment by moment.

— Gina Sannasardo

SAVOR THE KNOWLEDGE that all you have in life is a gift from God meant to be shared. Consider how you can give freely to others.

Prayer: Blessed Mother, I rejoice in your heavenly presence in my life. Thank you for giving your life to God so that divine abundance would reign for us all.

August 13

*"And God is able to provide you with every blessing in abundance,
so that you may always have enough of everything and may provide
in abundance for every good work." — 2 Corinthians 9:8*

Last year, my family suffered a devastating house fire. We were left with a fraction of what we had before the fire destroyed our house and almost everything in it. At the time of the fire, my husband and I were two weeks into a thirty-three-day preparation for a Marian consecration.

Despite our home being uninhabitable, having to relocate a family of five, replacing our belongings, working the insurance process, and selecting a contractor, we continued the consecration prayers. This journey to Jesus through Mary was our saving grace, given to us at a time when we most needed it. Through the overwhelming process of rebuilding our lives, our commitment to growing closer to Mary provided a constant reminder that we had everything we needed as long as we had Christ. Through Mary, we discovered that our relationship with Jesus was our most abundant blessing. He is enough!

— Meg Bucaro

WHAT COULDN'T you live without? Where does your relationship with God fit in?

Prayer: Blessed Mother, thank you for always walking with me; from the darkest of days through the happiest of days you never leave me. Guide me to always seek your Son, Jesus.

August 14

"I know how to be abased, and I know how to abound; in any and all circumstances I have learned the secret of facing plenty and hunger, abundance and want." — Philippians 4:12

In his *Spiritual Exercises,* St. Ignatius of Loyola encourages a healthy detachment and complete trust and dependence on the Lord. He stresses that no matter what we go through God is right there with us, giving us what we need. Ignatius learned this from the Blessed Mother, who was instrumental in his conversion. He saw that Mary enjoyed an abundance of grace because she had total trust and dependence upon the providence of God.

In reality, there is abundance of grace in recognizing that all will be well no matter what the outcome. If we can let go of our desired outcomes and trust in God's grace, the way Mary and St. Ignatius did, we will experience great freedom. God will provide all that we need, and we will not have to carry the burden of "it must go this way" any longer.

— Gail Krema

IS THERE A DESIRED outcome you can let go of today and trust in the Lord's presence instead?

Prayer: Mary, help me to let go and trust.

August 15
Solemnity of the Assumption of Mary

"God's temple in heaven was opened, and the ark of his covenant was seen within his temple." — Revelation 11:19

The Scripture readings for today speak of the Ark of the Covenant. In the Old Testament, the Ark of the Covenant was revered as the home of God's presence on earth. In parallel, we believe that Mary's immaculate womb was the sacred ark of God's new covenant in Jesus Christ.

On this day, we celebrate our Catholic belief that the Lord God blessed Mary with the fullness of his Son's resurrection, keeping her body from corruption, and bringing her — both body and soul — into heaven.

While our souls will meet God when we die, our earthly bodies will decay, until the Lord raises us up on the last day. This feast day of Mary is a beautiful reminder of God's promise to all of us: we will be reunited with our earthly bodies for eternity in a new heaven and a new earth.

— Dr. Mary Amore

SPEND SOME TIME today in prayerful reflection about this great mystery of our faith and the ways that Mary's life shows us the way to heaven.

Prayer: Mary, watch over me from heaven and help me to follow Jesus all the days of my life.

August 16

"The harvest is plentiful, but the laborers are few." — Matthew 9:37

An abundance of my wife's time and effort had been put into building a little garden. She had lined it carefully with rounded brickwork and filled the enclosure with small rounded stones and plants. Then the finishing touch was added: a statue of Mary carrying an armful of grain sheaves. Placed among the small plants and flowers, it appeared that Mary was coming in from the fields.

It is quite likely that Mary, and her young Son, had hands-on agriculture experience. Most families had a small vegetable garden. But when the fields were ready for harvest, anyone who could help did so. The grain was gathered, bound together as sheaves, and placed vertically in a stack with the heads aligned on top, allowing the grain to dry. It was backbreaking work, but also a time of joy in abundance. Jesus often used the examples of farming and harvesting to explain the abundance of the kingdom of God.

— Joseph Abel, PhD

QUIETLY CONSIDER the abundance you possess. Identify items that could be shared with others. Thank God for his abundant blessing to you by donating these items to those in need.

Prayer: Mary, I am part of God's harvest. As you once helped gather grain in harvests at Nazareth, gather me into God's kingdom.

August 17

"I myself am satisfied about you, my brethren, that you yourselves are full of goodness, filled with all knowledge, and able to instruct one another."
— *Romans 15:14*

My mother had a difficult life. After my dad left us, she rose to the challenge with abundant grace and worked two jobs in order to provide for her children. Mary reminds me of my mother, for Mary also knew the struggles that come with raising a child. Mary worked to provide a good home for Jesus. She ground wheat for bread, fetched water each day from the well, and cooked and cleaned for her family. As the mother of the house, Mary instructed Jesus in the Jewish faith and in the core values of life.

Mary's life inspires us to live abundantly. No matter what struggles we have or what our daily responsibilities may entail, we can turn to Mary to show us how to live each day to the fullest.

— Linda Brinkman

TAKE A PRAYERFUL MOMENT to remember your parents. Whether they are living or deceased, or represent a positive or negative presence in your life, thank the Lord for whatever good they brought you.

Prayer: Mary, teach us to honor the core values of our faith and to gently instruct our family members in the love and knowledge of Jesus.

August 18

*"Now to him who by the power at work within us is able to do
far more abundantly than all that we ask or think."*
— Ephesians 3:20

Mary knew that Jesus' miracles of abundance — from changing
the water to wine at Cana to multiplying the loaves and fishes to feed
thousands — would draw people to him. Mary also knows how much
her Son loves us. She lived everyday basking in God's goodness and the
wealth of his joy and peace. She invites us to turn to her and trust that
she will take all our needs and desires to Jesus. Mary knows that God
will never cease to provide for us. He is both able and willing to make
our lives far more abundant than we ask for, or could even imagine.

— Gina Sannasardo

How can you look doubt in the eye and confidently know God is at
work in your life right now? Invite Mary to be with you and feel assured of God's hand in your life.

*Prayer: Blessed Mother, help me never to doubt what the Lord has set out for me
to do. Remind me of how unlimited his abundant power is within us.*

August 19

"And why is this granted me, that the mother of my Lord should come to me?" — *Luke 1:43*

How often in our busy lives do we forget to share good news with our friends and families? So much bad news comes to us every day; we need to balance it with telling and sharing the good, especially with those we love. That is what friends are for — sharing, telling, and celebrating, not just for commiserating, supporting, and helping.

Good news only grows bright when it is shared. Generosity in sharing with others brings joy to all who hear it. Consider the events surrounding Mary and Elizabeth's meeting. How far did Mary have to travel? What were the obstacles on her journey, and, most importantly, why did she go? Mary had a message — good news to share — for her dear cousin Elizabeth and Elizabeth's husband, Zechariah. Even before Jesus was born, his mother began the family practice of sharing good news with others.

— Jill Bates, DMin

LET'S FOCUS ON abundant blessings and joy. Consider how you can celebrate and share good news with your friends today as Mary and Elizabeth did so long ago.

Prayer: Mary, I celebrate your relationship with your cousin Elizabeth and am grateful for your misison of abundant love.

August 20

"Then he said to the disciple, 'Behold, your mother!'" — John 19:27

My son recently told me that I was his second-favorite mom. Taken back, I could not wait to hear who No. 1 was. I have a close friend whom my child simply loves; I assumed it must be her. However, he surprised me when he mentioned, "Mary is my first favorite mommy!"

Why did it take a child to remind me that we are so blessed to have Mary as our No. 1 mother! She is our mother whether we ask her for prayers or not, whether we feel we know her or are just curious about who she is; Mary is mother to us all. Mary's greatest desire is for us to love her Son. At times, I wonder if I take this for granted.

We have an abundant blessing with Mary as our heavenly mother. If we seek a close relationship with Mary as a pathway to strengthening our relationship with Christ, we will experience abundance in our spiritual lives.

— Meg Bucaro

ASK MARY to be your No. 1 mother today. Thank her for her presence and prayers.

Prayer: Blessed Mother, thank you for always being present for me. Help me to learn that your presence is all I need to spur an abundant relationship with Christ.

August 21

"I came that they may have life, and have it abundantly."
— John 10:10

When I consider the Blessed Mother's life, abundance comes to mind. Mary's faith in God, her "yes" to his purpose for her life, was what brought her fullness and made her life complete. It is amazing to realize that Mary's love for Jesus helped to shape his earthly life among us, his ministry to each one of us.

In my own life, I am certain that my faith is what has brought an abundance to me. Like Mary, I have had my share of difficulties, yet my faith has brought me through even the most difficult times. With the eyes of faith I can see the beauty of nature in the created world around me. And in faith I am able to perceive the presence of God in loved ones and strangers alike. I am grateful to our Blessed Mother for showing me how to live life abundantly.

— Gail Krema

RECALL A TIME in your life when your faith helped you get through something difficult. Then reflect on the joy you've experienced in your faith. Has God given you a more abundant life?

Prayer: Mother Mary, thank you for your role in bringing abundance to our lives!

August 22

"You show me the path of life; / in your presence there is fullness of joy, / in your right hand are pleasures for evermore." — Psalms 16:11

Mary wants us to know how much we are loved. She knows that her Son provides for the birds in the air. Why then wouldn't he provide all we need and give it in abundance? Jesus is always with us, showing us the way, holding our hands so that we might have his peace, joy, and fullness of life. Because he is with us forever, his heaven is with us, too.

Mary lives in the fullness of Jesus' presence in eternity, and her heart overflows with his peace and love. She takes delight in her Son's glory and shares with us the rewards that await us.

— Gina Sannasardo

How CAN YOU CHOOSE to totally trust in God's plan as Mary did so that you can receive all that God wants to give you? Today, let Mary be the person in your life who brings you comfort.

Prayer: Blessed Mother, you know your Son's love for us and his desires for our lives to be abundant. Help us turn our gaze to him, just as you do.

August 23

"For it is the LORD our God who brought us and our fathers up from the land of Egypt, out of the house of bondage, and who did those great signs in our sight, and preserved us in all the way that we went, and among all the peoples through whom we passed." — Joshua 24:17

We stand on the shoulders of those who have gone before us. We are but a spiritual collage of the abundant gifts and talents of people whose lives have shaped and molded us through the years to be who we are today. Teachers, mentors, friends, and family — through these individuals we have learned grit and grace, and the resolve to endure even the most difficult of trials.

Like our ancestors, the life of our Blessed Mother has many lessons to teach us. Mary endured an abundance of hardships in her life, from an unexpected pregnancy to the violent death of her Son, yet Mary never wavered. She persevered because of her deep faith in God. As a result, she was crowned queen of heaven and earth. Where Mary has gone, we hope to follow.

— Linda Brinkman

TODAY, LET MARY rule your day as queen and experience the abundance of God's kingdom.

Prayer: Mary, yours is an abundance of grace and life lessons. Teach me the ways of the Lord that I may walk with him all the days of my life.

August 24

"Open my eyes, that I may behold / wondrous things out of your law."
— *Psalms 119:18*

Have you noticed the abundance of God's goodness and love in the world around you? Unfortunately, many people view the world through the eyes of desire instead of abundance. They selfishly want more of everything — clothes, shoes, furniture, money, and the latest in technology. People like this are never satisfied. They also find it difficult to truly connect with others.

Mary understood the essential gift of abundance in her life. She drew joy from being the handmaid of the Lord and the mother of Jesus. She lacked for nothing. Though no one would have counted her rich, she had everything she needed.

We can choose to enjoy simple hospitality rather than meet friends and family at restaurants or coffee shops. We can choose not to lose the personal touch and seek Mary's help in experiencing the abundance of life that God has given us in and through our relationships.

— Sheila Cusack

INVITE FRIENDS OVER for an evening of conversation. Reflect on the abundance you experience when you keep things simple.

Prayer: Mary, thank you for being God's example for me on how to recognize the abundant blessings in my life.

August 25

"You will be enriched in every way for great generosity, which through us will produce thanksgiving to God." — 2 Corinthians 9:11

I remember my dear grandmother telling me about the rejection she felt when her husband left her. She suffered immense pain, yet her deep faith in Our Lord and her devotion to Mary sustained her. She found help by turning to God in morning prayer for sustenance, and praying the Rosary daily. Through faith, my grandmother not only survived, she thrived. She found strength to return to work, and found fulfillment and joy again. God provided my grandmother with every grace she needed to live a meaningful life.

Mary's life was not easy either, but the Lord blessed her abundantly with the grace she needed to persevere through great difficulties in life. God gave Mary everything she needed to be a good wife to Joseph and mother to Jesus. We can trust that God will give us all we need to continue every good work.

— Gail Krema

PONDER THE GOOD WORKS you've been a part of and the abundant grace that you've received. What small thing can you do today to enrich someone else's life?

Prayer: Mother Mary, continue to inspire us to depend on God's grace to live a life of meaning and abundance.

August 26

"That you may suck and be satisfied / with her consoling breasts."
— Isaiah 66:11

The prophet Isaiah uses the metaphor of a loving mother to describe the abundant nature of the relationship of God to the children of Israel. The metaphor comes more fully to life in Mary's relationship to all of God's children. That, too, is abundant, both in terms of the number of Mary's children and the amount of grace flowing to them through her.

Mary's moment at the cross appears predestined. She approached Calvary as the mother of her only Son, Jesus. But the Mother of Christ left the cross a mother to us all. We are the ones Jesus gave to his mother. And we are the ones to whom Mary was given.

No doubt Mary welcomed her role as our mother just as she did being mother of Jesus.

Mary's deep love for us is manifested in the Scriptures, but also in her various apparitions at Lourdes, Fátima, Guadalupe, et al. She is with us always, most especially when we pray the Rosary.

— Bob Frazee

WHAT CAN YOU DO today to deepen your devotion to Mary?

Prayer: Blessed be the name of Mary, my mother.

August 27

"For you know the grace of our Lord Jesus Christ, that though he was rich, yet for your sake he became poor, so that by his poverty you might become rich." — *2 Corinthians 8:9*

Thinking abundantly can be a challenge at times. All we need to do is turn on the news to become surrounded with stories of what is lacking. We ought to worry about having what we need. Forget about abundance; we are lucky to have just enough. That's the message we hear every day in the world.

But that is not how God wants us to live. He came to show us his abundance. He became poor so that we might inherit his riches. The abundance of God and of the world are two different things. God may be asking us to accept something that at first doesn't make sense or isn't a part of the "plan" we had for our lives. Trust that God's abundance is that which will truly bring us joy no matter the outward appearance. Mary's life is a testament to that kind of abundance.

— Suzette Horyza

RECALL AN ABUNDANCE God brought to your life that you didn't expect.

Prayer: Mary, help me to be open to the abundance of God, even if it appears like poverty and want.

August 28

"I consider that the sufferings of this present time are not worth comparing with the glory that is to be revealed to us. For the creation waits with eager longing for the revealing of the sons of God." — *Romans 8:18-19*

Scripture assures us that all who carry heavy crosses in this life will be abundantly rewarded in the glorious kingdom of heaven. Mary's entire life was wrapped in suffering, culminating with the crucifixion of her Son, Jesus. Yet Mary's faith in God remained unshakable. At the end of her earthly life, God blessed Mary abundantly by bringing her, body and soul, into heaven. The body that bore and birthed and fed the Son of God was taken to heaven to reign beside her Son as queen.

Mary was a simple peasant girl ready to serve the Lord every day of her life. Her life inspires us to be open to doing God's will, even if that will involves suffering. If we remain faithful, God will abundantly reward us as he did Mary, with the glory of heaven.

— Lauren Nelson

THANK GOD TODAY for a hardship or difficulty you are experiencing. Seek Mary's help for a willingness to carry these crosses.

Prayer: Mary, help me to cheerfully accept my burdens with the knowledge that the glory of God's kingdom awaits me.

August 29

"And God said, 'Behold, I have given you every plant yielding seed which is upon the face of all the earth, and every tree with seed in its fruit; you shall have them for food." — Genesis 1:29

God has blessed us abundantly with every seed-bearing plant. August is harvest time in many places and we are invited to give thanks to the Lord for the abundance of food he has given us. Fields of corn and wheat dot the landscape, grapes are growing, and berries are ripe for picking.

Unfortunately, in the midst of this abundance of God-given gifts, many still struggle to put food on their table in this land of prosperity. This makes me wonder about Mary's life.

As a poor family in Nazareth, did the Holy Family hunger for food and the basic necessities of life, or were they able to survive on the products grown in the dry desert sun? Surely Mary fed her family with bread and water, but they also feasted daily on the abundance of God's love, goodness, mercy, and grace. They never lacked for any spiritual gift from God.

— Linda Brinkman

VISIT A FOOD PANTRY today and share your abundance with someone less fortunate.

Prayer: Mary, help me to be grateful for the abundance of food on my table, and help me to be of service to those who still hunger and thirst.

August 30

"Therefore, if any one is in Christ, he is a new creation; the old has passed away, behold, the new has come." — 2 Corinthians 5:17

Jesus tells us that in him and through him all things will come to new life as promised. Trusting this gave Mary the strength to stay the course in God's plan. The life that awaits us in heaven is unlike anything we have known.

Mary can be our guide in life. She nurtures Christ Jesus within us and teaches us how to live in the presence of the Lord just as he intended for us to do. From the moment of her birth, Mary lived her life according to God's way, his will, and his love. Mary's life shows us that God keeps his promises to us. Hope, joy, and abundance belong to those who believe in Jesus. Mary offers to be present with us every day so that we can let go of what holds us back from becoming new creations in Christ.

— Gina Sannasardo

HOW CAN YOU FIND new life in God and let the things of this world pass away? Ask Mary to show you how God is working in your life.

Prayer: Blessed Mother, we ask that you never leave us alone, but rather keep us company and journey with us from this life and into eternal life in Christ Jesus.

August 31

"For it is all for your sake, so that as grace extends to more and more people it may increase thanksgiving, to the glory of God." — 2 Corinthians 4:15

Here St. Paul suggests that the abundant graces poured out on each one of us and countless others can bring forth such thanksgiving and praise for the glory of God, that it actually spills forth outward into the world.

God's blessings were lavished on Mary. She did not take anything for granted, but was filled with gratitude for the abundance that had been given to her.

Many years ago, I kept a gratitude journal. Every evening I would look for three things that I was grateful for. Even on difficult days I was forced to look for the positive. That practice changed the way I looked at my life. Like Mary I found myself pondering the graces throughout my day filling my heart.

Gratitude can be contagious. When we express our thanks, it overflows and inspire others to focus their attention on what they are thankful for.

— Gail Krema

LIST THREE BLESSINGS you received today and express gratitude to God. Does it leave you with a desire for more, or help you to see your life of abundance?

Prayer: Mary, help me to appreciate all the grace in my life.

~ SELF-CONTROL ~

September 1

"The fruit of the Spirit is love, joy, peace, patience, kindness, goodness, faithfulness, gentleness, self-control; against such there is no law."
— *Galatians 5:22-23*

Recent studies have shown that human beings are influenced by their home environment. The manner in which family members treat one another at home is learned, then often repeated by the next generation. Mary's family life is a perfect example.

Mary's home was filled with God's love, joy, and goodness. Her peaceful and patient demeanor permeated every facet of her life. As a wife and mother, Mary practiced self-control in her behavior, emotions, and actions. As her Son, Jesus, grew, he learned from her example.

Mary's life can also be an inspiration for us. Her life in Nazareth offers us a beautiful portrait of how we are to live in this world. Because Mary walked with God each day, she lived a well-ordered and peaceful life.

— Sharon A. Abel, PhD

TODAY, TAKE CONTROL of your actions, emotions, behaviors, and desires. Fill your home with a Spirit-filled atmosphere. Yes, Jesus is watching.

Prayer: Holy Mother, I know that through baptism the fruit of the Spirit lies within me. Help me to remember that self-control navigates and leads me to fully integrating these fruits into my daily choices and behaviors.

September 2

"Let it be to me according to your word." — *Luke 1:38*

One dimension of self-control is the ability to accept what you cannot change. The youngest sibling in my family was born with severe Down syndrome. Back then, people were not accepting of these special children, and my mother was told by everyone that she should institutionalize my brother. The only person to support our family wholeheartedly was our parish priest. He encouraged Mom not to fear, but rather to trust in the Lord. My mom cared for her son though he never got out of diapers, never attended school, and could only communicate with family. One day when he was twelve years old, he just stopped breathing.

I believe that our parish priest was like the angel who told Mary not to be afraid because she had found favor with God. Mary's life inspired my mother to care for my brother. Mary knew what it was like to have a "special son," and my mother took her lead from her. My mom practiced the virtue of self-control on a daily basis.

— Bob Frazee

PRAYERFULLY REFLECT on a situation you cannot change. How can Mary's life inspire you to accept God's will?

Prayer: Mother Mary, I pray to you, help me to see God in the everyday challenges of life — be it done unto me.

September 3

"Be still, and know that I am God." — Psalms 46:10

At the Annunciation, Mary opened her life, her body, her soul to her God. She said "yes" to her beloved and gave God control over her life. Instead of trying to control him, or everything around her, Mary was content to control herself.

Can I trust that God's love will hold me when I need it most? That I can relinquish my (illusory) sense of control and count on his strength in place of mine? To learn from his wisdom? To hear his Word? Am I willing to be vulnerable, open, truly humble? How can I receive God's grace if I don't trust him?

We don't hear God in the hurricane in our minds. We don't feel God in the earthquake in our hearts. We don't learn from God in a life of distraction and fluttering. We hear God in stillness as a light murmuring sound or a small still voice. We exercise the greatest self-control when we learn to rely fully on him.

— Jane Zimmerman

SIT STILL for five minutes today. Listen to the noise that is within you, then ask Mary to help you learn to exercise genuine self-control and be still.

Prayer: Dear Mary, please help me to be still, so I can feel God's presence and store his treasures in my heart as you did.

September 4

"I can do all things in him who strengthens me."
— *Philippians 4:13*

Popular athletes and military leaders often use this verse to call upon power from a higher place to defeat an enemy or achieve a difficult task. Recently, though, I realized that Paul wrote these words from prison and spoke of the ability to remain strong, not because of our own power to control things, but from Christ, who is in control.

Mary is the perfect example of this source of self-control and empowerment. Time and time again, she placed her trust in God for all that she needed to move through any situation. Notice that Mary always accepted what was asked of her and drew her strength from knowing that it was God who was doing the asking.

— Deb Kelsey–Davis

HAS DOUBT OR FEAR OF DEFEAT caused you to take control in order to make a situation better for yourself? Are there times you decided to patiently trust God to work it out instead? What do these moments reveal to you?

Prayer: Mary, help me to remember that it is through your Son, Jesus, that I can endure life's trials. When I feel that I am doing it all on my own, give me the wisdom to realize the goodness that God has in store for me.

September 5

"And the angel said to her, 'Do not be afraid.'"
— *Luke 1:30*

There is a beautiful painting entitled *The Angelus* by Jean-Francois Millet. It depicts a man and woman working in the fields pausing at dusk to pray. Their postures evoke a feeling of deep reverence. I like to imagine our Blessed Mother teaching Jesus the prayers and rituals a young Jewish boy would learn growing up. A holy, prayerful life requires a certain amount of effort, including discipline and self-control.

Mary models these traits as she surrenders to the message of the angel, observes the purification rituals, attends Passover, and quietly walks the Way of the Cross with Jesus. Mary made time in her life for God, and she invites us to do the same.

Several years ago, I set the alarm on my cell phone to quietly chime at noon and 6:00 p.m. Hearing that soft chime is like a tap on the shoulder reminding me it's time to be with God — and Mary.

— Bob Frazee

A MORNING OFFERING, an examination of conscience, grace before meals, daily Mass, readings of the day are all ways of making time for God. Be creative and find what works for you.

Prayer: Mary, I pray to you for guidance. Show me the way to make time for God.

September 6

"For as the rain and the snow come down from heaven, / and do not return there but water the earth / ... / so shall my word be that goes forth from my mouth; / it shall not return to me empty, / but it shall accomplish that which I intend, / and prosper in the thing for which I sent it." — Isaiah 55:10-11

Mary doesn't use many words in Scripture. She speaks primarily with her actions, but her deeds always have purpose, and God is always at the forefront. It is clear that Mary practiced self-control throughout her life. I am sure Mary wanted to brag about her Son, Jesus, or perhaps scream when things went terribly wrong. She didn't. That is because Mary understood that what was happening was not about her, but rather was God's plan unfolding in her life.

Mary accomplished God's will for her by practicing self-control. When things don't go our way, we can choose to step back and allow the Lord to control the situation. Trust that the Lord will achieve his purpose.

— Lauren Nelson

How CAN YOU BE more mindful of your words today? What can you do to exercise self-control over what you say?

Prayer: Mary, put your hand on my shoulder and help me to have more control and to be more mindful of the words I use.

September 7

"You have put more joy in my heart / than they have when their grain and wine abound." — Psalms 4:7

Some of my greatest letdowns have come directly after the biggest celebrations in my life — like the day I turned twenty-one. So much anticipation built up to that day. Even with parties, laughter, and gifts, afterward, within days, I distinctly recall the emptiness and wondering, "What next?" Happiness seemed temporary. I was losing self-control and believed God had abandoned me; turns out, it was I who had strayed from him.

My devotion to Mary started out of a desire to emulate her trust in God. Her desires were not focused on the flesh or riches, nor were those the gifts she received. Yet, Mary's days were filled with hope and joy that endured even the most tragic of circumstances. As our mother Mary teaches us by example to place our desires and will into the hands of God, we should let God take control.

— Deb Kelsey-Davis

Is THERE SOMETHING in your heart today that is out of control?

Prayer: Mary, help me make choices that direct the desires of my heart toward God, as you did. Show me how to abandon my "self" to God in order to gain self-control arising from my free will and the grace of reason.

September 8
Feast of the Birth of Mary

"No temptation has overtaken you that is not common to man.
God is faithful, and he will not let you be tempted beyond your strength,
but with the temptation will also provide the way of escape, that you
may be able to endure it." — 1 Corinthians 10:13

Mary was conceived a sinless human being, but her life was far from perfect. Mary faced sadness, trials, and tribulations like we do. As the mother of Jesus, she endured horrific tragedies that would test her beyond human strength. Yet, Mary never wavered. Her deep faith in God helped her to practice self-control in the midst of chaos.

We often hear that God will not give us more than we can handle; for Mary this was true. Even as she watched her beloved Son suffer and die, Mary was in control of herself because she knew that God was with her. In moments of darkness and difficulty, we can ask Mary to help us trust in the Lord.

— Lauren Nelson

GIVE GOD CONTROL over your life — just for today. At the end of your day notice the good things that happen because of it.

Prayer: Mary, help me to put God in control of my life so I may walk through any obstacles knowing I am not alone when facing perils.

September 9

"But standing by the cross of Jesus [was] his mother." — John 19:25

I am somewhat of an "avoider" when it comes to suffering. Still, I find it even more painful to watch a loved one suffer. No doubt Mary felt the same as she stood at the foot of the cross. What did Mary feel at that moment? I can only imagine that it took a great amount of restraint and self-control to remain standing there in faith.

The opening line of an ancient Marian hymn is, "At the cross her station keeping." There's a haunting presence to that line. It's as if Mary was destined for her own moment at the cross.

Pain and suffering are unavoidable. Yet Mary's motherly presence at the cross challenges us to accept these painful moments with the grace of self-control. Rather than blaming God or others, Mary's life invites us to join her at the foot of the cross and resist the inclination toward anger.

— Bob Frazee

PRAYERFULLY REFLECT on a painful situation in your life. Freely give this experience to Mary and seek her help in carrying your cross.

Prayer: Mary, your heart was pierced with pain, yet you remained faithful to the Lord. Help me to follow in your footsteps and to carry my crosses with grace.

September 10

"He replied to the man who told him, 'Who is my mother, and who are my brethren?' And stretching out his hand toward his disciples, he said, 'Here are my mother and my brethren! For whoever does the will of my Father in heaven is my brother, and sister, and mother." — *Matthew 12:48-50*

"Who is my mother?" This was a situation in which Mary practiced great self-control. Instead of lashing out or taking these words personally, Mary chose to remain silent. She put his ministry before her own feelings, and allowed him to teach his disciples.

Mary's life as the mother of Jesus has much to teach us about self-control. The reality is that sometimes loved ones will disappoint us. When our feelings get hurt and we are tempted to react, Mary's life inspires us to practice self-control. Instead of engaging people when we are angry or disappointed, we can prayerfully give the situation over to the Lord.

— Dr. Mary Amore

RECALL A SITUATION where you felt betrayed or rejected. Would self-control have changed that response?

Prayer: Mary, you understand my pain. Help me to practice self-control when I am feeling betrayed and forgotten.

September 11

"Then the righteous will shine like the sun in the kingdom of their Father. He who has ears, let him hear." — Matthew 13:43

Mary was present with her Son, Jesus, through both light and darkness. She exemplified grace even during times of frustration and unexpected news. Drawing upon her strong faith in the Lord, Mary was able to exercise self-control when dealing with the miraculous events in her life — that is, situations that she encountered but did not understand. Mary never questioned God; rather she placed her complete trust in the ways of the Lord.

Mary can teach us how to deal with difficult situations and events in our lives that we don't fully understand. Instead of reacting in a negative way, we can follow Mary's example and prayerfully ponder things in our hearts as we give them over to the Lord. When we do, we will shine like the sun in the kingdom of our heavenly Father.

— Sheila Cusack

THINK OF A RELATIONSHIP or event in your life that could be improved if you practiced self-control. Seek the Blessed Mother's assistance in dealing with this situation.

Prayer: Mary, pray that I can exercise self-control in my dealings with people and events that are problematic for me.

September 12

"The beginning of wisdom is the most sincere desire for instruction / and concern for instruction is love of her." — Wisdom of Solomon 6:17

There's a story of a young sales clerk who was announcing a two-for-one special on giant chocolate bars. A rather overweight man stopped and stared at the counter. It was obvious that he was having an internal struggle as to whether he should buy the candy bars or not. The sales person waited, then finally inquired if the man would like a giant chocolate bar. He shook his head from side to side and said, "No, give me two."

Lightheartedness aside, Mary lived a life of self-control and self-discipline. Our Blessed Mother had definite priorities that led her to make specific choices. Remaining firm in her commitment to God all the days of her life, Mary gave us a beautiful example of how to exercise self-control.

Mary's life invites us to find balance by making life-giving and creative choices for ourselves while keeping our focus on loving and serving God. This is disciplined wisdom and self-control.

— Joseph Abel, PhD

USING THE SCRIPTURE above, take a few minutes and review the priorities in your life. How do they lead you to wisdom? Any needed changes?

Prayer: Mary, mother of God, may we embrace the self-discipline that leads us to wisdom.

September 13

"And the angel departed from her." — Luke 1:38

Have you ever wondered what happened to Mary after the angel departed from her? Young Mary had to deal with an unplanned pregnancy in a society that stoned women in that situation to death. Mary was not superhuman. She was a pregnant teenage girl filled with countless emotions: her life was in danger, Joseph would probably divorce her, and no one would believe her story. As the handmaid of the Lord, Mary practiced self-control in keeping her fears from dominating her soul. And through all of this, Mary remained faithful to God.

Each day we are faced with experiences that leave our hearts aching from disappointment or an unfulfilled dream: a job loss, an illness, a broken relationship, a marriage that failed. Whatever the situation, we can seek Mary's help in placing our complete trust in God. This is not easy, and it takes self-control. Mary can help us to let go of what we had planned in order to surrender our lives to the Lord.

— Dr. Mary Amore

WHAT ARE YOUR UNFULFILLED DREAMS? Seek Mary's help in giving these situations over to the Lord.

Prayer: Mary, help me to practice self-control in my dealings with my family and friends. Help me to seek to do the Lord's will at all times.

September 14

"I can do all things in him who strengthens me."
— Philippians 4:13

As a person in recovery from emotional overeating, I know that self-control is very misunderstood. To most, self-control is pulling up your bootstraps — a "super willpower," so to speak. That is not biblical. Each time we think that way and fail, we add to our belief that we can't control ourselves. Self-control is the fruit of living the life of Christ; it is he who gives us the strength to overcome our struggles.

Throughout the pages of Scripture, Mary continually demonstrated self-control. There were certainly times when she had to hold her tongue. Mary's ultimate act of self-control was not to rush in to try to save her Son from crucifixion or cry out with anger and bitterness at the betrayal he had suffered. Mary's self-control was the fruit of living a life of deep faith.

— Christine Grano

WHAT STRUGGLES have you had with self-control? Write down how you feel about those struggles and spend time with that in prayer.

Prayer: Mary, thank you for your quiet exhibition of self-control. Pray for me that my mind may be renewed about where self-control comes from. Please pray that I open myself to be empowered by the Lord.

September 15
Memorial of Our Lady of Sorrows

"And Joseph took the body, and wrapped it in a clean linen shroud."
— *Matthew 27:59*

All four Gospels mention the taking down of Jesus' body from the cross and the wrapping of him in a burial cloth. But none mention laying him in Mary's arms. Nonetheless, it's a powerful image: Mary in her sorrow, saying her final goodbyes.

Our tradition remembers this moment devotionally as the Thirteenth Station of the Cross and the Sixth of Mary's Seven Sorrows. These devotions, and the Bible, typically portray Mary as recollected and composed, a holy woman of immense interior strength disposed to a quiet demeanor. Still waters run deep.

Final goodbyes are difficult yet inevitable. At some point, Mary must have realized the inevitable conclusion Jesus was facing. There's a great deal of self-control in resigning yourself to the inevitable. As a hospice volunteer I've been present to those grieving loved ones. Words can bring some consolation, but mere presence and touch are much more comforting. Mary is here to be with us.

— Bob Frazee

JOIN MARY in her sorrow at the foot of the cross. Reach out to her, touch her, and be present to her as she mourns, and invite Mary to be with you.

Prayer: Mary, I ask for the privilege of being present to you in your time of sorrow.

September 16

*"For this very reason make every effort to supplement your faith
with virtue, and virtue with knowledge, and knowledge with self-control,
and self-control with steadfastness, and steadfastness with godliness,
and godliness with brotherly affection, and brotherly affection with love."*
— 2 Peter 1:5-7

Mary's life as the mother of Jesus is a perfect example of the kind of disciple that Peter describes. When Mary stood at the foot of the cross, she practiced the perseverance that comes from self-control. Mary lived a life of godliness and love.

The Blessed Mother encourages us to stay calm and not allow our emotions to get the best of us. This is easier said than done, and Mary is here to help us control our anger, resist the temptation for revenge, and practice self-control with our feelings and impulses. She is here to show us how to grow in love.

— Gina Sannasardo

How can I stay calm in a hurtful or tense situation? Today, ask Mary to help you practice self-control in your speech and actions.

Prayer: Beloved Mother, I ask you to be with me when I feel out of control. Calm my need to speak out or against someone; open my ears to listen to others and my heart to mutual affection.

September 17

"For God did not give us a spirit of timidity but a spirit of power and love and self-control." — *2 Timothy 1:7*

We all face situations where our emotions run high. If we have let our feelings carry us away, some of us may have been told, "You are too impulsive" or, "Think before you act!" I have certainly heard those words. Have you ever said something you later regretted or done something that you never would have if you could just exercise self-control?

Now think of Mary and the emotional crises she faced. Imagine how easy it might have been for her to lash out when she and Joseph had no place to stay in Bethlehem. Or how she must have felt about those who mocked and tortured her Son, Jesus. Yet, Mary resisted the temptation to react negatively. Her entire life was lived in the Spirit. That was her source of courage, power, love, and self-control.

— Deb Kelsey-Davis

WE ARE UNABLE to resist temptations of the flesh and mind on our own. Mary shows us that through God the fruit of the Spirit, self-control is available to each of us.

Prayer: Please help me, Mary, to live by the Spirit as you did. Guide me to draw upon the power that comes only from God to resist temptations and grow in self-control.

September 18

"Blessed are you when men revile you and persecute you and utter all kinds of evil against you falsely on my account. Rejoice and be glad, for your reward is great in heaven." — *Matthew 5:11-12*

We have to wonder what Mary felt when she heard about the slaughter of innocent children in Bethlehem shortly after the birth of her Son. What agony did she experience knowing that other young sons had been taken from the loving arms of their mothers only to be put to the sword?

Mary must have learned self-control in these moments of trial and tribulation. It was Mary's faith that helped her to maintain control of her emotions. She trusted God with everything. As our spiritual mother, Mary desires that we practice self-control, even if people insult us and persecute us for the sake of her Son. She wants us to know that God is in control.

— Larry Dreffein

ASK MARY TO SHOW YOU how to give your emotions to God and trust him in situations that upset you today.

Prayer: Mary, you trusted in the promise made to you and your people. Help me to trust in the promise of the Father to never leave us orphans. Help me to exercise self-control and live trusting in the promise of God.

September 19

"He who is slow to anger is better than the mighty, / and he who rules his spirit than he who takes a city." — Proverbs 16:32

Years ago, I learned a life and faith lesson in self-control from my father.

Dad and I were in a music store. I wanted to buy a newly released music album. I asked dad several times if he would buy it for me. He responded with a simple question: "Is this necessary?" I replied, "Yes, I really want this album." First came the faith lesson. Dad replied, "God provides you with all you need." The life lesson followed: "Is this something you want, or something you need?" I didn't get the album, but I got the life and faith lesson which I've passed on to my children.

Mary was a model of self-control. Her entire life was focused on serving God, and this helped form her decisions in life. Let us seek Mary's assistance to choose wisely.

— Sharon A. Abel, PhD

GOING SHOPPING SOON? Before placing each item in your cart ask yourself, "Is this necessary?" If not, estimate the cost of the items you do not buy and donate that amount to charity.

Prayer: Mary, help us to use God's gift of self-control to make life-giving choices which deepen our faith and reminds us that all we need in life you have already given.

September 20

"Every athlete exercises self-control in all things. They do it to receive a perishable wreath, but we an imperishable." — 1 Corinthians 9:25

Watch any great athlete and you will see discipline and self-control. For example, in baseball a batter considers the skill level of the pitcher, the ball-strike count, the game situation, and the umpire when deciding whether to swing.

Like a great athlete, Mary exercised discipline in decision making. When visited by the angel Gabriel, young Mary considered God's will, her ability to be a good wife and mother, and her desire to live her faith. These factors helped Mary make a holy and disciplined choice.

Every day we are faced with situations that demand that we make a choice. Do we exercise a disciplined approach to making a decision like Mary did, or do we choose by how we feel? It takes self-control to run faithfully toward an imperishable crown.

— Joseph Abel, PhD

REFLECT ON THE DECISIONS that need to be made today. How will you make these decisions into choices for God?

Prayer: Mary, you show us holy decision making in constantly choosing God's desires for you. Help me to use my power to choose God's desires for me.

September 21

*"And he rose and took the child and his mother by night,
and departed to Egypt." — Matthew 2:14*

My definition of self-control is dying to one's own self-interests in deference to another.

My guess is that by the time Mary gave birth to Jesus she thought the hard part was over. Then, she enjoyed the shepherds sharing angelic tidings of great joy and welcomed the Magi bearing gifts fit for a king.

No doubt Mary looked forward to bringing her new baby home to celebrate with the entire family and to settle down to a nice quiet life with Joseph. Surrendering to God, however, is not a one-time event. Another angel appeared, this time with an unwelcome message to go and stay in Egypt until further notice. The Holy Family fled for their lives as Mary practiced self-control and surrendered to the will of God once again.

Mary's life of grace invites us to cultivate a spirit of self-control and a readiness to do the will of God. When we face uncertain situations, do we demand to understand and know everything before we respond?
— Bob Frazee

CONSIDER THE WAYS you can seek God in the unknown and surrender a self-interest today as Mary did.

Prayer: Mary, remember me as I implore your help; give me the self-control to surrender and follow your example.

September 22

*"May the Lord direct your hearts to the love of God and
to the steadfastness of Christ." — 2 Thessalonians 3:5*

The ability to control our schedules, finances, and rules of the household — these are all good things, right? But I had fallen into the trap of believing I had self-control when what I was really trying to do was manipulate and control other people and my surroundings. When my relationships began to suffer, I pleaded with God for help. But even my prayers were an attempt to control God!

We need look no further than to our spiritual mother for the kind of positive peace and love that comes from a self-controlled heart. Mary was a listener, one who discerned and relinquished control to the will of God. Instead of trying to control her surroundings, she was content to control the things within her.

— Deb Kelsey-Davis

PRAYERFULLY CONSIDER the ways you can humbly invite Jesus to direct your heart and mind today, to let go of control, so that you may gain self-control guided by the Holy Spirit.

Prayer: Mary, help me to still my mind and open my heart to your Son, Jesus, that I may let go and let him provide me with the self-control needed to endure life's challenges.

September 23

"Finally, brethren, whatever is true, whatever is honorable, whatever is just, whatever is pure, whatever is lovely, whatever is gracious, if there is any excellence, if there is anything worthy of praise, think about these things."
— *Philippians 4:8*

This letter from St. Paul offers us a blueprint of perfection for us to dwell upon. If we really study this text, the attributes perfectly describe someone who practices self-control — the ability to choose wisely over the things of this world.

These characteristics also describe our Blessed Mother. Mary is a model of truth; she is honorable and right, accepting the joys and sorrows of life, but always choosing a steadfast faith in God. Mary is pure and lovely and good. If there is anyone worthy of praise, it is Mary, the mother of Jesus.

We can follow the life of the Blessed Mother by living a life worthy of praise. In times of difficulty, Mary can help us practice self-control.
— Lauren Nelson

SPEND TIME TODAY dwelling on the attributes listed in this reading. Reflect on how Mary can assist you to dwell on these things.

Prayer: Mary, keep me in your most pure heart. You are wonderful and good; help me to follow your example.

September 24

"Behold, your father and I have been looking for you anxiously."
— Luke 2:48

As a parent, this Scripture passage has always amazed me, because it is the only one that reveals Mary's emotion. The mother of Jesus is filled with great anxiety, and with good reason. Her twelve-year-old son has been lost for three days, missing in a world that bought and sold children like cattle and had no Amber alerts, milk cartons, or cellphones. Overwrought at the thought of losing her Son, Mary must have practiced great self-control as she and Joseph searched for him.

Mary's experience speaks volumes to us today, for our loved ones do not have to be physically lost to be lost in this world. We can lose family members to drugs and alcohol; we can lose them to the wrong set of friends, to atheism or a different religion. We can lose them in anger.

In these moments of loss, Mary invites us to surrender these painful moments into the loving arms of God and to let go of our fears and anxieties.

— Dr. Mary Amore

PRAYERFULLY REFLECT on one family situation that you can give over to the Lord. Seek Mary's help in trusting God, exercising self-control, and not worrying about the outcome.

Prayer: Mary, help me to control myself and surrender my loved ones to the Lord.

September 25

"For the grace of God has appeared for the salvation of all men, training us to renounce irreligion and worldly passions, and to live sober, upright, and godly lives in this world." — Titus 2:11-12

When I was a child, my favorite baby sitter was my mom's oldest unmarried sister. Aunt Mary watched us when my parents needed a date night. She had no experience with raising children and there were three of us to corral.

Aunt Mary was a gentle, quiet, calm, humble, and very self-controlled woman of faith. She cared for my grandmother, attended Mass, and prayed the Rosary daily. Simple and plain in appearance, Aunt Mary's upright and godly behavior was a good example for us. Auntie Mary brought calm and harmony every time she visited us. She was, I imagine, much like the woman she was named for — Mary, the mother of Jesus.

— Sharon A. Abel, PhD

TAKE CONTROL of your being today. Ask Mary to help you listen with an open heart. Think carefully before you speak and choose calm over anger or frustration when facing difficult people or situations.

Prayer: Mary, grant us the ability to listen well, to think before speaking, and to curb our negative emotions.

September 26

"For what does it profit a man, to gain the whole world and forfeit his life?"
— Mark 8:36

At the top of my list of indulgences are dark chocolate, a glass of wine, and traveling. You might wonder how something so small could be bad for you? Well, it doesn't hurt to have a few satisfying moments. It's when we *over*indulge or *self*-indulge that problems arise.

Losing self-control has taken me down the paths of gaining weight and prioritizing success over almost everything else. Failing to say "no" to myself even cost me contact with friends and compromised my relationship with God.

Mary reveals the power of saying "yes." She could have chosen to take a path that required less of her and brought her more immediate gratification. But Mary's faith was strong. Practicing self-control, Mary chose Christ over the world, and over herself.

— Deb Kelsey-Davis

THINK OF YOUR OWN weaknesses. We all have them. Are there things in your life that just might be separating you from God?

Prayer: Mary, help me to take my temptations and turn those struggles over to God as you did. Show me how to practice self-control so that I more fully may know the love of the Father and choose Jesus.

September 27

"Therefore gird up your minds, be sober, set your hope fully upon the grace that is coming to you at the revelation of Jesus Christ." — 1 Peter 1:13

Mary's life invites us to prepare our minds and fix our hope on the grace of God. Sinless from birth, Mary still had to look evil in the eye and practice self-control over temptations that came her way. As sons and daughters of Christ, our spiritual mother is here to help us keep sober and overcome all sin and temptation.

Because Mary completely focused on Jesus, she was able to say "no" to the things of this world even when they seemed attractive or better. She delighted in saying "yes" to the Lord's plan for her and extends her hands to us so that we may join her in saying "yes" to God.

— Gina Sannasardo

How can you practice self-control today? Ask Mary to always stay with you so that in moments of weakness she can be your strength.

Prayer: Beloved Mother, I come to you with hope and confidence that you will protect me from the false values of this world so that I may give myself totally to God.

September 28

"Behold, your mother!" — *John 19:27*

Although I am a cradle Catholic, I didn't put much effort into my faith until I was thirty-five years old and a priest friend encouraged me to pray each day. Since prayer was not part of my life, I began slowly and said a few Our Fathers, Hail Marys, and Glory Bes as I walked to work. A few weeks later, I discovered that there was a noon Mass near my work. I also tried to pray the Rosary occasionally. Now, thirty years later, prayer has become my lifestyle. I attend daily Mass, read Scripture, sit in silent meditation, and pray the Rosary often.

Prayer has drawn me into an intimate relationship with Jesus through his mother, Mary. I believe that's why Jesus gave us his mother from the cross. Jesus knew that Mary would lead us to him.

Prayer, like any relationship, evolves over time and takes some self-control. You can't pray if you don't make a conscious effort. Mary understands the daily demands of our busy lives, and she knows it takes self-control on our part to focus our energy on prayer.

— Bob Frazee

TODAY, PRAY ONE Hail Mary, one Our Father, and one Glory Be, or add a few minutes to your established prayer time.

Prayer: Mother Mary, guide me to your Son through a life of prayer.

September 29

"Not many days later, the younger son gathered all he had and took his journey into a far country, and there he squandered his property in loose living." — Luke 15:13

This Scripture reading about the prodigal son helps us to understand self-control and God's message to forgive. The father waited and watched for the prodigal son to return home. He practiced great self-control by not preventing the son from leaving home, dragging him back, or chastising him when he finally returned. The father loved his son and did not try to control him.

Mary exercised self-control as the mother of Jesus. As our heavenly mother, she invites us to keep our focus on God, but never seeks control. Like the father in the story of the prodigal son, Mary waits and watches for us to return home to our faith in God. When we do, she welcomes us without reservation.

— Sheila Cusack

ASK MARY FOR HELP today if you're feeling lost, far away, or in need of self-control. Has a lack of self-control meant leaving something or someone behind? How might you "return home" today?

Prayer: Mary, pray that I may exercise self-control in my relationships and encounters with others.

September 30

"He who is slow to anger is better than the mighty, / and he who rules his spirit than he who takes a city." — Proverbs 16:32

Patience is a virtue most of us struggle with almost every day of our lives. Culturally, we're expected to respond quickly, speak our minds, and go after what we want when we want it. The world is full of discourteous drivers, selfish people, perhaps even demanding family. It's hard to keep it together without losing your patience. In the heat of many moments, I've held my breath and asked God to give me patience — NOW!

Mary's whole life was a testament to patience and self-control. Consider her long journey to Bethlehem, her escape to Egypt to protect her Son, followed by waiting until it was safe to return to Nazareth. Mary's perfect patience made her strong and shielded her mind and emotions, guiding her to think and view the struggles in her life with calm acceptance.

— Deb Kelsey-Davis

HAS YOUR IMPATIENCE ever gotten the better of you? How has God shown you that being patient is not the same thing as being weak?

Prayer: Heavenly Mother, help me to grow in patience, that I may gain self-control, make better decisions, and open my heart to let Jesus in to guide me.

~ GENEROSITY ~

October 1

"For by grace you have been saved through faith; and this is not your own doing, it is the gift of God — not because of works, lest any man should boast." — Ephesians 2:8-9

How generous is our God! How great is the abundance of God's mercy and kindness. Our salvation is a gift of grace. We can't earn it. Therefore, we have nothing to brag about.

Mary was the recipient of God's enormous generosity. She was full of the grace of salvation because she opened her heart to fully receive all that God wanted to give her. She immersed herself in her mission as the mother of Jesus. Selflessly, she not only served as Jesus' mother, but as a faithful disciple of her Son in his mission of salvation. Mary shows us how to receive the generosity of God's love, mercy, and grace that await us.

— John Holmes

How can you respond more fully to God's generosity today? Ask Mary to help you open your heart fully to receive God's gifts.

Prayer: Blessed Lady, thank you for your example of God's generosity. Help me to follow, that I may find my true calling.

October 2

"Give, and it will be given to you; good measure, pressed down, shaken together, running over, will be put into your lap. For the measure you give will be the measure you get back." — Luke 6:38

Mary's life offers us a wonderful example of how to live an abundantly graced-filled existence. Mary generously gave her whole life to God in becoming the mother of Jesus.

Living a simple life in Nazareth, Mary generously devoted herself to her family and friends. At Cana, Mary was generous to the young wedding couple when she approached Jesus and asked him to save them from embarrassment. And when it came time for Jesus to pursue his public ministry, Mary was generous in helping him flourish. Even at the foot of the cross, our grieving mother was most generous. She gave her Son up to God's plan for our salvation, and accepted her role as mother to us all.

— Lauren Nelson

CONSIDER HOW YOU CAN be generous with your God-given gifts of time, talent, and treasure today.

Prayer: Mary, your generous heart overflowed with love for all. Help me to generously give of myself in loving service to others.

October 3

"He who is kind to the poor lends to the LORD, / and he will repay him for his deed." — Proverbs 19:17

The Jewish laws regarding generosity were well established by Mary's time. The Law taught her that everything was a direct blessing from God. Those who had been granted the means to give were chosen by God to give. Those who, due to reasons known to the Creator alone, were in need were placed by God in a position to receive.

Mary saw herself as among the givers who had been blessed with shelter, food, a family, a community, and faith. She would have felt a sense of obligation to share all she had with others.

But Mary took generosity even further, not just sharing what she possessed, but all of who she was. Mary's extraordinary generosity in giving her whole self to bear the Savior is a model of what it means to make a gift of self to God. Mary's life inspires us to share what we have been given. She also shows us how to become a gift.

— Joseph Abel, PhD

MAKE A CONSCIOUS donation today to someone less fortunate.

Prayer: O Mary, holy generosity was a way of life for you and your people. May my life show gratitude to God through my willingness to give myself and all I have to others.

October 4

"The tents of robbers are at peace, / and those who provoke God are secure, / who bring their god in their hand." — Job 12:6

Mary's life is a constant reminder to us that our God is faithful and that his promises can be trusted. Chosen by God to be the mother of our Savior, Mary generously cooperated with God's grace in bringing God's promise of salvation to fruition. As our heavenly mother, Mary generously intercedes for us, bringing our needs and petitions before her Son.

It is autumn, and where I live God's generosity is visible everywhere in creation. When I take a walk, I see the rich extravagance of the woods and the landscape around me. Beautiful crimson and gold trees, sapphire blue skies, and fresh air delight me and stir up within me a sense of all that God has given.

— Sheila Cusack

TAKE A NATURE WALK and invite Mary to walk alongside you. Know that she is here to help you on your spiritual journey to God.

Prayer: Mary, thank you for reminding me that our God is a generous God and that he will never leave me. Thank you for your care of my heart on my journey in life.

October 5

*"And a poor widow came, and put in two copper coins, which make
a penny. And he called his disciples to him, and said to them,
'Truly, I say to you, this poor widow has put in more than all those
who are contributing to the treasury.'"* — Mark 12:42-43

Big things don't always make a big difference. Often the littlest gestures can mean the world to others.

After my family suffered a devastating fire we had nothing. Not twelve hours later, people came forward generously giving us clothes and money for food. What touched my heart deeply was the generosity shown to us by an eight-year-old son of one of my friends who gave us the money from his piggy bank. He gave everything he had.

Mary was not a rich woman by any means, but her life inspires us to be generous to others nonetheless. Out of her poverty, Mary gave her life over to God. She invites us to do the same each day.

— Lauren Nelson

WHOSE LIFE can you touch with generosity today?

Prayer: Mary, your "yes" to God came from your heart. Teach me to give generously to others from my heart.

October 6

"I have compassion on the crowd, because they have been with me now three days, and have nothing to eat; and if I send them away hungry to their homes, they will faint on the way; and some of them have come a long way."
— *Mark 8:2-3*

The words of this Scripture passage tell us that Jesus was moved with compassion for his people because they were hungry. He generously took care of their immediate needs by transforming a few loaves of bread and some dried fish into a meal for the multitudes. God is always generous in his love and care for his people.

In her home at Nazareth, young Mary experienced the same generosity of God. When she willingly took on the role God had planned for her life, Mary was responding to God's generosity by choosing to live her life as the handmaid of the Lord. Mary gave herself fully to serving those in need and caring for her family. Mary's life inspires us to be generous in giving our time and loving service to others.

— Sheila Cusack

How can Mary's life help you to be more generous in spirit?

Prayer: Mary, thank you for being an example of sharing God's generous spirit with people I am graced to be with this day.

October 7
Feast of Our Lady of the Rosary

"For you formed my inward parts, / you knitted me together in my mother's womb. / I praise you, for I am wondrously made. / Wonderful are your works!" — Psalms 139:13-14

The feast of Our Lady of the Rosary was first established to honor Mary for the Christian victory in the battle fought at Lepanto October 7, 1571. Pope Pius V, with deep devotion to the Blessed Mother, rallied the faithful to pray the Rosary so that Mary would intercede on their behalf. For over five hundred years Mary's children have sought her help and protection in times of great distress through the gift of the Rosary.

Mary is generous in her desire to help us. Our Lady of the Rosary wants all of us to come closer to her Son, Jesus, so that we may experience his abundant love and generosity of grace on our spiritual journey. We are sons and daughters of the Father, wonderfully made in God's image. Let us not hesitate to bring our heartfelt needs to our heavenly mother, for wonderful are her works.

— Dr. Mary Amore

DO YOU NEED victory in your life? Pray at least one decade of this power prayer today.

Prayer: Mary, help me to honor you with prayer and to turn to you with my heartfelt needs and desires.

October 8

"Truly I tell you, this poor widow has put in more than all of them;
for they all contributed out of their abundance, but she out of her poverty
put in all the living that she had." — Luke 21:3-4

While calling attention to the widow's contribution in this Scripture passage, Jesus could have easily said the same things about his mother. Mary of Nazareth was a young woman of humble birth; yet she was rich in every way that matters. Through a generous act of faith, Mary gave her "yes" to the angel and became the mother of our Savior. She gave herself completely and without reservation.

Mary's humble life inspires us to give generously of ourselves to God. The Lord is not looking for the riches of this world; he seeks our human hearts. Even if we are broken or wounded the Lord desires to be one with us. He wants to give us everything, and to teach us how to do the same.

— Lauren Nelson

WHAT IS GOD ASKING of you today? Are you willing to say "yes" to God?

Prayer: Mary, help me to follow your example and to generously give all that I am over to Jesus by saying "yes" with my life.

October 9

"Give, and it will be given to you." — *Luke 6:38*

Teen participation in my parish youth-ministry program was dwindling. Parish demographics indicated that families with children and teens were becoming scarce. The parishioners were mostly seniors. My role on staff was to solve the issue.

A "Senior Helping Hands Project" became the new component of the teen program. Seniors who needed help to paint a room, clean a garage, move furniture, pack boxes, plant flowerpots, trim bushes, etc., signed up, and the teens provided the helping hands. Youth ministry went from talking about God to active discipleship. The teens gave up their weekend afternoons and recruited friends to help. The seniors loved the interaction with the teens and began funding future teen programs. Talk about generosity!

We often forget that Mary was a teenage girl when she said "yes" to becoming the mother of Jesus. She generously gave of herself with no expectations, and the gifts from God kept coming.

— Sharon A. Abel, PhD

MAKE A LIST of the gifts God has given you. How will you share these gifts with others today?

Prayer: Mary, help me to use wisely the gifts that God has given me in the service of others.

October 10

"For he who is mighty has done great things for me, / and holy is his name."
— *Luke 1:49*

Mary spoke these words of God's praise when she went to visit her cousin Elizabeth. In this exchange between two pregnant women, Mary's beautiful prayer reflects her understanding of God's generosity of grace in her life.

Like Mary, generosity can fill our spirits and move our hearts to be Christ-like in this world. I once witnessed a man step out of his car on a busy Los Angeles freeway to help a female motorist who was stalled in one of the lanes. He put up his hands to stop the traffic while he pushed the woman's car out of the lane and safely over to the shoulder. Another time I saw a woman get out of her car holding a towel. She bent down and scooped up a little turtle that was crossing a busy two-lane highway and safely placed the turtle in the grass on the side of the road. Generosity inspires the best in us.

— Sheila Cusack

RECALL A TIME when you acted generously toward another. How did this make you feel? Who can you be generous to today?

Prayer: Mary, help me to be your Son's hands and feet in this world, that I may give generously to those in need.

October 11

"Under the test of this service, you will glorify God by your obedience in acknowledging the gospel of Christ, and by the generosity of your contribution for them and for all others." — 2 Corinthians 9:13

Ever since I can remember, my mother gave generously of herself, even in the midst of her busy family life. Raising four children and working as a full-time music director, my mom always found time to care for family and friends when they were in need.

When the angel Gabriel announced to Mary that she was to be the mother of Our Lord, he also told her that her older cousin Elizabeth was pregnant. Scripture tells us that upon hearing this, Mary went with haste to visit Elizabeth. In the midst of all the things that Mary was experiencing in her young life, her generosity overflowed in love for her cousin Elizabeth.

— Christine Grano

WHEN WE SAY "YES" to God as Mary did, the Lord fills us with grace and generosity begins to flow. Take stock of your generosity today. Do you need a fill up of grace?

Prayer: Mary, help me to generously give of myself in service to others that I may glorify God through my deeds.

October 12

"Now the company of those who believed were of one heart and soul, and no one said that any of the things which he possessed was his own, but they had everything in common. There was not any one needy among them, for as many as were possessors of lands or houses sold them, and brought the proceeds of what was sold and laid it at the apostles' feet; and distribution was made to each as any had need." — *Acts 4:32,34-35*

This powerful passage from Acts reminds us that in the early Church those who followed the teachings of Jesus were of one heart and soul. They shared everything with one another. Even as the mother of Jesus, Mary would have shared whatever possessions she had with the followers of her Son.

Mary encourages us to be generous in giving. She inspires us to open our hearts and our spirits to the people among us, to share our belongings with those who have nothing, and to share our faith with those who hunger and thirst for God in their lives.

— Lauren Nelson

HOW CAN YOU BE of service to your brothers and sisters in Christ today?

Prayer: Mary, we are all of one heart and soul in your Son. Help me to follow your example of generosity in giving to others.

October 13

"Do not toil to acquire wealth, / be wise enough to desist. / When your eyes light upon it, it is gone; / for suddenly it takes to itself wings."
— Proverbs 23:4-5

The Jewish Book of Proverbs included short, pithy statements about how to conduct life well. They were bits of folk wisdom meant to be memorized. Mary likely knew this proverb by heart. She may have even taught it to Jesus as he worked with Joseph to learn his trade.

For Jews, both hard work and prosperity were considered blessings from God. Accumulating wealth was not the purpose of work, nor was wealth to be horded. Work was part of dignity and self-respect. Prosperity and riches were to be shared with the poor. As a faithful Jewish working family, the Holy Family would have exercised generosity by sharing their earnings through tithing to the Nazareth synagogue. Jesus was taught that through work God would bless him and the less fortunate.

— Sharon A. Abel, PhD

Do I work primarily to accumulate wealth? Is God remembered or forgotten in my choices about money?

Prayer: Mary, you taught your Son, Jesus, that work is a gift from God. Remind me to always bring my prosperity to the needs of the less fortunate.

October 14

"For every one who asks receives, and he who seeks finds, and to him who knocks it will be opened." — *Luke 11:10*

This Scripture reminds us of God's generosity. We simply need to bring our needs and wants to the Lord in faith and he will help us. Although the answer we receive may not be what we anticipated, when we trust in the Lord he always responds in generosity.

Mary turned to God with all of her needs. Surely Mary sought the Lord's help when fleeing to Egypt with baby Jesus, she turned to God when Jesus was lost in the Temple for three days, and most certainly Mary sought the Lord's help as Jesus was crucified. In all of these instances, God's love and grace were generously poured out upon Mary.

Our lives are no different. Each and every day we are faced with circumstances that are out of our control, situations that we cannot fix, and people we cannot change. Mary's life inspires us to bring all of our prayers and concerns to the Lord, for he will generously take care of us.

— Sheila Cusack

IN WHAT MANNER do we voice our questions to our generous God?

Prayer: Mary, walk with me and pray that my heart can be still, that I may hear your Son's answers to my prayers.

October 15

"If any man would come after me, let him deny himself and take up his cross daily and follow me." — Luke 9:23

My life has been touched by the generosity of good people who have given of themselves so that I might come to know and love Jesus and his mother, Mary. Teachers, priests, mentors, and friends have all helped to form me into a disciple of Christ, and have inspired me to pick up my daily cross and to follow Jesus. As members of the body of Christ, each of us is called to be generous with our life in some way — to deny ourselves and follow Jesus.

As a disciple of Jesus, our Blessed Mother heard her Son proclaim this challenge to his followers. No doubt Mary understood what Jesus meant, for she lived her whole life in this manner. From the moment of Mary's fiat to the angel Gabriel, Mary took up her "cross" by generously giving over her life to God.

— Christine Grano

WHAT ARE THE WAYS that the Lord has called you to be generous with your life? In what way can you take up your cross today?

Prayer: Dear Mary, please pray for me, that I might have the willingness to generously deny myself as you did, to bring Jesus into the world.

October 16

"In those days Mary arose and went with haste into the hill country, to a city of Judah, and she entered the house of Zechariah and greeted Elizabeth."
— *Luke 1:39-40*

Mary went in haste to the house of her cousin Elizabeth — a generous response to a need presented by the angel. As a young girl, Mary was able to assist her older relative in her final days of pregnancy. In spite of her own good, yet challenging, news, Mary went to care for her cousin. At the moment of her own need, Mary willingly went to serve the needs of another. Her choice to do so offers us a wonderful example of how to center our lives on others, rather than being self-centered.

Mary's life challenges us to be generous in our actions with others, most especially our family members. How do we show concern for others? How do we generously set ourselves aside to serve someone else?

— Larry Dreffein

CAN YOU RECALL a time when your generosity made a real difference in someone's life? How can you go in haste to serve someone today?

Prayer: Mary, you generously opened yourself to respond to the needs of another while you yourself had questions about where life would lead you. May I be generously open to God's grace in my life and recognize God's mercy as well.

October 17

"You shall remember the LORD your God, for it is he who gives you power to get wealth." — Deuteronomy 8:18

Jewish faith supports the acquisition of wealth, but it comes with a condition. A portion of one's wealth must be shared with the needy and less fortunate. In following this practice, a person's acts of love for the poor also displayed love for God and a recognition of his generosity.

Mary and Joseph would have followed the laws regarding tithing. They would have given ten percent of what they earned to others, not because they had to, but because it was the right thing to do. The needs of the less fortunate were never an afterthought. Every day presented opportunities to share their blessings with others in need. We can choose to follow Mary's example of generosity, not because we have to, but because it is still the right thing to do.

— Sharon A. Abel, PhD

HOW CAN YOU do more to respond to the needs of others? Make a plan. Start today.

Prayer: Mary, give me the grace to shoulder the responsibility to raise up the poor in our world. Because God has been generous to me, I have so much to give. Help me to remember that when I care for and love the needy, I also love Our Lord.

October 18

"He has filled the hungry with good things, / and the rich he has sent away empty. / He has helped his servant Israel, / in remembrance of his mercy."
— *Luke 1:53-54*

While most of us will never know the pains of hunger that come from a lack of sufficient food, the reality of life is that we all hunger for something. Some of us hunger for justice and equality in the workplace; others hunger for peace. Some people hunger for happiness, while others are in search of love and companionship. Whatever we hunger for, Mary assures us that the Lord will remember us with mercy, and will generously fill the hungry with good things.

Mary's Magnificat prayer of praise challenges us to reassess our priorities. Do we seek more wealth and possessions? Are we the rich that will be sent away empty? Or are we content with the blessings God has generously given us?

— Dr. Mary Amore

WHAT DO YOU HUNGER FOR in life? How can you refocus your priorities to seek the things of heaven instead of the things on earth? Seek Mary's help in desiring only those things in life that will lead you closer to the Lord.

Prayer: Mary, you generously gave of yourself to the Lord. Help me to hunger for the good things in life that will lead me to the heart of your Son, Jesus.

October 19

"When the wine failed, the mother of Jesus said to him,
'They have no wine.'" — *John 2:3*

In first-century Palestine, weddings were a weeklong celebration, and guests came from various towns and villages to join the festivities. At the wedding feast at Cana, Jesus and his closest disciples were invited, as was his mother, Mary.

Surely Mary had no idea what Jesus would do when she told him that the wine had run out. Jesus turned water into choice wine, more than the couple could ever have hoped for. He was generous to this newly married couple, just as he is generous to us each day.

As the mother of Jesus, Mary's life invites us to wait for and taste the generosity of the Lord's blessings in our lives. Her role in the wedding feast at Cana reminds us that our blessings cannot run short if we place our needs in the hands of her Son, Jesus.

— Sheila Cusack

TODAY, TAKE NOTICE of the people, places, things, and events that comprise your ordinary everyday existence. Count your blessings (if you can!) and be generous in thanking the Lord.

Prayer: Mary, help me to take time from the busyness of life to be grateful for this day with your Son, Jesus.

October 20

"The Pharisee stood and prayed thus with himself, 'God, I thank you that I am not like the other men, extortioners, unjust, adulterers, or even like this tax collector. I fast twice a week, and I give tithes of all that I get.'"
— *Luke 18:11-12*

The kind of generosity Scripture talks about is a fruit of our redemption, not a means to self-satisfaction. The Pharisee in this passage didn't talk about his generosity from a place of graced humility or as an outflow of the Spirit, but rather from a place of self-importance. We have all known people who give generously simply because they want to appear important to others. They seek affirmation for their good deeds.

Mary's life of humility reminds us that God looks at our hearts. We are called to give generously to others, but from a place of humble service to the Lord.

— Christine Grano

Do a heart check today — where does my generosity flow from? How can I be more generous to others in the name of Jesus?

Prayer: Mary, pray that I allow the Holy Spirit to continue the work of transformation in my life so that my generosity flows freely and from humble gratitude.

October 21

"Each one must do as he has made up his mind, not reluctantly or under compulsion, for God loves a cheerful giver." — *2 Corinthians 9:7*

The cause was just: poor women in our area could not afford treatment for breast cancer.

My friend, known for his generosity, owned a local restaurant where he frequently hosted fundraisers. He had lost a sister to breast cancer, as I had my mother. Together we hosted a breast-cancer fundraiser. Local ads, e-mails to customers, word of mouth, and phone calls got the word out, and donors came by the hundreds. The event was aglow with pink shirts, hats, signs, even a pink menu.

We went to every table and listened to the heart-wrenching stories people needed to share. Tables turned over four times. Funds were raised, cancer stories shared, and everyone gave from the heart. It was an amazing assembly of cheerful givers.

Mary's spirit rejoiced in the Lord not simply because she had found favor, but because she gave everything to God without a second thought. She wasn't looking for a return; she only wanted to please the Lord by giving. The result: Mary was filled with the joy of a cheerful giver.

— Sharon A. Abel, PhD

TODAY, WATCH FOR an opportunity to give spontaneously. Then do it.

Prayer: Mary, help me to give cheerfully and without counting the cost.

October 22

"Honor the LORD with your substance, / and with the first fruits of all your produce; / then your barns will be filled with plenty / and your vats will be bursting with wine." — *Proverbs 3:9-10*

Our family of second-generation Italians struggled for years and depended on the generosity of people, institutions, and the government for assistance. As a result, we sometimes overlooked the gifts God had given us.

Mary teaches us how to remain focused on God's gifts. The chosen mother of our Savior, Mary embraced the overshadowing of the Holy Spirit. Later, she was present when the Holy Spirit descended on the disciples gathered at Pentecost. Mary generously gave of herself all her life; first as the mother of Jesus, and then as a mother to the small community of believers from which our faith grew.

Mary's example has helped me to recognize the generous gifts that God has given me. I no longer look for generosity from other people. Instead, I try to respond to the needs of others out of love and gratitude to Jesus and his mother, Mary.

— Michael Grano

WHAT IS THE MOTIVATION for your generosity? Does it depend on other people, or the gifts of the Holy Spirit?

Prayer: Mary, please ask Jesus to help me to remember and honor his gracious generosity present in my life.

October 23

"One man gives freely, yet grows all the richer; / another withholds what he should give, and only suffers want. / A liberal man will be enriched / and one who waters will himself be watered." — Proverbs 11:24-25

This proverb invites us to reflect upon our own lives. Are we generous with God's gifts to us? Do we freely give to those less fortunate, or do we keep our material wealth to ourselves?

Mary led a simple and impoverished life, but her spiritual riches grew. As the mother of Jesus, Mary shared the most important person in her life with the world. She brought the gifts and blessings of God in her life to everyone she met.

Mary is here to help us grow richer in our spiritual lives, too. She invites us to freely share the gifts that God has given us, knowing that giving will always bring us more and not less.

— Lauren Nelson

IS THERE SOMETHING you have that you are afraid of losing? Who can you generously share that blessing with today?

Prayer: Mary, teach me how to be generous with the gifts that God has given me. Help me to lavishly pour out my love of God upon all those the Lord sends my way.

October 24

*"Now may the L*ORD *show mercy and faithfulness to you! And I will do good to you because you have done this thing." — 2 Samuel 2:6*

My sister is one of the most generous people I know. She gives her time, money, and, most importantly, love freely. She is constantly doing something kind; it comes very naturally to her.

Being generous is not always easy. Sometimes we want to store up and hold onto things, just in case. But that is not what God asks us to do. He wants us to trust him and know that he will be generous with us, because he loves us. Generosity flows from knowing that we are heirs to God's kingdom and are loved by a truly generous God.

Mary's "yes" to God was one of the most generous acts in human history. Through her generosity, God could be even more generous to us and give us the most precious gift of all — salvation in his Son, Jesus.

— Suzette Horyza

TODAY, LOOK FOR SIGNS of God's love for you. Consider giving something you'd rather keep to someone else.

Prayer: Mary, show me how much God loves me. And help me to model my life after yours by being generous in spirit.

October 25

*"He gives power to the faint, / and to him who has no might
he increases strength."* — Isaiah 40:29

The Lord is so generous with his children. I have been amazed by this time and time again. Whenever I am afraid or anxious, if I seek the Lord's help, my fears fall away. I am humbled by the Lord's abundant love and care for us, even in the smallest matters.

Mary intimately knew the Lord's generosity, and she modeled his goodness to all she met. Mary never sought attention for herself; her entire life was devoted to helping others come to know and love her Son, Jesus. Mary is here to help us come to know that the Lord gives abundant strength to the weak, and power to the faint. As our heavenly mother, Mary gently guides us to the pathway that leads to Jesus.

— Dr. Mary Amore

NAME THREE WAYS that the Lord has helped you on your spiritual journey in the past week.

Prayer: Mary, help me to follow your Son, Jesus, that I may grow strong in his knowledge and love.

October 26

"The point is this: he who sows sparingly will also reap sparingly, and he who sows bountifully will also reap bountifully. Each one must do as he has made up his mind, not reluctantly or under compulsion, for God loves a cheerful giver." — *2 Corinthians 9:6-7*

I have a friend who epitomizes a cheerful giver. Every time we meet, she brings me something — fresh veggies from her garden, a warm batch of cookies, a prayer card. She is delighted to give them to me. I know she does the same for many other people as well. Her faith has produced generosity in her, and many people are blessed by her gracious giving.

Mary did not sow sparingly. She gave her entire life to God. When Mary accepted her role in the Incarnation, she was filled with joy. Her generosity in giving herself over to the redeemer of this world was cheerful.

— Christine Grano

ARE YOU A CHEERFUL GIVER? Do you find joy in giving? Take time to think about those people in your life who have blessed you with their generosity, and then give thanks to God and to one of them.

Prayer: Mary, pray for me that the Lord may instill within me a joyful and generous spirit.

October 27

"I have become a stranger to my brethren, / an alien to my mother's sons."
— *Psalms 69:8*

Two small American flags were taped to the armrests of his rusty wheelchair and a medal was pinned to his tattered army jacket. On the ground was a bowl with a sign: "Help Me." He had lost a leg. He was poor, alone, homeless, and asking for help. My fear prevented me from helping the vet. I went home feeling guilty and asked Mary for guidance. Mary calmed my fears and inspired me to do the right thing and help my brother.

The next day, I decided to make "a bag of blessing." The gallon-sized bag contained socks, snacks, a bottle of water, grooming products, and food coupons for free meals. I put a sticker on the front which read, "A Bag of Blessings," and included a Scripture verse. I went back and gave the bag to the vet. He smiled and thanked me for my generosity. Now I always carry "a bag of blessing" in my car.

— Sharon A. Abel, PhD

CONSIDER MAKING UP "a bag of blessings" for your car. Offer it to the next homeless person you meet.

Prayer: Mary, please continue to help me overcome my fears and inspire me to follow your example of generously sharing myself with others.

October 28

"Then he ordered the crowds to sit down on the grass; and taking the five loaves and the two fish he looked up to heaven, and blessed, and broke and gave the loaves to the disciples, and the disciples gave them to the crowds. And they all ate and were satisfied. And they took up twelve baskets full of the broken pieces left over." — Matthew 14:19-20

How often do we think we won't have enough but end up with plenty? Did Mary think she had "enough" to mother the Son of the Most High and to bear the disgrace of a premarital pregnancy? When we take on a new job, or suffer a divorce, or contend with a serious illness, do we feel we have enough to handle it?

But then, someone with a generous heart — a neighbor, a friend, a sister, a colleague, a stranger — offers something. We feel supported, loved, encouraged, and we move forward. Generosity takes many forms, and it always brings with it the gift of courage — inner strength that comes from a caring heart.

— Jane Zimmerman

ARE YOU AFRAID of not having enough of something that you need? In what ways can you show generosity today?

Prayer: Mary, give me the courage to accept the gift of generosity and to give generously, even when what is received or given seems small.

October 29

"And Zacchaeus stood and said to the Lord, 'Behold, Lord, the half of my goods I give to the poor; and if I have defrauded any one of anything, I restore it fourfold.' And Jesus said to him, 'Today salvation has come to this house, since he also is a son of Abraham'" — Luke 19:8-9

The story of Zacchaeus challenges us to examine our lives. Are we honest in our dealings with people, or have we taken advantage of the goodness of others?

Years ago, I cashed a check at our local bank. When I got home, I noticed that the cashier had given me fifty dollars too much. I immediately went back to the bank and returned the excess cash. God's generosity is more than sufficient for us to do the right thing.

Mary's life bears witness to the generosity of God. The abundance of grace that filled Mary's gentle soul allowed her to willingly become the mother of Jesus. Mary invites us to follow in her footsteps and do what is right so that salvation can come to our spiritual houses, too.

— Dr. Mary Amore

IS THERE SOMETHING you can give to make something more just? If you owe something to someone, repay at least some of it today.

Prayer: Mary, help me to give generously and honestly of myself in loving service to others.

October 30

"Pray at all times in the Spirit, with all prayer and supplication. To that end keep alert with all perseverance, making supplication for all the saints."
— *Ephesians 6:18*

Over my life, I have had many people ask me to pray for their needs; likewise, I have asked others to pray for me and my family. What always amazes me are the people who pray for me even when I don't ask.

Recently, I got a text from someone who told me that she had been praying for me. At Christmastime, another person gave me a baby quilt that she crocheted for my soon-to-be grandson and told me that she prayed for him with each stitch.

When we come to Mary with our prayer needs, her generosity overflows as she intercedes for us. She never stops praying for us. As a mother, Mary knows what we need and will pray to her Son on our behalf.

— Christine Grano

REFLECT UPON those individuals in your life who have been generous with their prayers for you. Offer prayers for their needs.

Prayer: Mary, thank you for your generosity in praying for me. Please pray that I, too, will be generous in my prayers for those in need.

October 31

"Blessed be he by the LORD, whose kindness has not forsaken the living or the dead!" — Ruth 2:20

I pulled up to the drive-through window to pay. The cashier handed me my order then waived me on, saying, "Have a great day!" "Wait," I said, "I owe you three dollars and sixty-five cents. Here's four dollars." "No need," she replied, "the gentleman before you paid for your order, too. He told me to tell you to have a great day." I was dumbfounded. A stranger had just paid for my breakfast.

The next morning, I returned to buy a cup of coffee. I told the cashier I wanted to also pay for the order behind me. "Tell them to have a great day," I said. Once again, I drove away thinking, "What a pleasant way to start my day." Passing on the generous blessing I received the previous day to a new recipient was a blessing, too. Generosity can become contagious.

Mary's Jewish faith taught her that God was always present, actively participating in all of life. This meant she needed to be alert, or she might miss some of the generous blessings God showered upon her. The same is true for us.

— Sharon A. Abel, PhD

WHAT GENEROUS BLESSING can you pass on to another person today?

Prayer: Mary, help me to be watchful and look for God's generous blessings each and every day.

~ GRATITUDE ~

November 1
Solemnity of All Saints

"We give thanks to you, Lord God Almighty, who are and who were, / that you have taken your great power and begun to reign." — *Revelation 11:17*

St. John the Apostle, author of the Book of Revelation, gives us this song of praise sung by saints in heaven. John is the beloved disciple who took Mary into his home after the Crucifixion. Perhaps it was Mary's gracious heart that inspired St. John and the other apostles to offer prayers of gratitude for all that Jesus had done for them. Mary used similar images when she proclaimed God's goodness to Elizabeth in her magnificent prayer of praise, the Magnificat.

It is this same prayer of gratitude that the saints sing eternally in heaven. As Queen of Heaven, Mary inspires all of us to proclaim with awe and gratitude God's mighty deeds. Everything is a grace and a blessing.

— Lauren Nelson

DO YOU HAVE a favorite saint? Today, thank God for giving us these models of love and thankful praise. How can your life inspire others to offers prayers of gratitude to God for his wondrous deeds?

Prayer: Queen of All Saints, teach me to be gracious like you. Fill my heart with gratitude that I may offer praise to God every day of my life.

November 2

"O give thanks to the LORD, for he is good; / for his mercy endures for ever!"
— *1 Chronicles 16:34*

How often do we give thanks? Every day, or only on special days, or when we want something? Do we give thanks to God for everything in our lives, good or bad, or do we only give thanks when things are going well?

We need to recognize that everything in life is God's gift. He is the one who created everything. To feel gratitude, we need to start noticing these blessings, big or small, ordinary or extraordinary, and be grateful no matter what else is going on in our lives. And we need to say thank you!

Pope Francis has called Mary the "model of gratitude." She said "yes," with no complaints. She devoted her life to Jesus and expected nothing in return. Her deep love for her Son helps us to realize the Lord's goodness and love for us. Like Mary, we should all take note of what we have been given and the Lord's faithfulness to us. Then, like her, we will be able to live in peace and gratitude.

— Mary L. Kostic

HOW DOES MARY'S LIFE invite you to live as a disciple of gratitude?

Prayer: Mary, help us to write our own prayer of gratitude to Our Lord. Help us to be humble, appreciative, and grateful.

November 3

"And Mary said, / 'My soul magnifies the Lord, / and my spirit rejoices in God my Savior, / for he who is mighty has done great things for me, / and holy is his name." — Luke 1:46-47,49

I imagine this graced encounter with her cousin Elizabeth took Mary by surprise. Yet it affirmed what the angel Gabriel had foretold — her elderly relative was indeed pregnant. Mary's hymn of praise speaks of her humility and gratitude to God for choosing her to bear the Christ.

Mary was able to thank God for her life — just the way it was, with such uncertainty. She was an unmarried pregnant girl, who certainly would have been looked down upon. She could not have known how her life and the life of her child would unfold, yet she proclaimed unshakable faith in, and gratitude to, her God of goodness, justice, and mercy.

Mary's "yes" to God's plan for her life is the best example we have to trust in God's plan for us as well. Her praise and gratitude inspire us to focus on the graces in our lives.

— Gail Krema

PRAYERFULLY CONSIDER all you have to be grateful for in your life, and write your own hymn of praise.

Prayer: Blessed Mother Mary, inspire us always to be grateful to God.

November 4

"Therefore let us be grateful for receiving a kingdom that cannot be shaken, and thus let us offer to God acceptable worship, with reverence and awe."
— *Hebrews 12:28*

Mary's faith in God never wavered. She trusted in a God whose love and care could get her through anything. Her faith got her through the unknown, wondering what it would be like to bear and raise this Son of God. This same faith nurtured her relationship with her husband, Joseph, and guided her through the everyday tasks of caring for her family.

Her days might have appeared to be ordinary, yet she knew better: Mary maintained a heart filled with gratitude and awe. She knew with certainty that God was there throughout her life, in her love for others; in the trial, torture, and crucifixion of her beloved Son; and most especially in his resurrection. Mary's unshakable faith invites us to live with awe and gratitude to our loving God.

— Gail Krema

HAS THERE BEEN A TIME in my life when I questioned my faith? How did God show me that he was right there to provide for me? Write a note to God expressing your feelings.

Prayer: Mary, at times we are unaware that God is right there with us in our pain. Help me to acknowledge his continued presence with reverence and awe.

November 5

"Rejoice always, pray constantly, give thanks in all circumstances; for this is the will of God in Christ Jesus for you." — 1 Thessalonians 5:16-18

Paul reminds us that we are called to be prayerful people. In all we experience, we are invited to express gratitude to the Lord. In challenging times, prayer helps us embrace the moment and move through it with grace. When the issues resolve, gather what you have learned from the experience and offer thanks to God for helping you grow stronger from it. Focus on the blessings received, not on what may be missing in your life. We are covered in God's goodness, so it is only right and just that we honor and call those moments to mind in praise and thanksgiving.

Mary's life was no different. Mary faced difficult moments, yet she remained thankful to God. In Luke, Mary sings her gratitude to God, and his love and protection remained with her throughout her life. In return, she stayed faithful, full of gratitude for his tenderness.

— Nanci Lukasik–Smith

WHAT SONGS OF GRATITUDE can stem from your heart today?

Prayer: Holy Mother, when I am facing difficult moments, remind me of God's faithfulness. Keep my eyes focused, so that I will not become distracted from his love.

November 6

*"Enter his gates with thanksgiving, / and his courts with praise! /
Give thanks to him, bless his name!"* — Psalms 100:4

Mary is our example of living in the glory of God. She is a model of grace and gratitude. Mary was graced from the moment of her conception, and she blessed the holy name of God every day of her life by her words and actions. Mary shared this grace with her Son, Jesus.

Mary's life of grace and gratitude invites us to be hospitable to strangers. Mary shared her gift of hospitality with her cousin Elizabeth and with the wedding couple at Cana. Mary gave of herself to others in grateful response to God for the abundant blessings she received from him. Today, seek the help of Mary as you cultivate a spirit of gratitude for the abundant blessings in your life.

— Sheila Cusack

How CAN YOU MAKE your home a dwelling place for gratitude and grace, a place where hospitality welcomes all who enter?

Prayer: Mary, help me to express my gratitude to God by sharing my life and my home with those God sends my way.

November 7

"For he who is mighty has done great things for me, / and holy is his name."
— *Luke 1:49*

It's interesting to note that the words "gratitude" and "grace" stem from the same Latin root. Gabriel greeted Mary as "full of grace," and she broke forth into her great prayer of thanksgiving, the Magnificat, upon seeing her cousin Elizabeth.

Our tradition teaches that all we have comes as a free gift from God. Even the good we do is a response to God's grace in us, to God's initiative. In 1 John 4:19 we hear, "We love, because he first loved us."

On occasion, I am tempted to take credit for my good deeds, kindness, or displays of virtue. I want others to think well of me. However, the appropriate response is gratitude and praise, thanking God for his free gifts, even in helping me carry out his will.

Mary exemplified this attitude throughout her life. Even when Mary plays a central role, her demeanor is always humble. Mary recognizes that God has done great things for her.

— Bob Frazee

LET US IDENTIFY and praise God for the great things he has done for us and be conscious of what God continues to do.

Prayer: My spirit rejoices in God my savior.

November 8

"Give thanks in all circumstances; for this is the will of God
in Christ Jesus for you." — 1 Thessalonians 5:18

In light of this Scripture passage, we have to ask ourselves, Was there anything Mary could have been grateful for as she stood at the foot of the cross? No one knows what she was experiencing at that tragic moment, but perhaps she whispered a prayer of gratitude to God from the depths of her broken heart for the gift of being the mother of Jesus. Surely she was grateful that John would now take care of her.

Mary reminds us to be grateful to God is all circumstances, even in the midst of darkness and tragedy. We are called to model Mary's life of faith and offer prayers of gratitude for every moment of every day, for all of life is a gift from God.

— Lauren Nelson

WHAT PROBLEMS are you experiencing now? Imagine that Mary is standing next to you. What is she urging you to be grateful for in this moment?

Prayer: Mary, I know God wants us to be grateful even in the midst of our difficulties. Stand with me when I am hurting and take me into your gracious heart, that I may be grateful for all of life.

November 9

"I thank my God always when I remember you in my prayers."
— *Philemon 1:4*

I often receive prayer requests. It is a challenge to balance the needs of others with our own spiritual needs, yet remembering others promotes devout stability. To pray for others reminds us that we are all part of the Body of Christ.

A friend was diagnosed with cancer, which had spread throughout her body. During this time, she would say, "I just don't have the energy to pray for myself." I encouraged her to take time to sit with God and be silent, to hear his whisper. In the meantime, I shared her story with a group of prayerful friends and together we took on the role of praying for her.

Often, we call upon Mary for her prayerful assistance. Those moments when we cannot pray for ourselves, we ask her to lift us to the Father. She guides, leads, and raises us to him.

— Nanci Lukasik-Smith

WHO CAN YOU PRAY FOR today? Who can you ask to pray for you?

Prayer: Mary, prayerful mother, we ask for your holy guidance in lifting our loved ones in prayer. Thank you for being our advocate in times of personal struggle and lift us toward the heavens so we can serve others on earth.

November 10

"Let the word of Christ dwell in you richly, as you teach and admonish one another in all wisdom, and as you sing psalms and hymns and spiritual songs with thankfulness in your hearts to God." — *Colossians 3:16*

We often take our blessings for granted, such as our loved ones, prosperity, health, and safety. How different our world might be if we honored one another with gratitude for our qualities, uniqueness, gifts, talents, and perspectives. This would truly build self-esteem and could even eliminate contemptuous language and bullying.

Imagine Our Lady delighting in the gift of her Son, particularly when she found him in the Temple preaching to the elders. Was she in awe of his wisdom? I imagine Mary teaching and admonishing Jesus with love and tenderness while singing praises of God's love in her heart.

— Dr. Barb Jarvis Pauls

How CAN I BETTER appreciate the blessings in my life? How can I admonish those around me to be grateful for their blessedness? How do I express my gratitude?

Prayer: Blessed Mary, Holy Mother of God, pray for me to acknowledge my gratitude for the presence of Christ in my life and the lives of others.

November 11

"Give thanks worthily to the Lord, / and praise the King of the ages, / that his tent may be raised for you again with joy." — Tobit 13:10

Two nine-by-twelve-inch pans filled with casseroles usually did the trick. When I was a child, feeding a large family meant planning for a banquet every night, and leftovers were rare. When they did appear on the table, it left my siblings confused. On one rare leftover night, as we prepared to say grace, a younger sibling asked, "Wait, didn't we thank God for this last night?"

Mary cooked for her family, and I imagine she, too, rarely had leftovers. Yet I'm sure she prayed with gratitude every night, even if the bread was stale and the portions meager. Mary saw everything as a gift from God

Mary's gratitude to God produced joy in her life. When gratitude is lacking in us, joyfulness gives way to listless boredom. Mary shows us that the path to joy is gratitude. The more grateful we are to God the more joy will dwell in our soul.

— Joseph Abel, PhD

BE WATCHFUL and attentive to God's blessings throughout this day. As you notice them, thank God … twice!

Prayer: O Mary, we pray with you. Help us to be grateful for all of God's grace and blessings.

November 12

*"I will give thanks to the LORD with my whole heart; / I will tell of
all your wonderful deeds." — Psalms 9:1*

The poignant words of the psalmist offer us a portrait of the life of the Blessed Mother. No matter what difficulties Mary experienced, her heart remained grateful to the Lord. As a young girl, when she was asked to be the mother of Jesus, her heart echoed a song of praise and gratitude in spite of her life being in jeopardy. Mary was able to see past the fear of the situation by offering thanksgiving to God for the blessings of being chosen.

Mary has much to teach us about the virtue of gratitude, for it should not just be about our blessing, but also about our challenges in life. We should seek to see God's hand in all situations, even those that might seem frightening at first.

— Lauren Nelson

CONSIDER YOUR OWN LIFE. How can you proclaim your gratitude to God for his wondrous deeds? Is there a particular situation in your life that seems fearful? How can you see the good within it?

Prayer: Mary, your gracious heart proclaimed God's greatness to the world. Help me to proclaim to all the good deeds that God has done for me.

November 13

"For everything created by God is good, and nothing is to be rejected if it is received with thanksgiving." — *1 Timothy 4:4*

Mary surely taught Jesus that God created the world, and that it was good. The mother of Jesus lived with a grateful heart, dwelling on the goodness of the world. She never criticized those who opposed Jesus even to the point of crucifixion. Our Blessed Mother received everything with heartfelt gratitude, and she instilled in Jesus that same grateful appreciation for the world and all its glory.

Like Mary, my own mother instilled in me the importance of looking for and acknowledging the good in others. She taught me that whenever I think anything good about a person I should tell them, as we all need to hear of our own goodness. We all need affirmation.

We can look to the Blessed Mother as an example of how to notice goodness in our lives and in others, and to always be thankful. Mary modeled acceptance of others. She did not reject anyone or any situation because she trusted in the goodness of God.

— Gail Krema

TODAY, TRY PUTTING ON the lens of gratitude; choose to see the good in those you encounter, and offer words of affirmation.

Prayer: Mary, help us to focus on the goodness of God's creation and always to be grateful.

November 14

"And let the peace of Christ rule in your hearts, to which indeed you were called in the one body. And be thankful." — Colossians 3:15

Paul tells us to allow Christ's peace into our hearts while we work and live with others. Living as one in the Body of Christ, we are called to live in harmony with others.

Mary lived a deep level of gratitude to God, and she understood peace, even when she carried pain in her heart. Warned by Simeon that "a sword will pierce through your own soul" (Lk 2:35), she continued to allow God's love to rule her actions. Like Mary, we seek the peace of Christ to rule our hearts and minds as we express gratitude for our role as faithful followers.

— Nanci Lukasik-Smith

LET US SEEK Mary's help in restoring peace to our heart, that we may live in a spirit of gratitude for all of God's blessings.

Prayer: Mary, bring your Son's peace into our hearts and minds, focus our attention on gratitude that we have been grafted to the vine of God, and help us to retain inner peace as we continue our service on earth.

November 15

"Every good endowment and every perfect gift is from above."
— James 1:17

Meister Eckhart, a Dominican theologian and mystic in medieval Germany, said that if the only prayer we ever say is "thank you" it will be enough. In gratitude one has the sense of receiving a gift beyond what was earned. How much of what we receive do we actually earn or deserve? The abundance of the earth, family, friends, work, and God's grace are not the result of my doing or being. They are there often without my asking.

To say "thank you" is to acknowledge that I have been blessed. It recognizes, as Mary did, that the Almighty has done great things for me. What relationship do I have with God? With Mary? With other people? Those I know, and those I don't? With the earth and its fruits? With the cosmos?

— Jane Zimmerman

SEEK MARY'S HELP in seeing all of life as something the Almighty has done for you. Spend some time reflecting on the blessings in your life, both large and small.

Prayer: Mary, please open my eyes to the myriad gifts I receive every day, without my having earned them.

November 16

"Therefore let us be grateful for receiving a kingdom that cannot be shaken."
— *Hebrews 12:28*

There's a story of an Irish mineworker during the great potato famine who ate his lunch alone every day. Stealing away from his co-workers, he would make the Sign of the Cross, say a prayer, and then open his lunchbox. The other workers wondered why he was hiding his lunch. They assumed he had some delicious morsels and didn't want to share. Finally, someone grabbed and opened his lunchbox to find that it was filled with potato peels. While his children were given the potatoes for their lunches, he took the peels.

Blessings come from God in many ways. For this Irish father, the ability to feed his children was a blessing. Mary, too, saw her life as rich in blessings not of this world. She exhibited gratitude by giving to those who could not give in return — a very important lesson for all of us to learn.

— Joseph Abel, PhD

MAKE A SINCERE ACT of gratitude this day. Identify someone you can lift up who is unable to repay you. Act on their behalf.

Prayer: O Mary, you showed us that the path of gratitude lies in service to others. May we exercise true gratitude to God by lifting others up.

November 17

"Let the word of Christ dwell in you richly, as you teach and admonish one another in all wisdom, and as you sing psalms and hymns and spiritual songs with thankfulness in your hearts to God." — Colossians 3:16

Mary understood the blessings she received in life. From the moment of her fiat to the angel Gabriel to the moment she became our spiritual mother at the foot of the cross, Mary accepted all of life with a grateful heart and praise of God.

Each day we are given opportunities to experience the grace of God in the people we encounter. Yet, often we relate to others harshly and without thought. We admonish without grace and fail to be grateful for the blessings we have in life. Mary inspires us to reach out to people with kindness and respect. Her motherly presence can help us accomplish all of our tasks with a heart filled with gratitude, for all of life is a gift.

— Sheila Cusack

HOW CAN MARY'S EXAMPLE help you to remain in a state of gratitude?

Prayer: Mary, pray for me that I may live with gratitude in my heart as you did in your home at Nazareth. Help me to be grateful for people in my life who bring God's grace.

November 18

"Every good endowment and every perfect gift is from above, coming down from the Father of lights with whom there is no variation or shadow due to change." — James 1:17

The world's abundance is too large for me to grasp. Here in North America, our churches are large, our infrastructures speak volumes of our wealth, mega-grocery stores and department stores provide more goods than we need. If I have more, shouldn't I be more grateful?

I frequently look to Mary, Virgin Most Prudent, to put this all in perspective. Through her, we have been given Jesus, the perfect gift, and this gift invites our eternal gratitude. This handmaid of the Lord inspires us to be grateful for every good and perfect gift in our lives, most especially our families, and for the life of faith that the Lord has given us.

— Alice Smith

Do you say "thank you" often? Have you experienced a variation or a shadow that makes you doubt the Lord's perfection?

Prayer: Mary, my heart is filled with gratitude when I look at the abundance that surrounds me. Help me to thank Jesus each day for every good gift in my life.

November 19

"Let the word of Christ dwell in you richly, as you teach and admonish one another in all wisdom, and as you sing psalms and hymns and spiritual songs with thankfulness in your hearts to God." — Colossians 3:16

If we allow the word of Christ to take hold in us, we can truly live with gratitude to God. If his word and teachings abide in our minds and hearts, our natural response will resemble the old, familiar hymn "How Can I Keep from Singing?"

Mary's life was one long, continuous hymn of praise and gratitude to God. From the moment of her encounter with the angel Gabriel, Mary's soul resonated with a song of thanksgiving to the Lord for his marvelous works. In her home at Nazareth, Mary surely taught Jesus hymns of praise and thanksgiving to the Lord.

Whether we are praising God with song, saying "thank you" to the grocery clerk, or waving to the driver who lets us merge on the busy highway, Mary encourages us to make our lives sing with hymns of praise and gratitude.

— Gail Krema

WHAT HYMN OF GRATITUDE comes to your mind? Let the lyrics wash over you and continue to speak to your heart throughout this day.

Prayer: Mother Mary, help us always to have a grateful heart and to express our gratitude to God and to those in our lives.

November 20

"Give thanks to [God], bless his name." — *Psalms 100:4*

The painting often referred to as the "Madonna of the Streets" by Roberto Ferruzzi (1853-1934) reminds me of a conversation I had with a homeless person I once met while working in a hospital. I was asked if I had children. Did I live in a house? Have furniture? A kitchen? Are there cabinets?

With each question I felt as if I was an onion, its many layers being peeled away. I was uncomfortable, and this brought me to an awareness of my surroundings. Had I taken for granted the things that God had given me? A healthy family, a warm home, a place to lay my head at night, a sense of safety. These were all wonderful gifts. How humbled I felt. I was looking at things with new eyes.

Mary lived a humble life in Nazareth, and she was aware of countless blessings from God. Her life inspires us never to take anything for granted, for all is a gift from above.

— Eugenia Callison

LOOK AROUND. What can you see with new eyes? When was the last time you actually felt grateful for the essential elements of life?

Prayer: Dear Madonna of the Streets, grant us an awareness of all the goodness that God has set before us.

November 21

*"Every good endowment and every perfect gift is from above,
coming down from the Father of lights with whom there is
no variation or shadow due to change." — James 1:17*

Mary is our mother and intercessor. When we are in need of help, Mary invites us to present our prayer requests to her, as heartfelt gifts, and she will bring them to her Son. Mary wants to help us because she desires her children to be close to her Son, Jesus.

Mary is our own perfect gift from Jesus, and we should be grateful for her presence in our lives. Jesus gave us the gift of his mother at the moment of his death so that we might have a heavenly mother to care for our hurts and comfort us on our spiritual journey as only a mother can. With grateful hearts let us turn to Mary with our needs and petitions, trusting that she will bring our prayer requests to her Son.

— Lauren Nelson

DIRECT YOUR THOUGHTS this day to being grateful to God for the many gifts you have been given. Seek Mary's help in bringing your intentions before the throne of our Lord Jesus Christ.

Prayer: Mary, thank you for being our heavenly mother and for bringing our needs to your Son. You are a precious gift from him to us.

November 22

"We know that in everything God works for good with those who love him, who are called according to his purpose." — Romans 8:28

If all situations flowed as described above, we would have many blissful and grateful moments in our lives. Unfortunately, things don't always go so smoothly. When we fail to work together, we lose the opportunity for personal growth and development in Christian love. That's why God likes to throw us out of our comfort zones, so that we might work together for good.

Mary certainly participated in working together for God's purpose. She willingly and gratefully embraced motherhood under unique circumstances. Her modest acceptance shows us the example to follow when we are participating in a holy life. Following Mary's example of working with others opens our lives to be filled with grace, even down to the tiniest details.

— Nanci Lukasik-Smith

DO YOU FIND IT GRATIFYING to work with others for a common goal? Can you thank God even when you find it difficult to work with certain people?

Prayer: Mary, when I'm working with others, gently remind me that my love for God should be at the forefront. Guide my words and actions that they may be gentle, offering gratitude to all.

November 23

"And they sang responsively, praising and giving thanks to the LORD / 'For he is good, / for his mercy endures for ever toward Israel.' / And all the people shouted with a great shout, when they praised the LORD, because the foundation of the house of the LORD was laid." — *Ezra 3:11*

Jesus, the fruit of Mary's womb, came forth as the new foundation for the house of the Lord. For nine months, Mary protected and cared for this baby in her womb. When Mary visited her cousin Elizabeth, who was also with child, Elizabeth responded with thanksgiving to God that the mother of her Lord should visit her.

As Christians, our hearts should be filled with songs of praise and thanksgiving to the Lord each day for the marvelous gift of Jesus and Mary in our lives. Without Mary's role in salvation, there would be no foundation for the Lord's house. Let us turn to Mary with grateful hearts, praising her willingness to dedicate her life to the Lord.

— Lauren Nelson

WHAT ARE YOU MOST GRATEFUL FOR? What aspects of your faith life cause your heart to sing with joy? Spend some time in prayer today thanking the Lord for his goodness.

Prayer: Mary, help us to build our faith, that we may live each day with a grateful heart, praising the Lord for his wondrous deeds.

November 24

"Behold, I will rain bread from heaven for you; and the people shall go out and gather a day's portion every day." — Exodus 16:4

The Lord takes care of his people. In gratitude, Mary lovingly baked and shared bread with Jesus and Joseph. The bread would have been blessed and shared by Mary's family in the opening Sabbath evening prayers, which speak of gratitude to God for the covenant.

Mary invites us to partake in her Bread of Gratitude recipe:

Ingredients

- 6 days of creation and work; 1 day of rest
- creation of humanity, male and female, in the likeness of God
- the covenant with Abraham
- passing over from slavery to freedom
- the promised land gained, lost, and to be restored
- the Temple in Jerusalem and its hope
- a legacy of faith in the mighty deeds of God
- a child born in a stable

— Joseph Abel, PhD

LET US BRING Mary's bread to our table of thanksgiving. What ingredients would you add to your bread of gratitude?

Prayer: Mary, in your home you led the weekly Sabbath prayers of gratitude. May we follow your example and live with prayerful gratitude.

November 25

"O give thanks to the LORD, call on his name, / make known his deeds among the peoples! — 1 Chronicles 16:8

When our children were smaller, they attended the local Catholic school. This parish community was unique, as many of the families had transferred from other parts of the country. It was a melting pot coming together in our faith community.

After the morning drop-off, instead of darting off to get daily chores completed, many parents gathered to pray and share in fellowship. During this time, bonds were formed and friendships made, with God at the center of the gathering. We recognized his wondrous deeds among the families, which he brought together in support and friendship.

When Mary visited Elizabeth, we read of her initial expression of gratitude to God for her mission of motherhood. The coming together of parents from the school and parish mirrored the familial bond shared by Mary and Elizabeth.

— Nanci Lukasik-Smith

IN YOUR DAILY MEETINGS, how can you invite God into your activities and make known his splendid deeds to others?

Prayer: Mary, as I work through my day, please remind me to call upon God in gratitude for those he brings into my life. Let the warmth of the Father's love shine through me. Help me to be grateful for friendships, and let others see your goodness through my actions.

November 26

"Now there are varieties of gifts, but the same Spirit."
— 1 Corinthians 12:4

Mary grew up celebrating her faith in God. In the face of the mysteries of life she couldn't understand, she remained grateful for the gifts God had given her. As a young mother and wife, Mary reflected patience and wisdom as she lovingly raised her Son.

After Jesus took on his public ministry, Mary needed the divine gifts of compassion and trust in God as she witnessed her Son brutally murdered. Mary never wavered in her gratitude to God. She persevered in loving and trusting the Lord every day of her life, in spite of difficulties and trials.

Mary's life has much to teach us about living with gratitude. Every situation, every person, and every event is an opportunity for us to use the gifts God has given us to offer praise and gratitude to him.

— Sheila Cusack

OFFER A PRAYER of thanksgiving to Mary today for her inspiration and guidance in your life

Prayer: Mary, thank you for helping me to live my life with a heart filled with gratitude.

November 27

*"I will give thanks to the LORD with all my heart; / I will tell
of all your wonderful deeds."* — Psalms 9:1

Jewish traditions and teachings are built on a profound sense of gratitude. Mary's childhood home would have grounded her and prepared her for the Jewish practices of giving thanks throughout the day for all the blessings God bestowed upon her.

In addition to morning and evening prayers, Mary's household would have offered prayers of gratitude to God throughout the day. Ingredients for bread, fresh well water, a visiting neighbor all became opportunities to pause for a moment to offer God gratitude for such blessings.

This Jewish notion of gratitude was built on remembering what God was actively doing in her present moment of life. Watching for God's daily intervention and giving thanks was Mary's religious lifestyle, not an isolated ritual. Mary's gratitude, when merged with her deliberate watchfulness, resulted in thanking God for every blessing he sent her way. Let us follow the way of Mary and practice gratefulness for every moment of our ordinary day.

— Sharon A. Abel, PhD

WHAT DO YOU TRULY VALUE in your life? What would make it easier for you to acknowledge God's daily blessings in your life?

Prayer: Mary, grace me with your understanding of gratitude. Help me to be vigilant so that I may recognize God's daily blessings.

November 28

"Have no anxiety about anything, but in everything by prayer and supplication with thanksgiving let your requests be made known to God."
— *Philippians 4:6*

Imagine a life without anxiety, free of fears and worries. Doesn't that sound wonderful? St. Paul tells us that we do not need to live with anxiety; the way out is prayer. I tend to worry, yet I know in my heart that God wants me to hand my concerns over to him, trusting that all will work out. Of course, when I'm able to do this, I feel immense gratitude that "God has this."

Mary is our model for turning things over to God in prayer, with a grateful heart, trusting that all will be well. She knew great anxiety in her life, yet she was able to trust in the Lord completely. In turn, she always exhibited a calm, loving peacefulness to all. Her entire life was a prayer of gratitude to God. Mary wants this for all of us. Jesus also urges us not to worry or be anxious, but to trust in the heavenly Father — such a gift.

— Gail Krema

WHERE IN YOUR LIFE are you experiencing anxiety? Prayerfully hand this over to the Lord with thanksgiving, asking for what you need.

Prayer: Mary, help me to pray always, handing my anxieties over to God, and to be thankful.

November 29

"I thank you that you have answered me / and have become my salva-tion. / The stone which the builders rejected / has become the cornerstone. / This is the LORD'S doing; / it is marvelous in our eyes. / This is the day the LORD has made; / let us rejoice and be glad in it." — *Psalms 118:21-24*

As a young girl growing up in a patriarchal society, Mary had no voice. Metaphorically, she likely would have been considered a stone the builders rejected. Yet, the Lord raised her up to be the mother of Jesus. Mary's life would become the firm foundation for the chief cornerstone of salvation. With heartfelt gratitude, Mary dedicated her entire life in thankful service to the Lord.

God has a plan for each of us; like Mary, every day we can cooperate with God's plan of salvation. Our good works on earth and the blessings that come to us each day are gifts from God, and our hearts should rejoice with gratitude.

— Lauren Nelson

SELECT ONE PERSON in your life that you are grateful for. Prayerfully give them to the Lord this day, thanking God for their presence in your life.

Prayer: Mary, help me to follow your example by giving thanks to God for all he has done for me. Help me to see the ways that the Lord is working in my life.

November 30

"In every way and everywhere we accept this with all gratitude." — *Acts 24:3*

A heart of gratitude does not have space for protests or complaints. There's a popular expression: "have an attitude of gratitude." But what does this attitude represent? For some, it is merely to be grateful for the good things that happen in their lives. For others, it is to be grateful for everything, both the good and bad.

Mary knew how to be grateful for the good as well as the bad. Mary knew her Son's special place in the world and was grateful for every facet. The joys of raising Jesus, the challenges of watching his ministry, and the sufferings of his death were all vital parts of our redemption. She was aware that suffering would be in their future. In grace and gratitude, Mary accepted the course intended for her life, and modeled this attitude for others.

— Nanci Lukasik-Smith

AM I GRATEFUL for all of life, or only for the good and happy things?

Prayer: Holy Mother, open my eyes to see that the joys and trials placed before me only bring me closer to our heavenly Father. Let me share in the sufferings of Christ with a thankful heart, always placing myself in his presence.

~ PATIENCE ~

December 1

"Restore us again, O God of our salvation, / and put away your indignation toward us. / Show us your merciful love, O Lord, / and grant us your salvation." — *Psalms 85:4,7*

We can only hear God if we tune into his channel of communication: silent prayer. Moving away from the tinsel activity of our lives and placing ourselves in prayerful silence allows us to get in touch with God's presence within us. This silence restores our weary spirit in grace and love. Cultivating the discipline of silent prayer does not happen overnight, it takes patience and perseverance on our part.

As a young woman in Nazareth, Mary prayed to the God of Abraham, Isaac, and Jacob every day. She walked with the Lord, and when the angel Gabriel came to her, she was open to doing God's will. Mary is here to help us develop a healthy prayer life. Seek her assistance each day and she will show you the pathway to her Son.

— Dr. Mary Amore

TODAY I INVITE YOU to turn off your television, pour a cup of hot tea, and just sit at the kitchen table in prayerful silence. Seek the Lord's presence; he's been patiently waiting for you.

Prayer: Mother Mary, take me by the hand and lead me to your Son, Jesus, that he may show me the way to salvation.

December 2

"They have no wine. Do whatever he tells you." — John 2:3,5

Have you ever hosted a party and realized you don't have enough food or drink? Your house is full of people and you begin to panic. How can you fix this situation — before the guests find out?

This is exactly what happened at the wedding in Cana. Mary noticed the problem and went to Jesus. She simply noted what was wrong and left it for him to solve, trusting that Jesus would handle the situation. She urged the servants to trust him the same way. She knew her Son's time had come to begin his public ministry.

Mary has much to teach us about waiting. She waited thirty years for Jesus to begin his ministry, prayerfully preparing herself and Jesus for this moment. Mary knew the heart of Jesus, and she trusted him not only to address the wine shortage but to bring about the long-awaited kingdom of God.

— Nanci Lukasik-Smith

DO YOU HAVE a holy longing in your heart? Seek Mary's help that she may lead you to her Son.

Prayer: Holy Mother, during the busyness of this Advent season, please help me to be patient with others and with myself. Help me to slow down so that I may not forget the importance of this season.

December 3

"Be patient, therefore, brethren, until the coming of the Lord. Behold, the farmer waits for the precious fruit of the earth, being patient over it until it receives the early and the late rain. You also be patient. Establish your hearts, for the coming of the Lord is at hand." — James 5:7-8

St. James addresses a community of believers that is waiting for the coming of the Lord. He urges them to make their hearts firm: to be steadfast and to persevere in their faith.

Mary's life is a beautiful example of perseverance and steadfast faith. From the moment of the Annunciation to the end of her Son's life, Mary endured countless difficulties, but she persevered in her faith in the Lord. Mary invites us to take it one day at a time. As our heavenly mother, she desires that we remain firm in our faith, for the coming of the Christ Child is near.

— John Holmes

Do you struggle with being patient? Seek the help of our Blessed Mother this Advent as you wait with steadfast faith for the coming of the Lord.

Prayer: Mary, help us to cultivate patience in our spiritual life that we may persevere in steadfast faith in your Son, Jesus.

December 4

"More than that, we rejoice in our sufferings, knowing that suffering produces endurance, and endurance produces character, and character produces hope."
— Romans 5:3-4

Perhaps one of the most popular Marian devotions today is the novena to Our Lady Undoer of Knots. This novena seeks Mary's help untying the knots in our lives. The image associated with this devotion shows Mary patiently undoing knots in the ribbons of our lives.

Undoing knots is not easy. It takes patience and perseverance. Just undoing a twisted shoelace, straightening a headphone cord, or untying a knotted chain frustrates me. Yet Mary waits patiently for us to turn to her so that she can unravel the knots in our lives and straighten our pathway toward Jesus.

— Lauren Nelson

WHAT KNOTS can Mary undo for you? In what ways can Mary's life inspire you to live with patience, waiting for the Lord to act?

Prayer: Mary, you are always undoing the tangles I bring to you. Be gentle and help me to find the patience I need to let you undo my knots — and to help others undo theirs.

December 5

"But Mary kept all these things, pondering them in her heart."
— *Luke 2:19*

Advent is my favorite time of year because it forces me to wait patiently. Candidly, patience is not a strong suit of mine. In many areas of my life, I struggle to wait — like answered prayers, people, challenging processes, problems.

We cannot think of Advent or Christmas without reflecting on Mary. How did she do it? Mary pondered things in her heart. During Advent, like our Blessed Mother, I try to pause, go inward, and center myself on Christ.

This takes time. It means getting out of autopilot mode and focusing on the Christ Child in my life. When I take this time, I inevitably become more patient. Yet it is work — at first. Taking five minutes out of a busy morning is not easy, but it's worth it. I become more patient with my children, my students, my parents, my friends, and even perfect strangers taking their time at the checkout line or on the highway.

— Meg Bucaro

HOW CAN YOU IMITATE Mary's patient approach as we continue through Advent? Pray for her to help you center yourself on Christ.

Prayer: Mary, help me to follow your example of quietly centering myself on God as I wait for the coming of the Christ Child in my life.

December 6

"I came not to call the righteous, but sinners." — Matthew 9:13

According to a traditional Hebrew story, Abraham welcomed an older man traveling alone. Abraham washed the old man's feet and offered a meal. The old man began eating without saying any blessing. Abraham asked him, "Don't you worship God?" The traveler replied that he had no need of a god. Incensed, Abraham threw the old man out into the cold night.

Later that night, God called to Abraham and asked where the stranger was. Abraham explained that he had forced him out because of his lack of worship to God. God answered: "I have suffered him these eighty years although he dishonors me. Could you not endure him one night?"

Because of her life situation, Mary knew how quick the faithful servants of God can be to judge and punish. She also knew something else: God is not simply patient with people like the old traveler, he comes to seek them out.

— Joseph Abel, PhD

TURN TO MARY for help in finding the patience to minister to your friends, family, and the people God sends your way. Gently call to mind any resentments you hold. Forgive, and ask God for the grace to patiently endure.

Prayer: O Mary, may our patience show forth as we see God patiently seeking the lost.

December 7

"Be patient, therefore, brethren, until the coming of the Lord. Behold, the farmer waits for the precious fruit of the earth, being patient over it until it receives the early and the late rain." — James 5:7

Patience is a difficult virtue to cultivate, especially in today's society, saturated with technology and the instant gratification it produces. We do not have to wait for information; knowledge on any subject is instantly available at our fingertips. In a way, the Internet has almost eliminated the need for patience.

Mary's life beautifully demonstrates why patience is a necessary virtue on our spiritual journey. From the moment of Jesus' conception in her womb, Mary waited. She waited patiently for nine months for Jesus to be born. Her ability to wait on God was tied to her deep faith. Mary believed that the Lord was directing her life.

Today, instead of pushing through our agendas, let us model our lives after Mary.

— Lauren Nelson

DO YOU STRUGGLE with patience? What situation can you turn over to the Lord and wait for a response?

Prayer: Mary, help me to put aside my desire for instant gratification and wait patiently for the Lord to act in my life.

December 8
Solemnity of the Immaculate Conception

"Mary said, 'Behold, I am the handmaid of the Lord; let it be to me according to your word.' And the angel departed from her." — Luke 1:38

From the moment of her creation in the womb of her mother, St. Anne, Mary had no sin. Her immaculate soul was perfectly open to receive the Holy Spirit. Growing up, Mary lived the simple, ordinary life of a young Jewish girl, waiting patiently for the fulfillment of God's promise to humanity.

When the angel Gabriel visited Mary and asked her to be the mother of Jesus, Mary didn't try to rationalize the situation, nor did she question God's plan; rather, she surrendered her will to the Lord. In doing so, she participated in the fulfillment of God's long-awaited promise of salvation.

When we experience things in our lives that are upsetting and unplanned, instead of trying to make sense out of chaos, Mary invites us to join with her in patiently praying to let be done according to God's word.

— Dr. Mary Amore

CONSIDER YOUR OWN LIFE. Call to mind a situation or event that you can prayerfully surrender to the Lord.

Prayer: Mary, help me to be patient, that I may joyfully wait for the will of God to unfold in my life.

December 9

"Blessed is she who believed that there would be a fulfillment of what was spoken to her by the Lord." — Luke 1:45

One season, our college cross-country coach gave us a new strategy: begin the 3.1-mile race at the back of the pack. All competitors blew past us as the race began. "Patience!" our coach told us. If we maintained a healthy but slower pace in the first mile, we would have enough energy and stamina to pass competitors, one by one, over the next two miles. We would finish strong and win.

I have often thought of this in the context of my spiritual life. How often do we think that we would be better off with an immediate "win"? I pray for a miraculous cure for my friend dying of cancer, or that the Lord saves another friend's marriage before the divorce is final. Really, I'm demanding an immediate answer.

Sometimes, like Mary, we need to stay in the back of the pack. We need to allow time for God to act, in his way. Pregnant as a virgin? Surely Mary yearned for immediate answers. Yet she knew God knew what he was doing.

— Meg Bucaro

Do you demand instantaneous answers in life? Seek Mary's help to cultivate patience.

Prayer: Lord, grant me the patience of Mary today, to rely on you completely.

December 10

"In those days a decree went out from Caesar Augustus that all the world should be enrolled. And Joseph also went up from Galilee, from the city of Nazareth, to Judea, to the city of David, which is called Bethlehem, because he was of the house and lineage of David, to be enrolled with Mary his betrothed, who was with child." — Luke 2:1, 4-5

When my daughter was ready to give birth to our first grandchild, we made sure everything was perfect for the arrival of our long-awaited baby. We patiently decorated the nursery, washed and folded baby clothes, and placed them in a scented tissue-lined drawer. Prenatal classes were attended.

Mary was not as fortunate. About to give birth, Mary was forced to leave home to complete a Roman census. Jesus was born and placed in a manger, surrounded by strangers. Throughout this entire ordeal, Mary never lost hope; she practiced great patience in waiting for the Lord to act in her life.

— Dr. Mary Amore

LET US TURN TO MARY and ask her for patience, that we may never give up on God, for he is always at work in our lives.

Prayer: Mary, help me to be more patient and to persevere in my faith life.

December 11

"'My son, do not regard lightly the discipline of the Lord / nor lose courage when you are punished by him. / For the Lord disciplines him whom he loves, / and chastises every son whom he receives.' / It is for discipline that you have to endure. God is treating you as sons; for what son is there whom his father does not discipline?" — Hebrews 12:5-7

Practicing patience can be difficult, especially in times of trial. Yet Scripture invites us to endure trials as "discipline." This is easier said than done. When life is filled with pain and sorrow, we turn to the Lord for immediate help, and when it seems he does not answer to our prayers, we can easily become despondent.

Mary teaches us about the virtue of patience. Following the birth of Jesus, Mary was forced to flee to Egypt, fearing for the life of her Son. When Jesus was lost in the Temple for three days, Mary waited patiently, drawing upon her deep faith to see her through. She wants us to practice patience so we can endure all trials that come our way.

— John Holmes

Is THERE A RELATIONSHIp with a friend, relative, or coworker that is unsettling? Seek Mary's help in practicing patience with this situation.

Prayer: Holy Mother, help us to recognize that patience is necessary for the good of our relationship with God and one another.

December 12
Feast of Our Lady of Guadalupe

"O daughter, you are blessed by the Most High God above all women on earth; and blessed be the Lord God, who created the heavens and the earth.... Your hope will never depart from the hearts of men, as they remember the power of God." — Judith 13:18-19

When Mary appeared to Juan Diego, a peasant of little stature, she brought a message of hope and encouragement to the poor, letting them know that they are loved by God. The image of Our Lady of Guadalupe challenges us to look beyond the outer trappings of wealth, status, and lifestyle, and to recognize and respond to the presence of God in all people. Mary's message of hope challenges us to cast off our robes of entitlement in order to help the poor, the displaced, and those forgotten by society.

— Dr. Mary Amore

PRAYERFULLY REFLECT on the ways that you can treat people with mercy and compassion, regardless of their social status or situation.

Prayer: Dearest Mother, through Juan Diego you assured all people of God's love for the poor and marginalized. Help me to treat all people as my brothers and sisters in Christ.

December 13

"We who are strong ought to bear with the failings of the weak, and not to please ourselves; let each of us please his neighbor for his good, to edify him."
— *Romans 15:1-2*

In his Letter to the Romans, St. Paul expresses how important it is that we recognize differences. Often, we adopt an attitude that I am doing my part, either in a relationship or at work, and why isn't he or she doing more? This lack of patience with people's faults can lead to serious problems in relationships. Harmony comes from the God of endurance and encouragement. Patience leads to greater understanding and a community speaking with one voice.

Mary modeled patience, endurance, and encouragement. She was certainly patient after the Annunciation, as Joseph grappled with his decisions. She endured as she gave birth in a stable and had to flee into Egypt. She would later remain present, enduring her Son's passion and death. Mary teaches us to accept the faults and failings we encounter in ourselves and others.

— John Holmes

HAVE SOMEONE'S FAILINGS annoyed you today? Ask Mary to help you be patient with that person.

Prayer: Dearest Mother, help us to adopt a presence to others in our lives, which models yours. May we be an encouragement to others to be patient for the sake of the Kingdom.

December 14

"Better is the end of a thing than its beginning; / and the patient in spirit is better than the proud in spirit. / Be not quick to anger / for anger lodges in the bosom of fools." — *Ecclesiastes 7:8-9*

Why do we become discontented so quickly? We switch from one project to another; we change jobs or pursue new career paths before we have fully seen what could become of our lives. Yet Scripture tells us to wait, for the best is yet to come.

Mary knew the value of waiting. She persevered through difficulties. She didn't give up or change course. Mary was no fool; she placed her entire life in the hands of the Lord.

At times in our lives we stray from Jesus due to impatience; perhaps God is not answering our prayers as quickly as we'd like. Mary is here to urge us to wait. God is working in our lives. Let us be patient and keep vigil with our Blessed Mother.

— Lauren Nelson

WHAT IS CAUSING you discontent right now? Take a moment to be patient and to listen for God's voice to direct your path.

Prayer: Mary, help me to practice patience with the people and activities in my life. Help to know that your Son will always answer me; I just need to listen patiently for his answer.

December 15

"Every one then who hears these words of mine and does them will be like a wise man who built his house upon rock; and the rain fell, and the floods came, and the winds blew and beat upon that house." — Matthew 7:24-25

Scripture reminds us to build our lives around the Lord. He is our rock, enabling us to withstand every storm. Today it is easy to build our lives around the latest movement on social media or the most popular show on television. When we do this, we build on sand.

Brick by brick, Mary patiently built her spiritual house on loving and pleasing the Lord. Mary wants us to do the same. She invites us to reassess our priorities and to rebuild on the solid rock of Jesus Christ. This is not an easy task; it takes patience and perseverance to shore up our spiritual lives. But Mary is here to help us.

— Dr. Mary Amore

LET US SEEK Mary's assistance in turning away from the people and events that prevent us from building our spiritual house on the Lord. Consider your own life. Where are your priorities?

Prayer: Mary, you are the mother of Jesus. Help me to build my life around his life-giving words and actions.

December 16

"If it seem slow, wait for it; / it will surely come, it will not delay."
— *Habakkuk 2:3*

It is amazing how quickly Advent seems to fly by. One week we are lighting the first candle on our Advent wreath, then, before we realize it, the final purple candle is lit. It is a time of joyful anticipation, a time of waiting, wondering, and reflecting on the birth of our Savior. It takes great patience to slow things down so we can savor the moments of the great feast of Christmas.

With our homes decorated with trees and holiday sparkle, Christmas is a time for gathering with friends and families to share past memories while making new traditions. Mary invites us to slow down and to savor these precious moments. She waits patiently while we work through the challenges of humanity. As our spiritual mother, Mary invites us to slow down and to stay focused on the precious gift of the Christ Child.

— Nanci Lukasik-Smith

SEEK MARY'S HELP in refocusing your priorities this holiday season.

Prayer: Blessed Mother, guide me to practice the virtue of patience in everything I do today. When I become impatient and intolerant of others, remind me of the graces of God and fill my heart with joy.

December 17

"Let us then cast off the works of darkness and put on the armor of light; let us conduct ourselves becomingly as in the day." — Romans 13:12-13

In our instantaneous world, patience is not something many of us revere. On a daily basis we are bombarded by constant texts, tweets, and e-mails. Couples enjoying a meal together at a restaurant keep their cellphone on the dinner table just in case they get a more important communication.

Mary invites us to turn away from the incessant chatter of our modern world and join with her in joyful expectation of the coming of the Christ Child. In first-century Palestine, Mary didn't have the technological distractions of our world; hers was a time of prophecy and fulfillment. Mary chose to make her relationship with God a priority. She prayed, trusted, and waited. She prepared her heart for God's call.

This season, let us walk with Mary; let us throw off the works of darkness and distraction and conduct ourselves properly as we wait for the light of the Christ Child to come into our world.

— Dr. Mary Amore

TODAY, TURN OFF YOUR PHONE and sit in silence for ten minutes.

Prayer: Mary, help me to tune out the distractions so that I can wait in joyful expectation for the coming of Christ.

December 18

"Therefore do not throw away your confidence, which has a great reward.
For you have need of endurance, so that you may do the will of God
and receive what is promised." — Hebrews 10:35-36

As Scripture reminds us, trials and afflictions come with being a disciple of Christ. We need to endure our sufferings patiently, with steadfast confidence that we are doing God's will.

Patience and endurance were hallmarks of Mary's life. In her role as the mother of Jesus, she endured an uncertain future, death threats from Herod, becoming a refugee, and, ultimately, the gruesome death of her child. But Mary endured. Her steadfast faith never wavered, even in the most difficult trials. Her life inspires us today.

— John Holmes

WHAT TRIALS might you be enduring? Is uncertainty causing you restlessness and angst? Do you feel out of the flow of Divine Love?

Prayer: Heavenly Mother, you give us an example of patience and endurance. Help me to stay grounded in God's love that I may endure the trials of discipleship.

December 19

"Comfort, comfort my people, says your God. / Speak tenderly to Jerusalem, / and cry to her / that her warfare is ended, / that her iniquity is pardoned, / that she has received from the LORD's hand / double for all her sins."
— *Isaiah 40:1-2*

Good Catholic guilt: none of us want it, all of us have it. What are we to do? This reading from Isaiah beckons us to let go of guilt because our expiation is at hand. Salvation is ours. Do we believe this?

Mary certainly did. Throughout her life, Mary waited patiently for these words of Isaiah to be fulfilled. She trusted in the Lord. Her patience came to fruition when the angel Gabriel visited her and asked her to be the mother of Jesus. Mary's life inspires us to trust in the life-giving words of the Lord. She wants to comfort us and remind us that Jesus gave his life so our sins could be forgiven.

— Dr. Mary Amore

WHAT ACTIONS IN YOUR PAST are troubling your soul? Consider confessing these sins so that your heart may be ready to receive the gift of the Christ Child.

Prayer: Mother Mary, your sinless womb carried the long-awaited promise of salvation for all of God's people. Help me to turn away from sin and to follow Jesus.

December 20

"Wait for the LORD; / be strong, and let your heart take courage; / yes, wait for the LORD!" — *Psalms 27:14*

As she waited for Jesus, Mary dug deep into her inner strength. As most new mothers, Mary was probably very scared of the unexpected. During that time, women went through birth surrounded by female members of their family. Mary was all alone; she only had Joseph to rely on to help her with the birth of her Son. Surely Mary practiced patience as she taught Joseph about childbearing.

There are times in all our lives when our patience with God wavers, when we get scared and nervous and fearful of what is to come. At these times, let us to turn to our Blessed Mother, for Mary understands our feelings of uncertainty, and she is here to help us wait for the Lord with strength and patience. In the end, our patience will give way to joy, the same joy that Mary experienced when Jesus was born.

— Lauren Nelson

TODAY, IF YOU EXPERIENCE anxiety or nervousness, take a moment and seek Mary's motherly help.

Prayer: Mary, your patience and strength inspire me. Help me to find those gifts within myself.

December 21

"The wolf shall dwell with the lamb, / and the leopard shall lie down with the kid, / and the calf and the lion and the fatling together, / and a little child shall lead them." — Isaiah 11:6

Isaiah portrays a world where everyone gets along, where peace and gentleness coexist in spite of great diversity. How far are we still from this vision of paradise? We deceive ourselves that we are the best, we are the ones with the truth, we are better than everyone else. Those seeking to change the world desire instant gratification, and they are not willing to wait for God's vision of the world to unfold.

Mary beckons us to wait in joyful expectation for the Lord to act in our lives and in the world. Mary did not fear the future, nor did she try to control her own destiny; rather, Mary waited patiently for God's will to unfold. She placed her complete trust in the Lord, and she invites us to do the same.

— Dr. Mary Amore

How does patience fit into your spiritual journey? Consider the ways you can wait patiently for the Lord to work in your life.

Prayer: Mother Mary, help me to be patient so that all of my actions may reflect the will of God.

December 22

"My son, if you come forward to serve the Lord, / remain in justice and in fear, / and prepare yourself for temptation. / Set your heart right and be steadfast, / incline your ear, and receive words of understanding, / and do not be hasty in time of calamity. / Await God's patience, cling to him and do not depart, / that you may be wise in all your ways."
— *Sirach 2:1-3*

Trials are a part of life, and we must prepare for them. Scripture offers encouragement as well as a challenge. Sincerity of heart, patience, and steadfastness are the keys to facing life's problems. Yet remaining patient in crushing misfortune seems a tall order.

Clearly, Mary placed enormous trust in God. Like gold tested in the fire, Mary's faith grew stronger with each crushing event. Mary's life challenges us to reassess our level of faith and our commitment to patiently endure the trials of life. Mary is here to help us persevere and not lose hope when life is difficult.

— John Holmes

HAS YOUR FAITH been tested in the fire? In times of trial, seek Mary's motherly help to increase your faith in the workings of the Lord.

Prayer: Mother Mary, help us to continue to find ways to connect with you and your Son in times of trial. Then we will grow in faith and trust, patiently enduring life's trials.

December 23

*"The voice of my beloved! / Behold, he comes, / leaping upon
the mountains, / bounding over the hills."*
— *Song of Solomon 2:8*

One of the most joyous occasions for our family is to walk into church on Christmas Eve and see all of the wonderful decorations. The trees, while simple, are full of white lights, the Nativity scene is in front of the altar, and everything is draped in cloths of white and gold.

Patience is part of our preparation for Christmas. Advent is about waiting. We reflect on Mary's nine months waiting for the birth of Jesus, on Joseph and Mary's long journey for the census. Even the Wise Men waited patiently to see the Christ Child, and the grace of patience protected them as they traveled from afar.

Mary displays grace in her ability to wait. She understands that things should not be rushed. This season is meant to give us joy.

— Nanci Lukasik-Smith

ASK MARY TO HELP YOU appreciate the joy and beauty of the birth of the Christ Child.

Prayer: Mary, as we near the end of this holy season of waiting, help me to slow down. Grant me patience in my daily activities that my heart may be ready to welcome the Prince of Peace.

December 24
Christmas Eve

"[She] wrapped him in swaddling cloths, and laid him in a manger, because there was no place for them in the inn." — Luke 2:7

There's a Polish tradition of setting an extra place at the Christmas Eve table for the "stranger." As the family gathers to eat, they wait to welcome any unexpected visitor who may drop by on this special evening.

On that first Christmas Eve, Mary, pregnant and about to give birth, was refused lodging because there was no room for her and St. Joseph. They were strangers and no one welcomed them. What must have gone through Mary's mind at that moment? Surely her great faith in the Lord gave her the patience to endure this difficult situation and the hope to believe that God would take care of her.

Our lives as Christians invites us to wait patiently, for one never knows when or how Christ may appear. He may come in the person of a stranger who is homeless and looking for a place to sleep, in someone recently released from prison looking for employment, in a friend diagnosed with a terminal illness.

— Eugenia Callison

How WILL YOU receive Christ when he knocks at your door?

Prayer: Mary, help me to be open to the presence of your Son, Jesus, in the strangers I meet each day.

December 25
Christmas Day

"And they went with haste, and found Mary and Joseph,
and the baby lying in a manger." — Luke 2:16

Mary rested with the Christ Child in total peace and harmony with the world. For nine months, she patiently waited for the birth of her Son, and how she savored this moment. We hear in Scripture that the shepherds went in haste to see this newborn king. To their surprise they found a little baby lying in a manger, guarded by Joseph and Mary. This beautiful scene of the nativity of Jesus invites us to slow down and savor the special moments in life.

If we take time to slow down and enjoy the beauty of God's design in the littlest things, we, like Mary, will take great delight in the simple things in life. We will delight in the beauty of the birth of our Savior.

— Gina Sannasardo

THIS CHRISTMAS SEASON, breathe in God's goodness. Prayerfully gaze on the image of the baby in the manger, just as Mary did on the day of his birth. Invite the Blessed Mother to be with you and to draw you closer to her Son, Jesus.

Prayer: Blessed Mother Mary, how you adored your Son. Help us to make room for the Christ Child to be born in our hearts, that our lives may be changed forever.

December 26

"For to you is born this day in the city of David a Savior,
who is Christ the Lord." — *Luke 2:11*

This Christmas proclamation is appropriate not only for today but for every day of the year: unto us, you and me, a child was born. Born into poverty, Jesus was placed in a wooden crib. Christ's road would take him from the wooden manger to the wood of the cross. As we celebrate the birth of Jesus, what message does his life bring to us today?

We need only to look to Mary for the answer. Mary gave birth to the gift of God's divine love. Later, Mary would embrace God's unconditional love as she watched her beloved Son brutally crucified for us. But love endured; it did not die on the cross. Love triumphed over death. Mary's life as the mother of the Christ Child challenges us to follow the way of love, even if it takes us to the cross. For unto us, you and me, he was born.

— Dr. Mary Amore

CHRISTMAS IS MORE than gifts and holiday parties. Jesus is the long-awaited fulfillment of the promise. Let us seek Mary's help in remembering, celebrating, and honoring the gift of God's love in our lives.

Prayer: Mary, help me to love Jesus, who gave his life that I might live forever.

December 27

"And when they saw him they were astonished; and his mother said to him, 'Son, why have you treated us so? Behold, your father and I have been looking for you anxiously.'" — Luke 2:48

Three whole days missing their Son! They certainly felt some anxiety. Mary and Joseph's initial reaction was one of astonishment. No doubt Mary was surprised by what she witnessed in the Temple. As any mother would, Mary posed a question. Jesus explained. Mary exhibited great patience in accepting, though not understanding, her Son's explanation.

— John Holmes

ARE THERE SITUATIONS at home or at work which may trigger a reaction or really try our patience? Is a lack of understanding of the other person part of the problem? By merely being in that moment, not fully understanding, maybe we can exhibit the kind of patience Mary did.

Prayer: Dearest Mother Mary, thank you for your example of patience in the midst of anxiety. Help me to stay in the moment and not react impatiently.

December 28
Feast of the Holy Innocents

*"A voice is heard in Ramah, / lamentation and bitter weeping. /
Rachel is weeping for her children; / she refuses to be comforted
for her children / because they are not." — Jeremiah 31:15*

As Mary and Joseph fled for their lives in the middle of the night, did Mary realize the carnage she would leave behind? Was she aware of the massacre of the innocent little boys that would take place and the inconsolable cries of their grieving mothers all because Herod wanted to destroy her Son, Jesus?

As a refugee in Egypt, Mary waited patiently for the Lord's plan to unfold as she clung to her faith on a daily basis. Her life was not without struggle and pain, yet Mary patiently endured her trials because she knew the Lord was with her.

We can turn to Mary for patient strength and the fortitude to help us move through the challenges of life with the knowledge that we are not alone. Mary is here to lead us to her Son, Jesus.

— Dr. Mary Amore

CALL TO MIND a difficult situation you are facing. Share your sobbing and lamentation with Mary. Ask her to give you patient endurance.

Prayer: Mary, help me to not give in to the difficulties in life but rather to place my trust and hope in the Lord.

December 29

*"And behold, the star which they had seen in the East went before them,
till it came to rest over the place where the child was. When they saw the star,
they rejoiced exceedingly with great joy; and going into the house they
saw the child with Mary his mother." — Matthew 2:9-10*

Two thousand years ago, three kings saw a star rising in the East, shining over Bethlehem. Under that special star they found Mary swaddling her infant, Jesus. Here in this place the fulfillment of the long-awaited promise of salvation came to pass in the birth of Jesus.

Today, we won't find the baby Jesus in a manger with his mother, Mary, under a starry sky. Our newborn King can be found in the world around us — in the poor, the homeless, the forgotten, and the marginalized. If we are patient and seek the presence of Christ, we will find him wherever we look. Mary is our guiding star, and she will lead us to an encounter with her Son, Jesus.

— Alice Smith

WHERE HAVE YOU ENCOUNTERED Jesus lately? How did you respond to him?

Prayer: Dear Mary, help me to be patient on my spiritual journey. Guide me to your Son, Jesus, as I gaze at the stars.

December 30

"Now when [the Wise Men] departed, behold, an angel of the Lord appeared to Joseph in a dream and said, "Rise, take the child and his mother, and flee to Egypt, and remain there till I tell you; for Herod is about to search for the child, to destroy him." — Matthew 2:13

Talk about patience. Mary and Joseph had no idea when they would be able to return home for Egypt, their place of exile. Mary surely survived this move by placing her complete trust in the Lord, waiting patiently for his plan to unfold.

I would not have been as patient as Mary; most likely I would have taken matters into my own hands — usually cause for great concern. Most of us lack patience; we fail to see that God has a plan for us.

— John Holmes

MARY HAS MUCH to teach us about patience and letting God's plan unfold in our lives. Reflect on one situation in your life that requires patience. Seek Mary's help in waiting for the Lord's will to be done in this particular situation.

Prayer: Holy Mother, teach me to remain calm in the turmoil of my daily life. May I patiently accept all of life's events as they come my way.

December 31
New Year's Eve

"Therefore, if anyone is in Christ, he is a new creation; the old has passed away, behold, the new has come." — *2 Corinthians 5:17*

The old year is about to pass away, and we eagerly wait for the new year to come. The end of a year is a sacred time, a time to reflect on all that has transpired during this past year. Mary spent a good portion of her life in this prayerful, grateful reflection.

As we look forward to a new year, our hearts are filled with hope for the possibilities of new life that await us. Mary was filled with similar hopes and dreams as she looked upon her newborn Son. Perhaps she imagined what he would become as the years went on.

Mary's prayerful and reflective stance invites us to take some quiet time to thank the Lord for his goodness, and to place our trust and future in his loving care.

— Lauren Nelson

CONSIDER MAKING a spiritual resolution to draw closer to Mary and Jesus in the coming year.

Prayer: Mary, as this year comes to a close, help me to be patient with myself and with God. Teach me not to expect instant change, but rather transformation at a slow and steady pace.

Contributors

Joseph Abel holds a PhD in Educational Psychology, a Master of Pastoral Studies Degree, and a Master of Divinity. Joe has served as an adjunct professor of humanities at Benedictine University and is certified as a professional life coach. He is a member of the board of directors of Mayslake Ministries.

Sharon A. Abel holds a PhD in adult education and a Master of Pastoral Studies. A former Joliet diocesan consultant in adult formation, Sheri also worked as an online author for the Center for Ministry Development. She currently serves as the director of Program Initiatives at Mayslake Ministries.

Dr. Mary Amore holds a Doctor of Ministry Degree in Liturgical Studies and a Master of Arts in Pastoral Studies. A published author and national presenter, Dr. Amore is the host of the television show *Soul Snackin' with Dr. Mary Amore* sponsored by Mayslake Ministries and is the full-time executive director of Mayslake Ministries.

Jill Bates holds degrees from De Paul University, Loyola University, and a Doctor of Ministry from the Graduate Theological Foundation. Jill has worked in the areas of adult faith development, ecumenism, and chaplaincy. Led by the Holy Spirit and nourished in the community, she finds personal enrichment in her current role as spiritual director at Mayslake Ministries.

Betty Bentley has been involved in ministry for the past twenty years serving the Church at both the parish and diocesan levels. In addition to her role as office coordinator for Mayslake Ministries, Betty enjoys developing and presenting retreats for youths who are preparing to receive the Sacraments of Reconciliation, Eucharist, and Confirmation.

Father Tom Borkowski has a MEd in Special Education from the University of Missouri, a MDiv from the Pontifical College Josephinum, and has undertaken post-graduate studies in Carmelite spirituality and contemplative prayer. His background includes education and ministry with persons with disabilities, pastoral ministry and counseling, adult faith development, and co-dependency and recovery counseling. He is a spiritual director with Mayslake Ministries.

Linda Brinkman is a former elementary and high school teacher. Linda holds a Certificate in Spiritual Direction from the Siena Retreat Center in Racine, Wisconsin, and is also a licensed social worker.

Meg Bucaro is the mother of three, a college speech instructor, and a past member of the Rockford Diocesan Pastoral Council and Catholic MOMS (Ministry of Mother's Sharing). Meg is a member of the Mom's Ministry Team at Mayslake Ministries.

Eugenia Callison holds a Master of Arts in Pastoral Studies and a Certificate in Spiritual Direction. An accomplished music therapist who works with individuals with emotional and social needs, Eugenia serves Mayslake Ministries as a spiritual director specializing in the spiritual needs of military families.

Katie Choudary holds a Bachelor of Arts in history and a Master of Education. A stay-at-home mom, she and her husband are the proud parents of three young children. Katie serves as a catechist in the Catechesis of the Good Shepherd Program and is a member of the Mom's Ministry Team at Mayslake Ministries.

Betty Crane serves as a spiritual director with Mayslake Ministries. She received her spiritual director training through Christos in Minnesota. Betty also is a psychotherapist who works primarily with adults seeking assistance with relational issues, recovery from abuse, and marital concerns. Betty is eager to help others ignite and integrate their spirituality with a healthy psyche in order to know and to sense God more fully in their lives.

Sheila Cusack is an affiliate spiritual director at Mayslake Ministries. A registered nurse by profession, Sheila's spiritual areas of interest focus on end-of-life issues, hospice, grief, and health concerns.

Deb Kelsey-Davis, RN, MHSA, is a clinician, a family caregiver expert, author, and speaker who holds a graduate degree in Health Services Administration and a Lay Ministry Certificate. Passionate about addressing the emotional, practical, and spiritual needs of family caregivers, Deb offers programs and videos on the topic of caregiving at Mayslake Ministries.

Mary Beth Desmond is a registered nurse holding master's degrees in both nursing and spirituality. Currently finishing her doctoral degree in nursing, Mary Beth serves Mayslake Ministries as a spiritual director.

Larry Dreffein is a teacher, pastor, and administrator following the call of the Gospel in the footsteps of St. Francis of Assisi for the last fifty years. An accomplished spiritual director at Mayslake Ministries, he has accompanied many on their journey, listening to the call placed in their lives and helping them discern its meaning and direction.

Bob Frazee holds a Master in Pastoral Studies from Catholic Theological Union. His passion is adult spiritual formation. Bob has served as an RCIA catechist, an instructor in the Joliet Diocesan Lay Formation program, and as an adjunct to the Emmaus Program at CTU. Bob is an affiliate of Mayslake Ministries and specializes in contemplative prayer practices.

Christine Grano is a certified spiritual director, retreat leader, and presenter for Mayslake Ministries. An accomplished pastoral musician, Chris is also trained in Christian Lay Counseling & Inner Healing Prayer. Her faith life and ministry is deeply rooted in twelve-step spirituality. Married and the mother of two adult children, Christine is a new grandma.

Michael Grano is the husband and soulmate of Christine Grano, and a spiritual director and retreat facilitator for Mayslake Ministries. Mike holds a special devotion to the Blessed Mother, which has guided him in his spiritual and professional life as a financial planner.

Chris Hannighan-Wiehn, a former schoolteacher, currently serves as a faith-formation director in a suburban parish of Chicago. Chris is also a spiritual director at Mayslake Ministries. She feels blessed to journey with people as they reflect on their relationship with the Lord.

John Holmes holds a Certificate in Spiritual Direction from Hesychia School of Spiritual Direction in Tucson, Arizona. A certified lay minister of the Archdiocese of Chicago, John is retired from pharmaceutical sales and spends time with his wife of forty-seven years, their three sons and five grandchildren. He is a Vietnam veteran and leukemia survivor. John's ministry focus is spiritual direction and hospital ministry.

Suzette Horyza has been a retreat director for nearly three decades. Professionally, she is a tour director taking groups traveling throughout the United States and Canada. Her writing inspiration comes from God being her tour guide throughout the many journeys of life. Suzette serves as tour director of Mayslake Ministries "On Holiday with God" day trips.

Dr. Barb Jarvis Pauls holds a Doctorate of Ministry in Pastoral Counseling and a master's in counseling psychology. Barb is currently in private practice and also ministers as a spiritual director, adjunct presenter, and pastoral counselor at Mayslake Ministries. She specializes in bereavement, marriage enrichment, and family-systems therapy.

Mary Kostic holds a Bachelor of Science in Elementary Education and a MAT from the University of Pittsburgh. She has been involved in parish ministry for over twenty-five years and holds a certification in the Liturgy Certification Program of the Diocese of Joliet. A board member of Mayslake Ministries, Mary is married, has three adult children, and five grandchildren, and lives in Naperville, Illinois.

Gail Krema is an affiliate staff member of Mayslake Ministries. She earned a Certificate in Advanced Spirituality and Spiritual Direction from the Institute of Spiritual Leadership, an MA in Spirituality from Loyola University Chicago, and a BSN from the College of Saint Teresa. She is passionate about Ignatian spirituality, and does volunteer work with the Ignatian Spirituality Project, which provides retreats for homeless individuals who are currently living in a shelter and working on recovery from addiction.

JoAnne McElroy holds a Master of Arts in Spirituality from the Institute of Pastoral Studies at Loyola University and a post-graduate Certificate in Spiritual Direction. She came to spiritual direction through her desire to listen more deeply to God's presence in her life. She delights in her grandchildren, nature, the arts, and dream work. JoAnne is a spiritual director with Mayslake Ministries.

Lauren Nelson is the director of communications at Mayslake Ministries. Married and the mother of two young girls, Lauren holds an undergraduate degree in theology and enjoys teaching religious education for first and second graders.

Deborah O'Donnell, a former board member of Mayslake Ministries, has a master's degree from Ball State University and serves Mayslake Ministries as a Christian life coach. Owner of Rodas Life Coaching, Deborah's passion is to help individuals recognize their God-given gifts and strengths so as to achieve success in their chosen career path.

Gina Sannasardo is a young wife, mom, Catholic-school educator and Christian life coach (CPC, ELI-MP). Gina is a team member of the Mom's Ministry Program at Mayslake Ministries. Her passion in ministry is about helping others experience God's love!

Alice Smith holds a Master of Science in Home Economics Education. Her ministry — What's New with You and Jesus — examines family life in relationship to Jesus, weaving Scripture and prayer into family stories resulting in a spiritual legacy. Alice is a member of the board of directors of Mayslake Ministries and acts as co-host on Mayslake Ministries television program *Soul Snackin' with Dr. Mary Amore.*

Nanci Lukasik-Smith holds a Certificate in Lay Leadership and a Certificate of Catholic Theology from the University of Notre Dame S.T.E.P. program. A religious educator for over twenty-five years, Nanci serves Mayslake Ministries on the Mom's Ministry Team.

Jane Zimmerman, RN, MSN, has a Certificate in Spiritual Direction from Claret Center and is working on a Master of Arts for Spiritual Direction. Certified to offer training and assessment related to intercultural competency, Jane is skilled in assisting in meditation and healing.